Simple Line Tattoo Designs

Great inspiration for artists, amateurs and professionals, people who have no idea for their first tattoo and more.

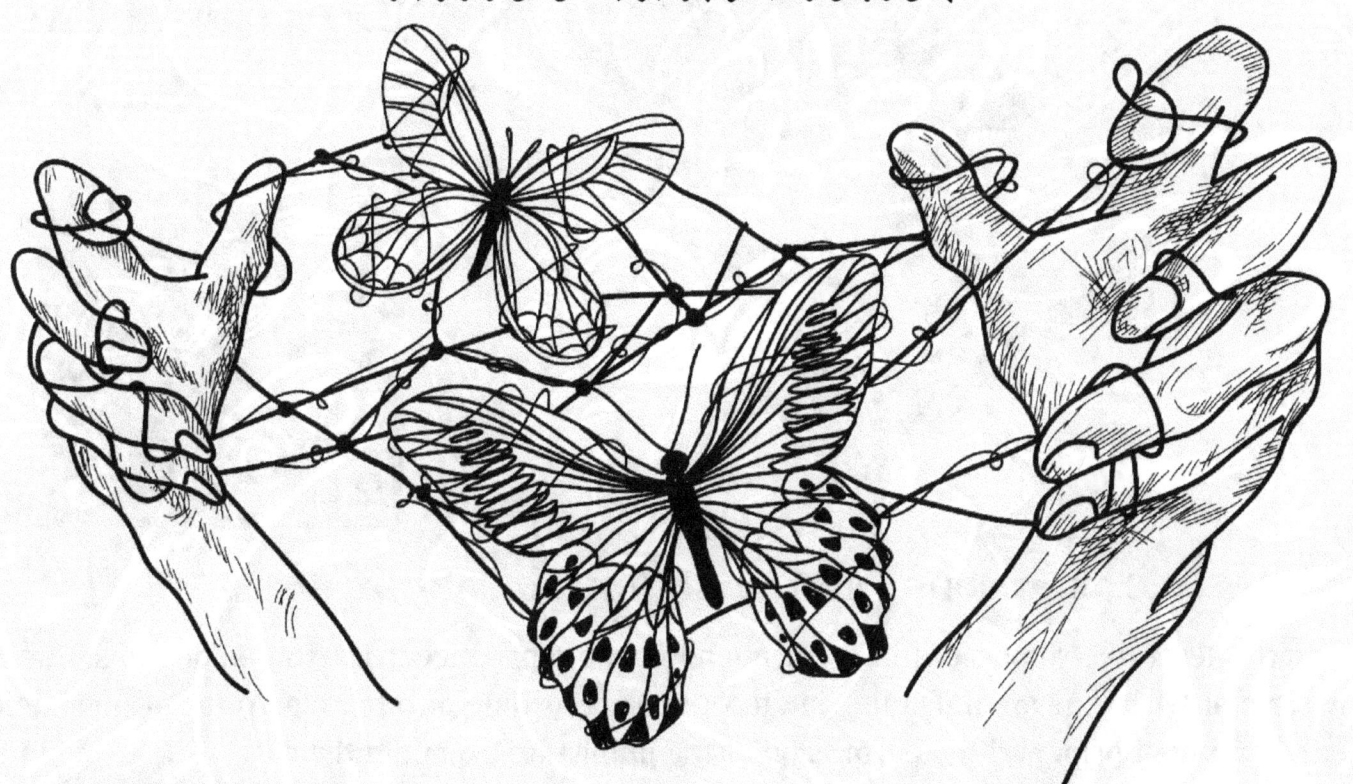

Over 1530 Simple Line Tattoo Designs

This Book Belongs to

The Big Book of Small Tattoos.

600 Minimalist Tattoos.

Download The Free eBook

Copyrights © 2024

J. Fabian Rama and Rama Tattoo Coloring Press

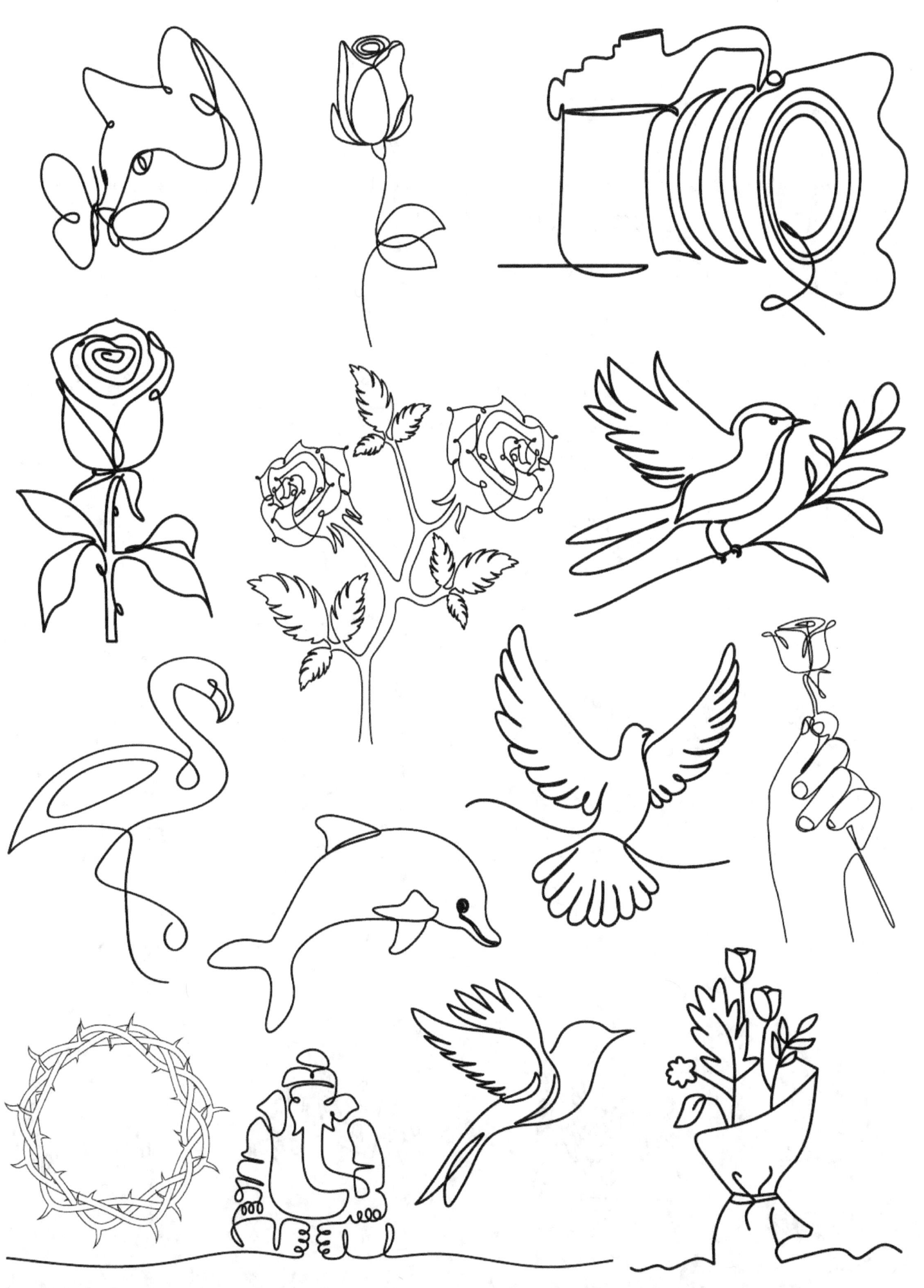

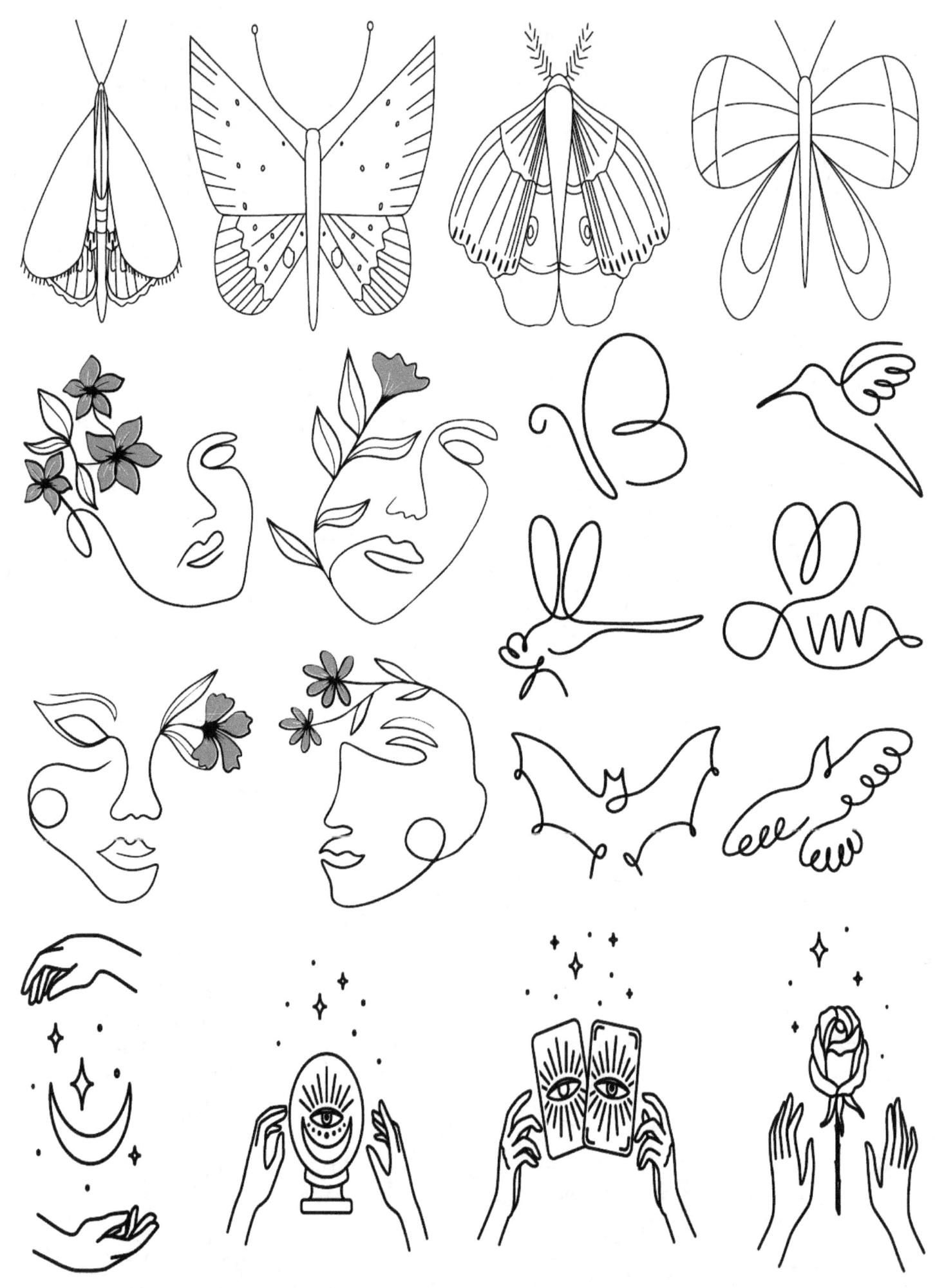

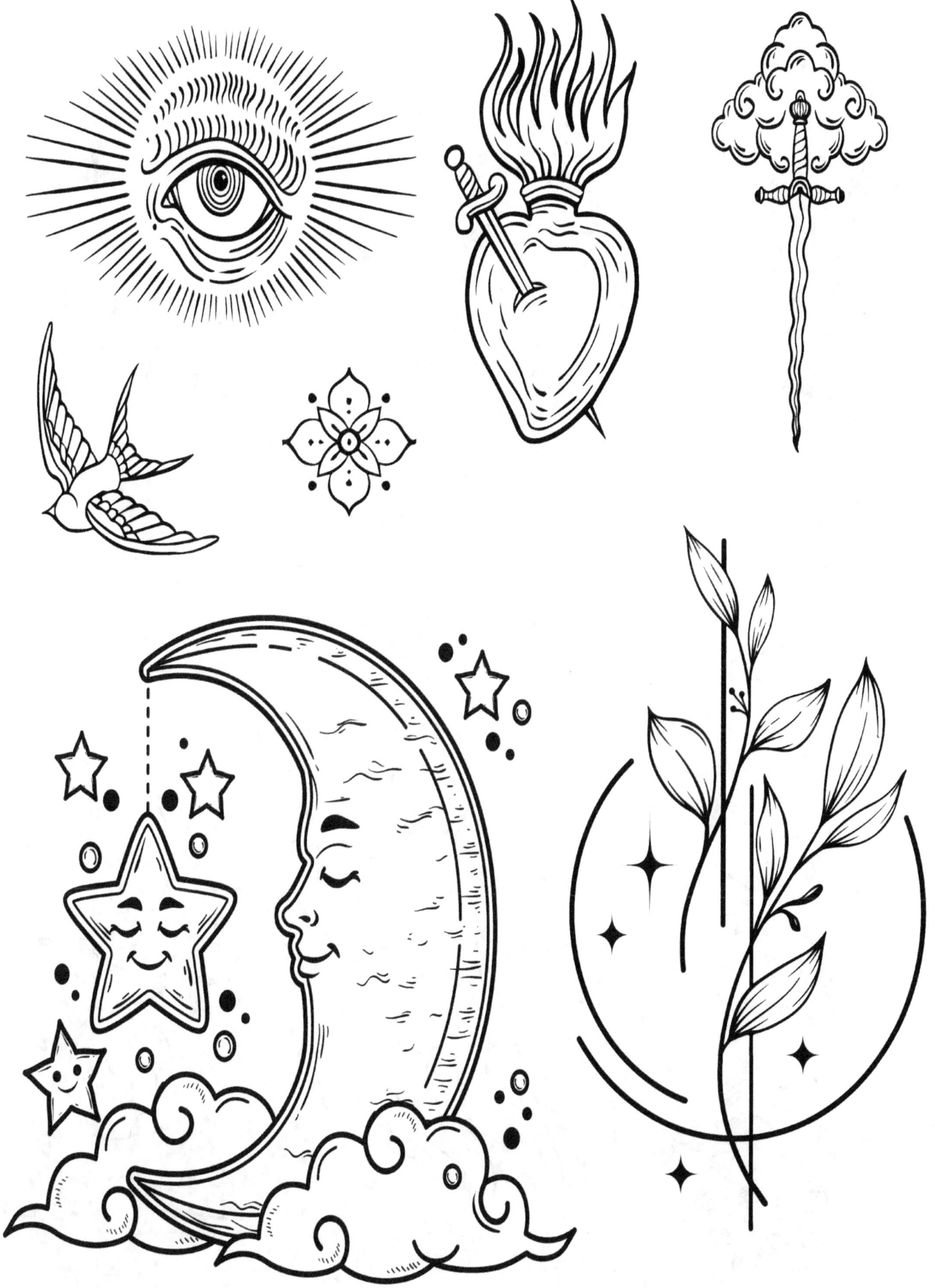

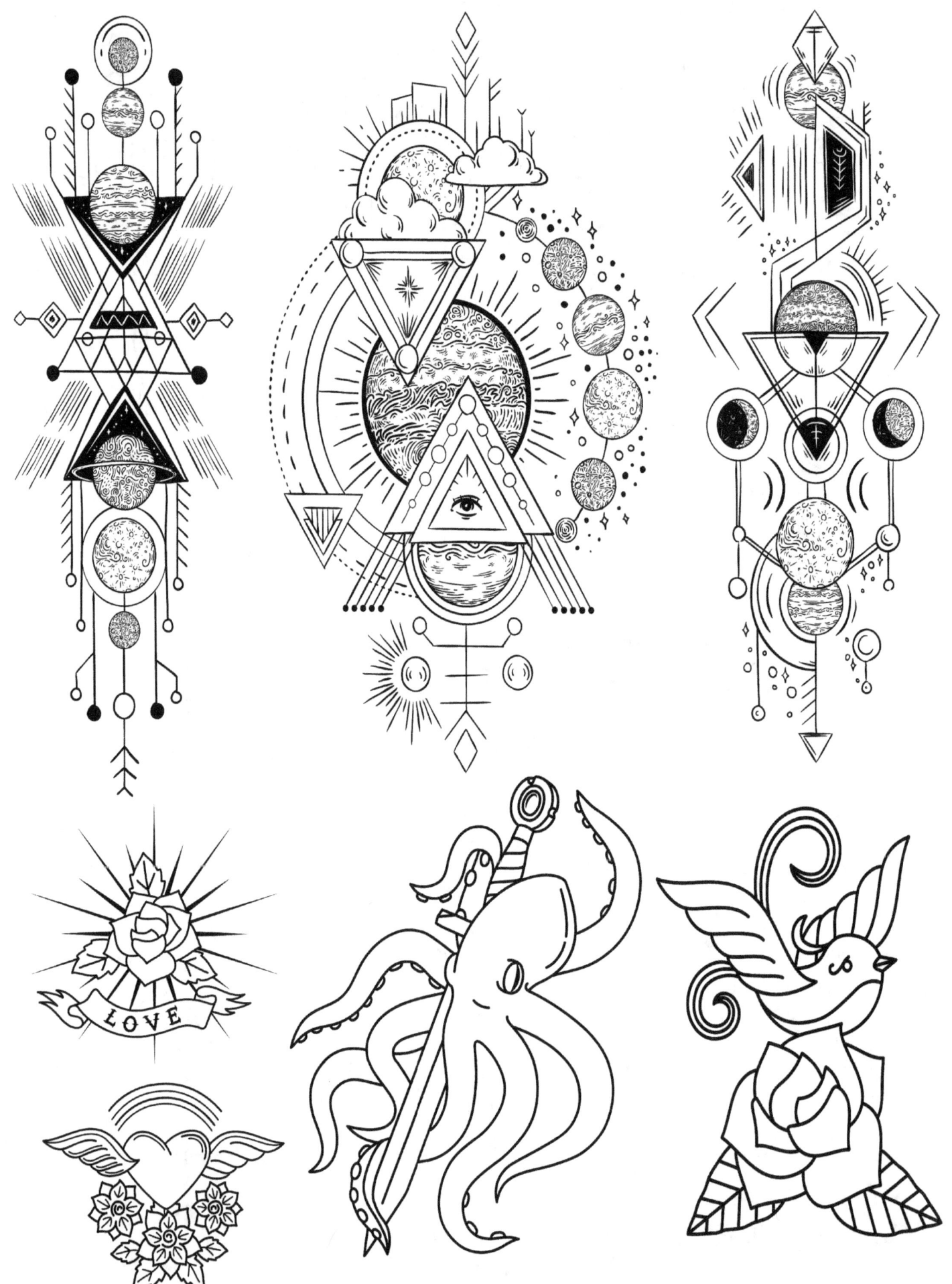

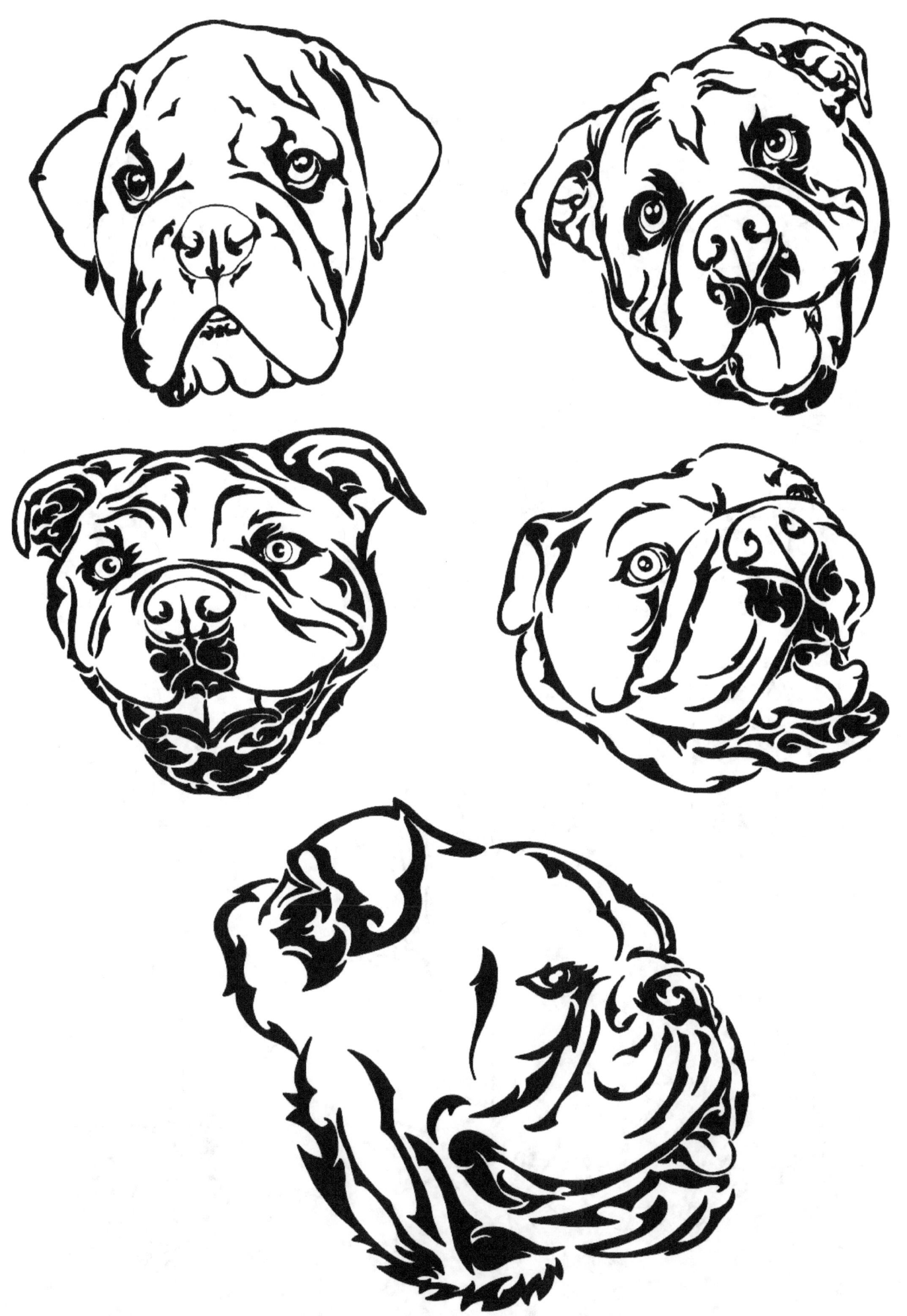

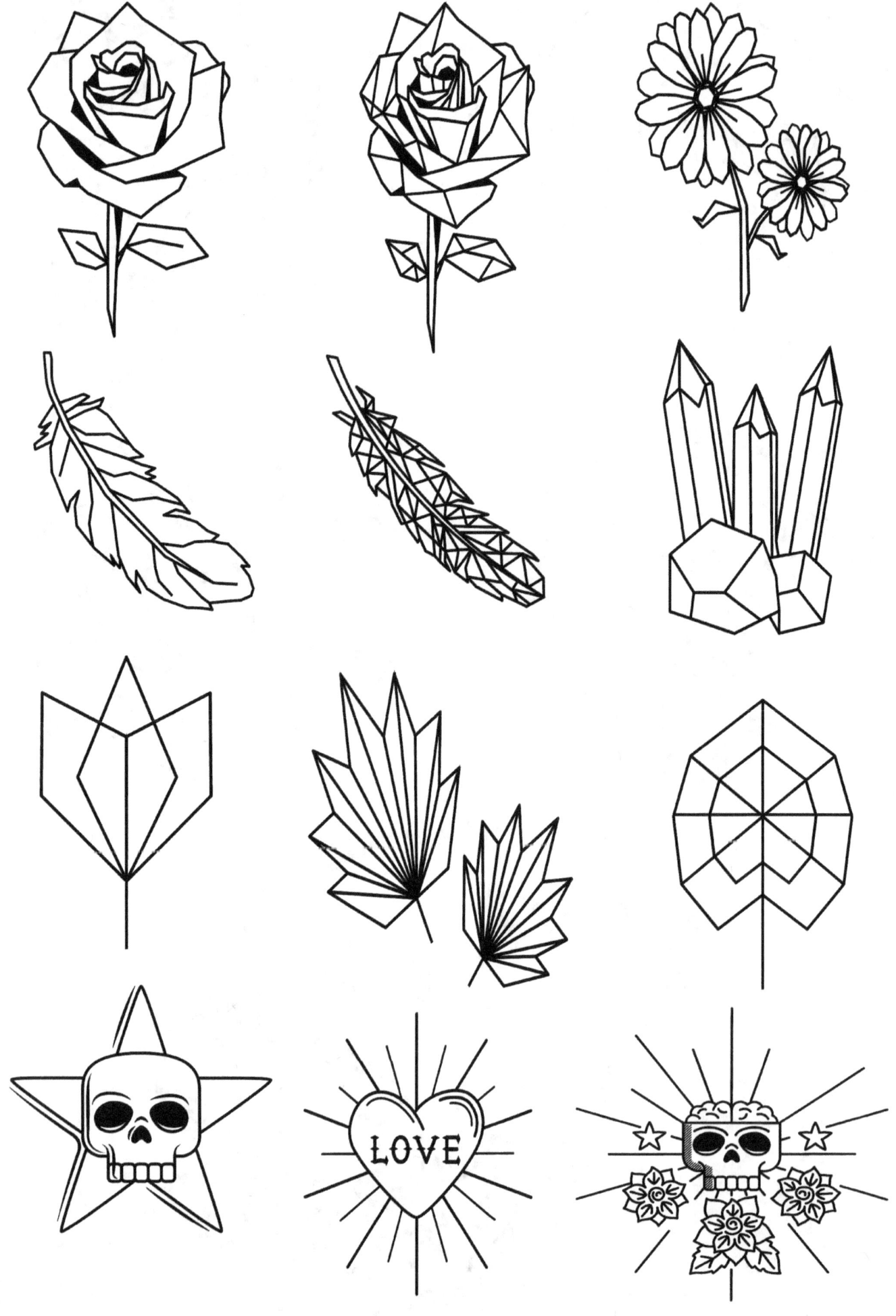

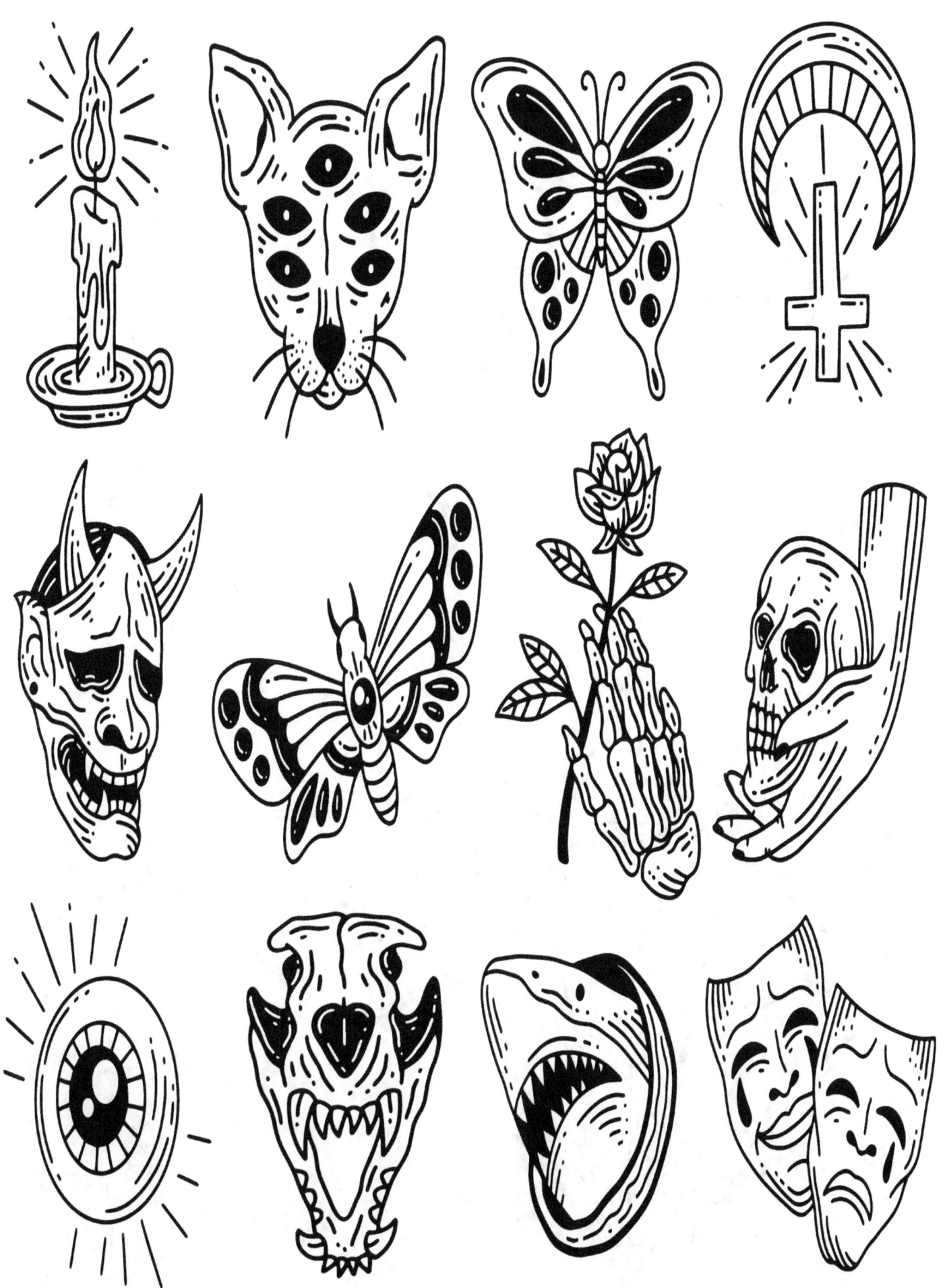

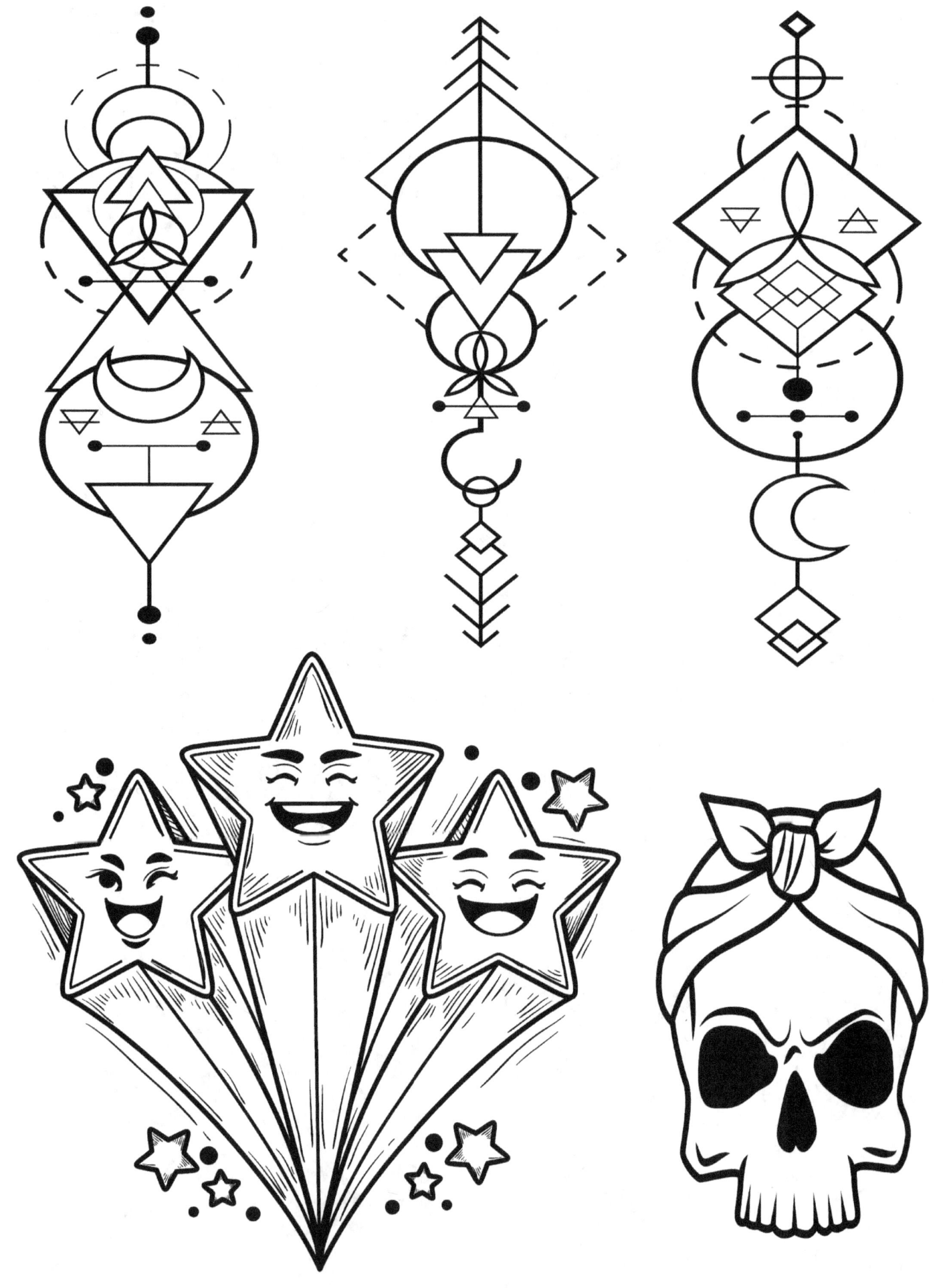

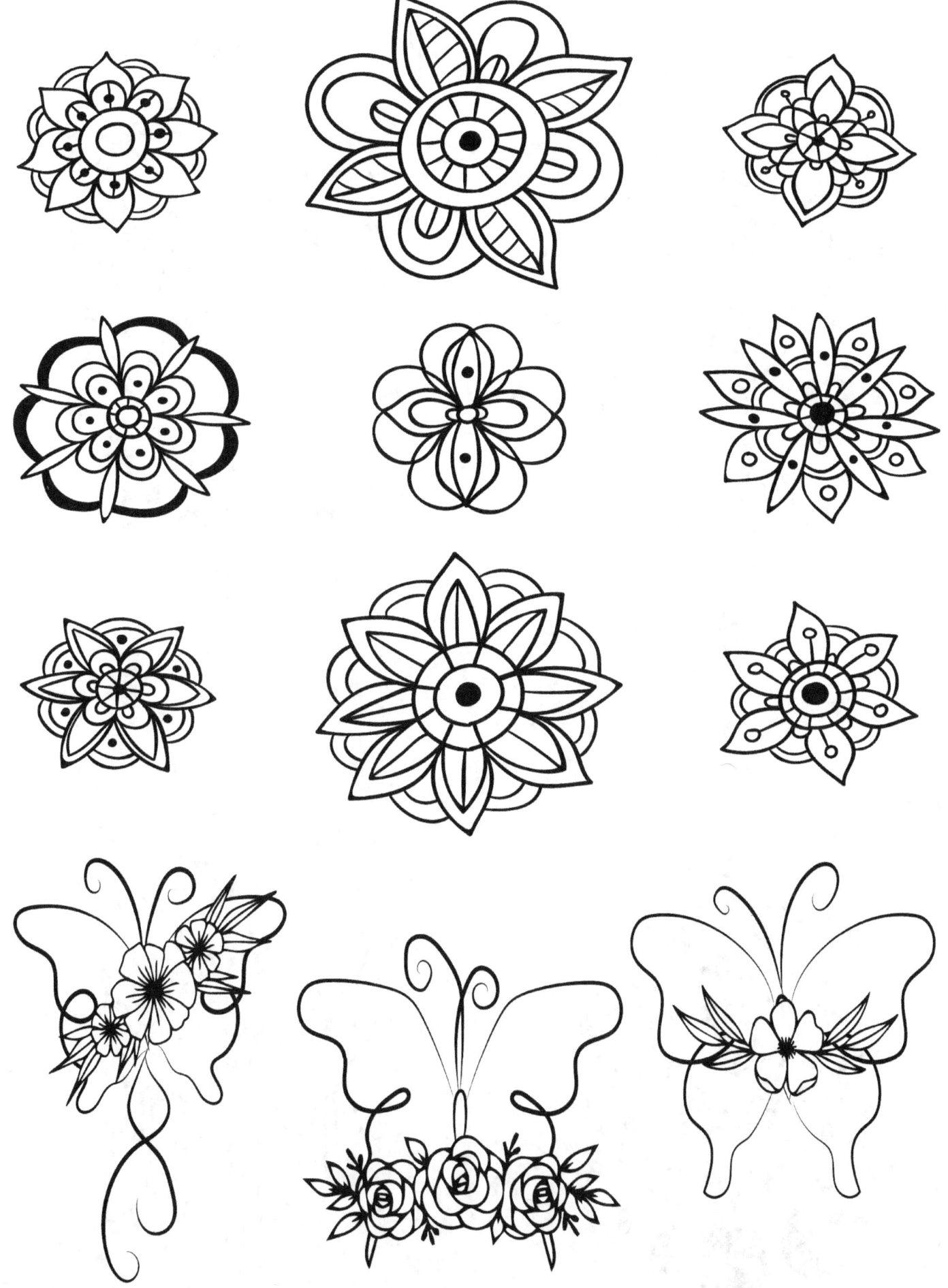

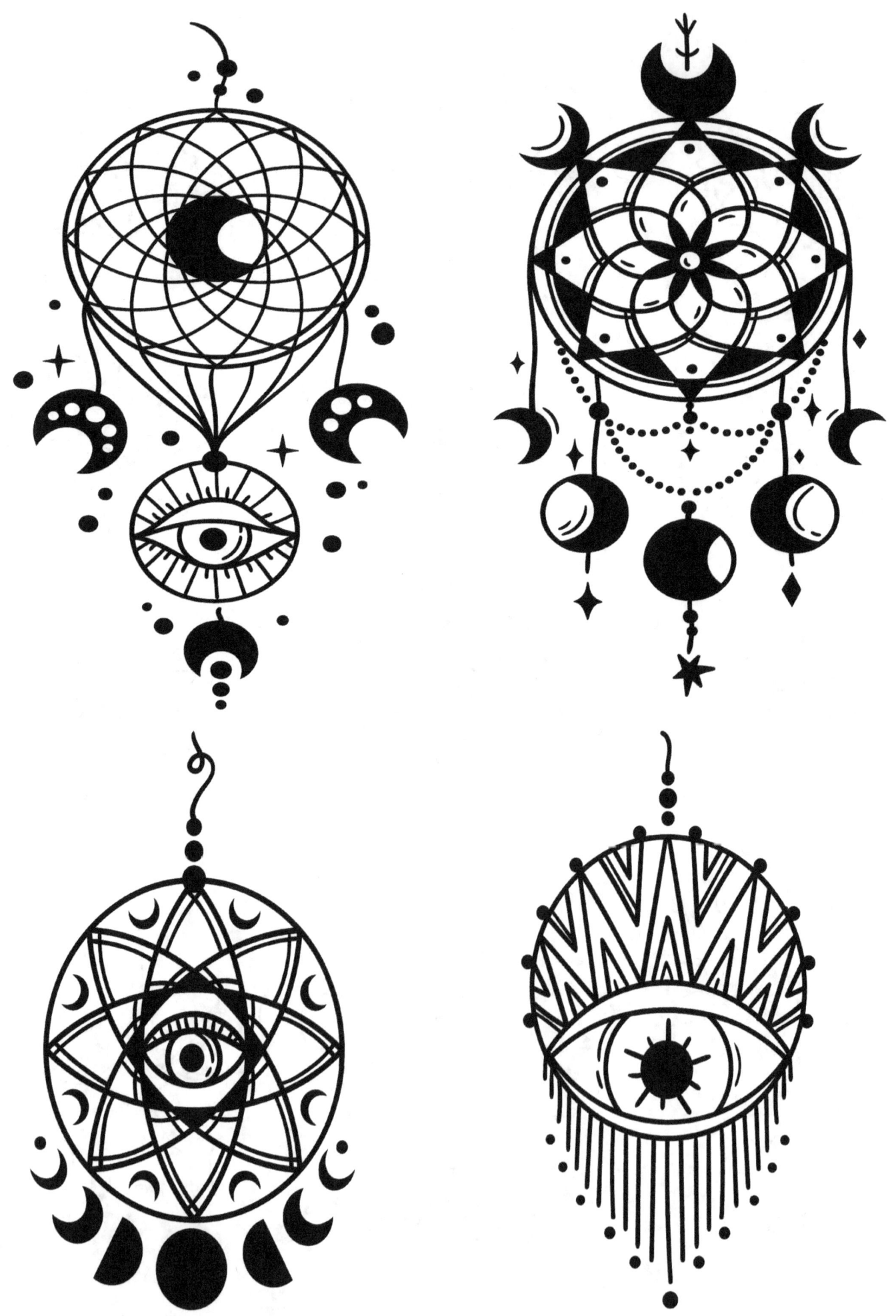

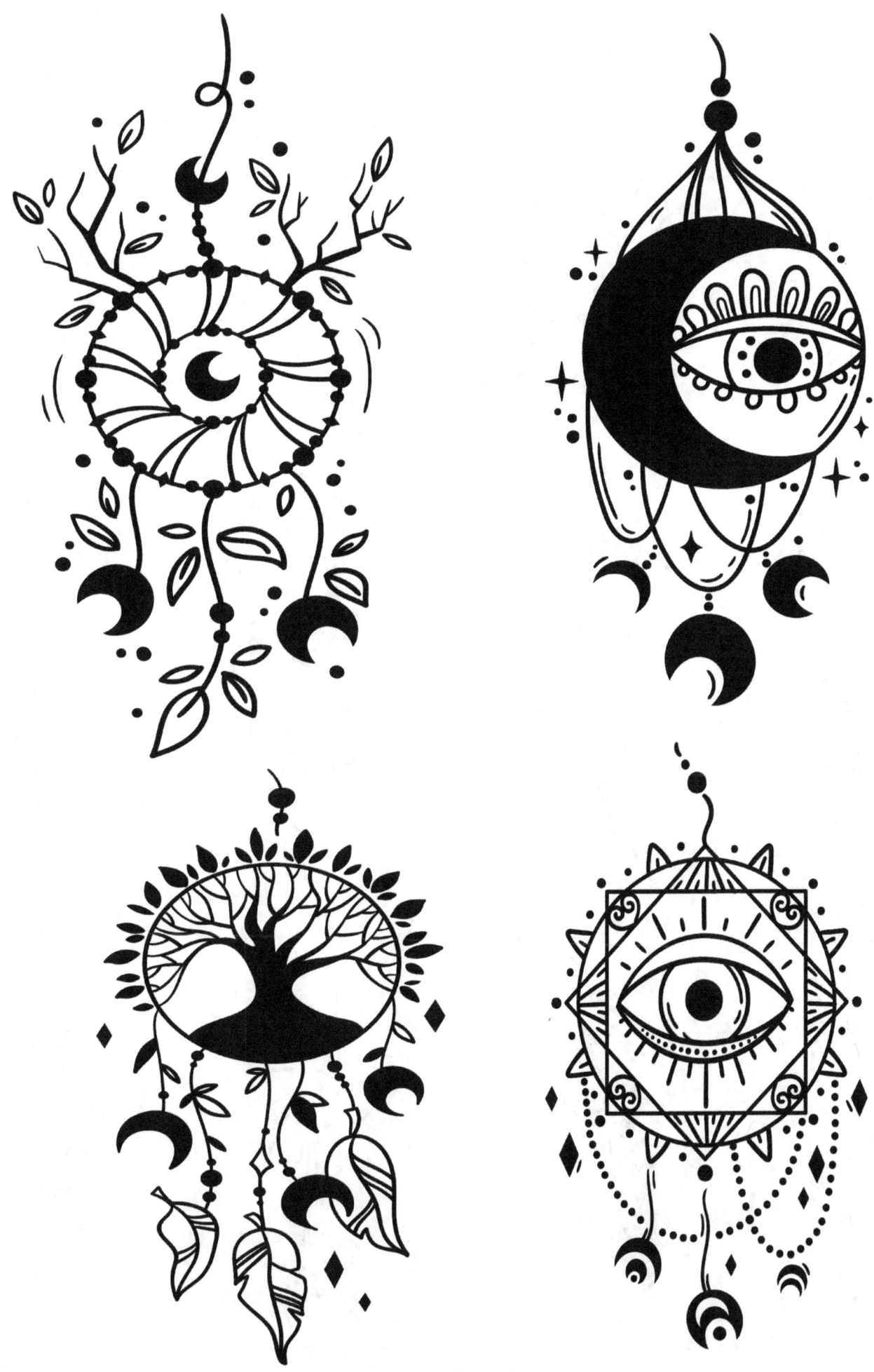

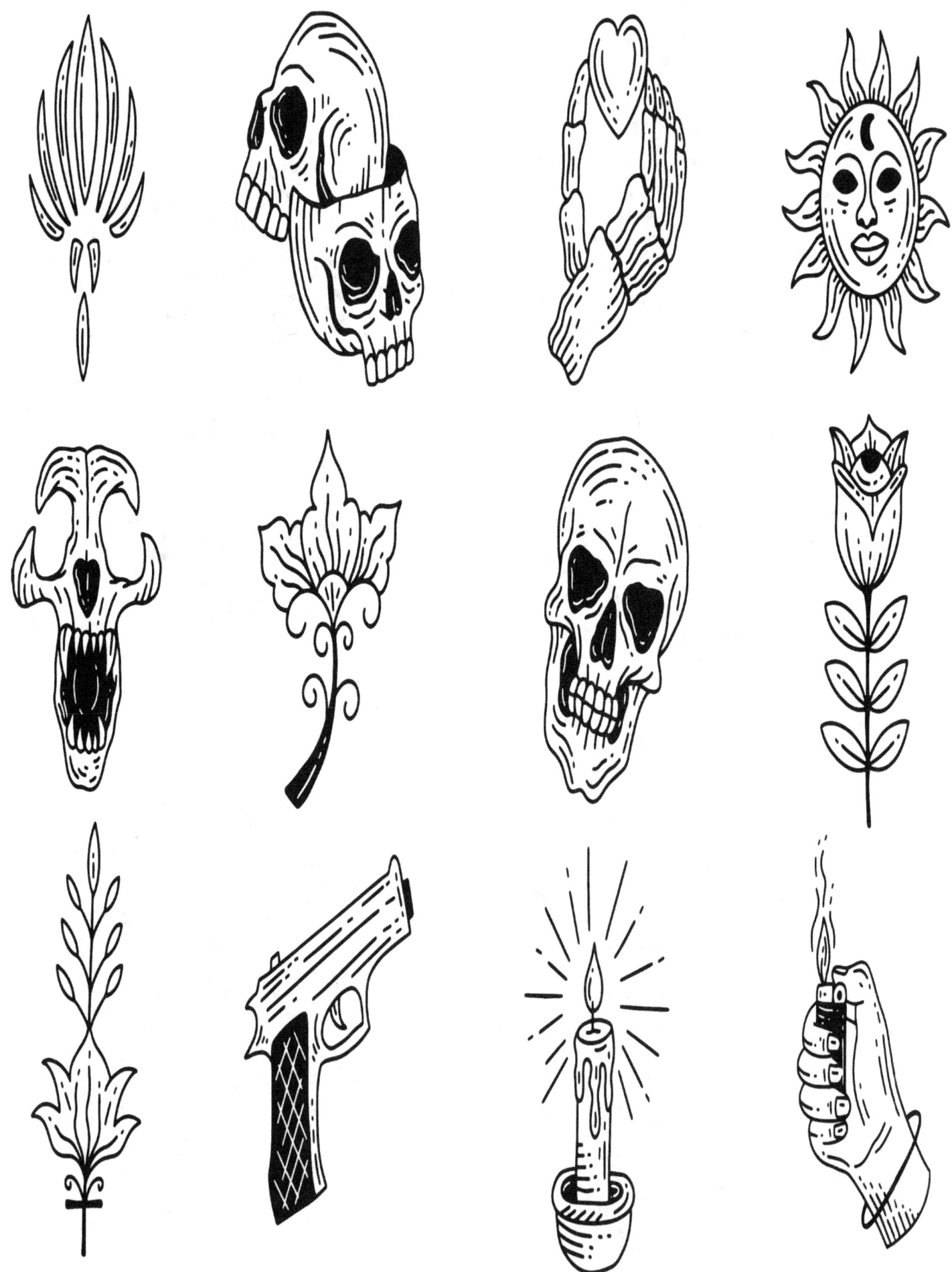

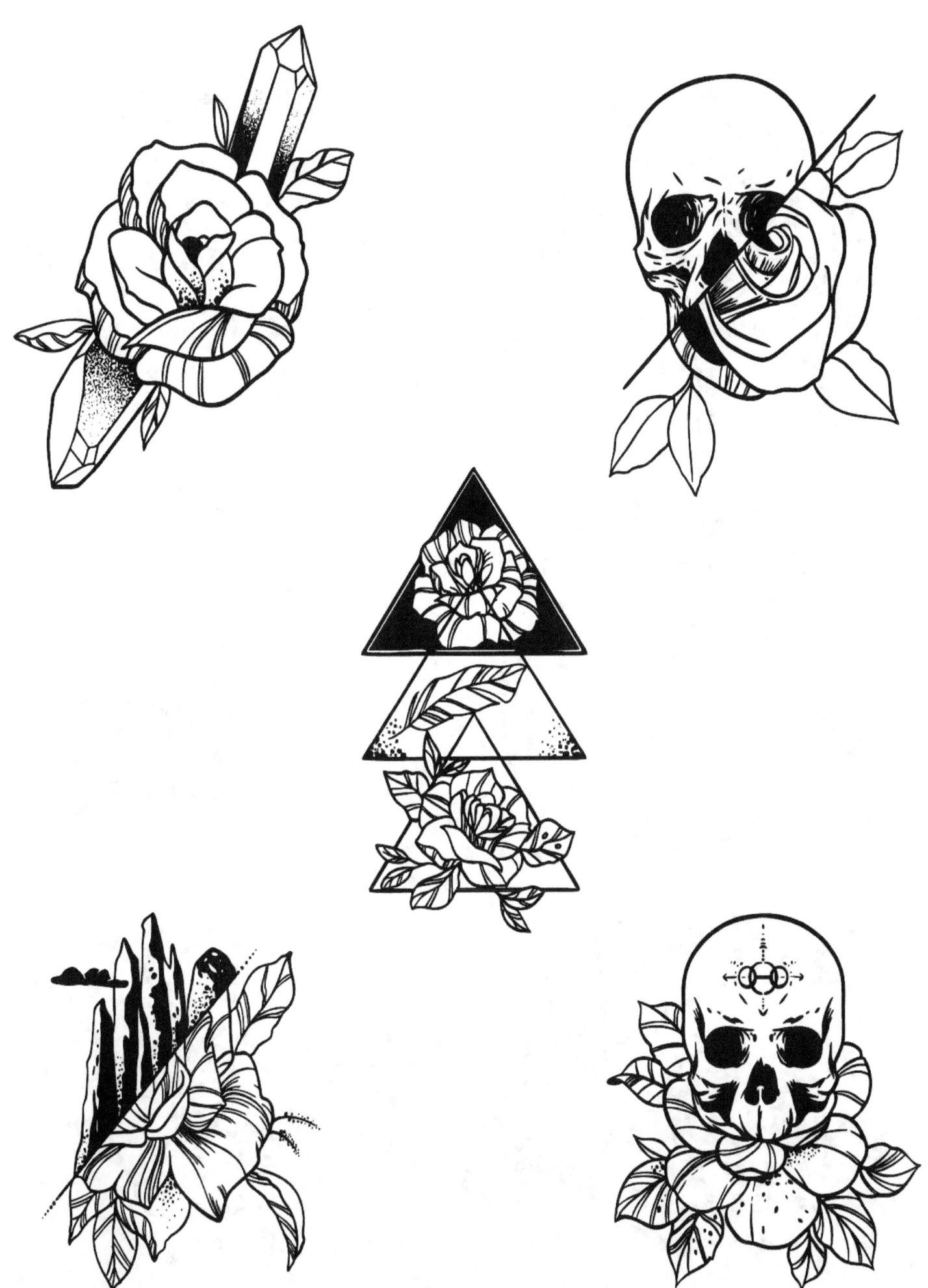

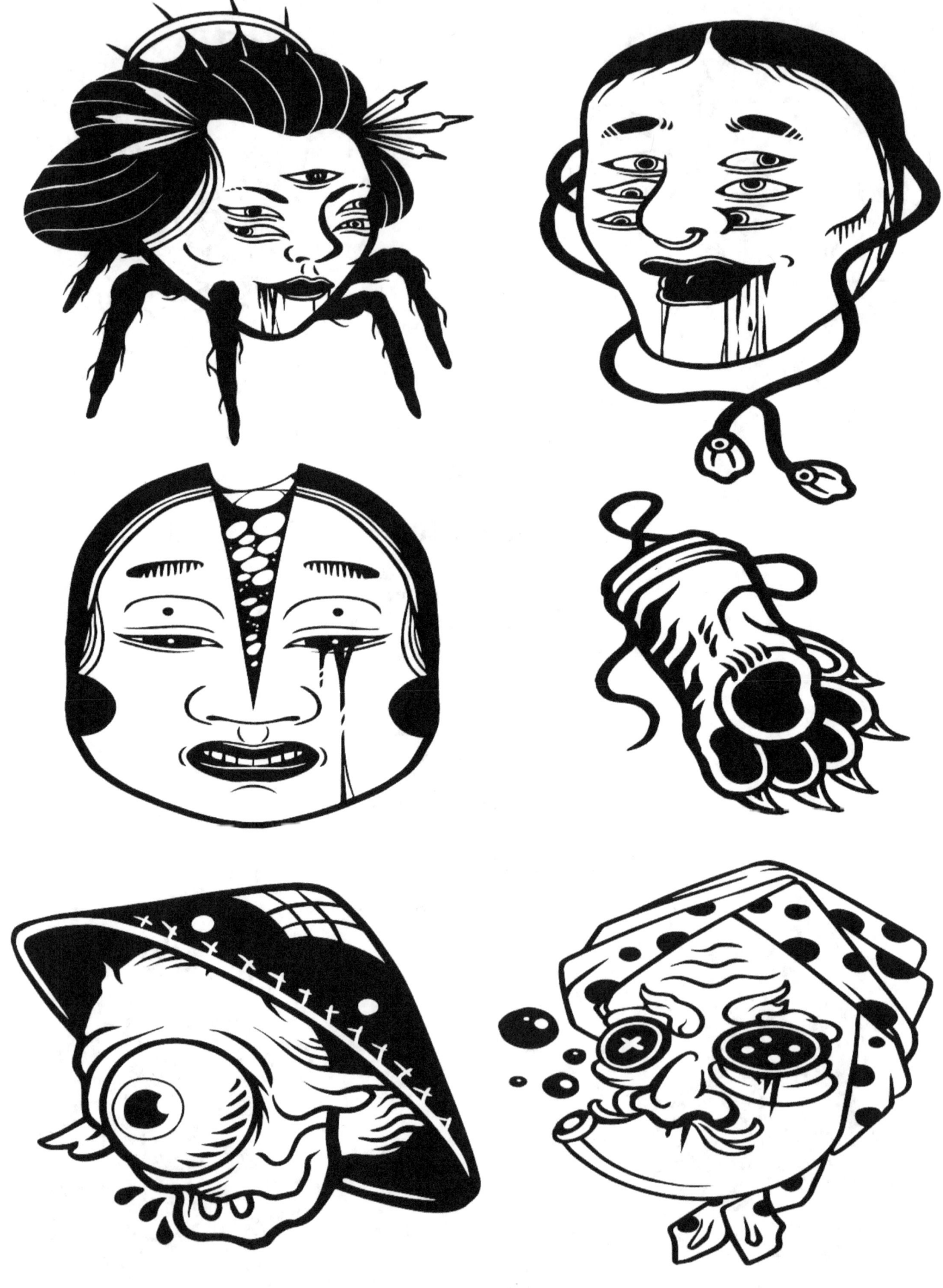

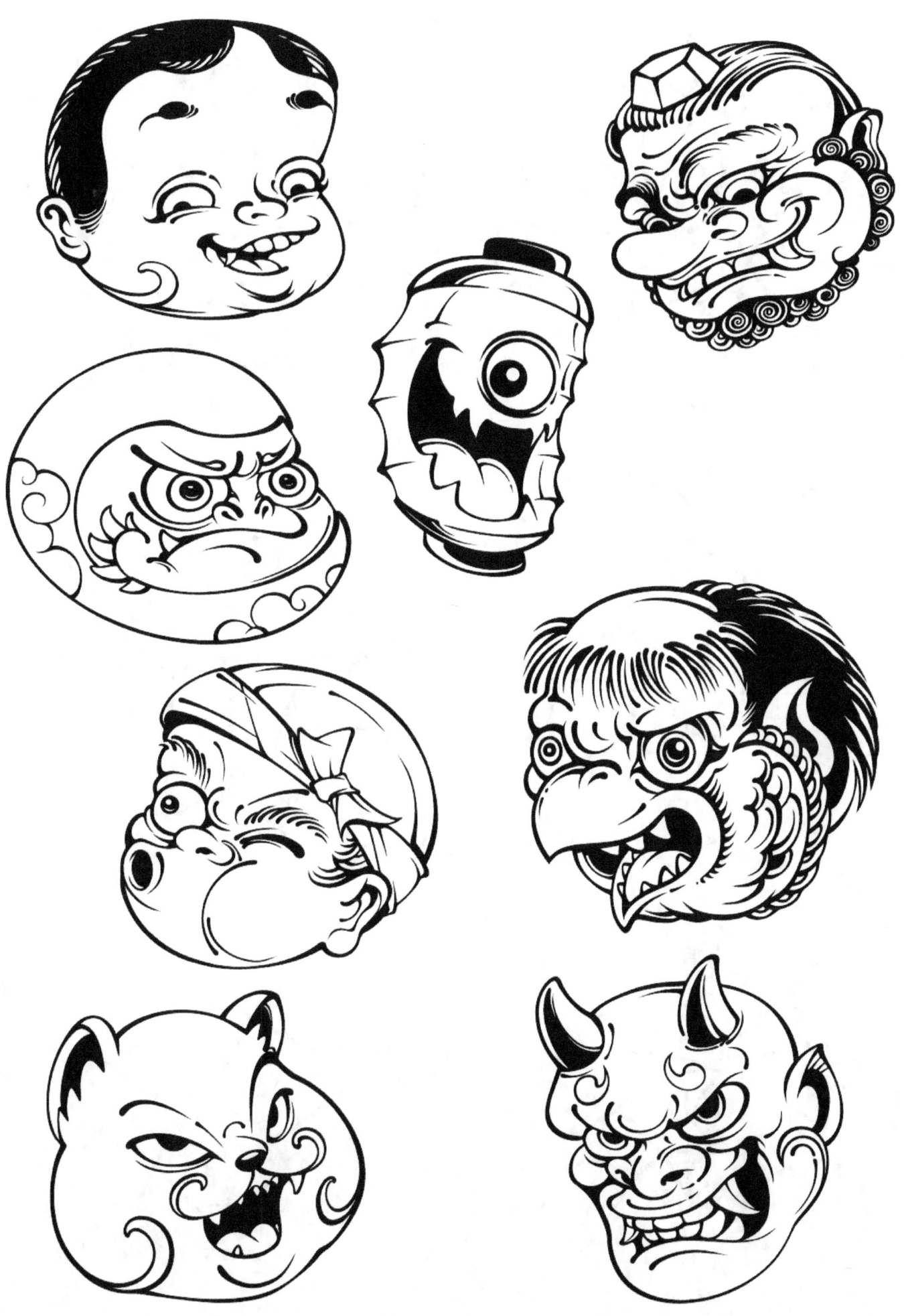

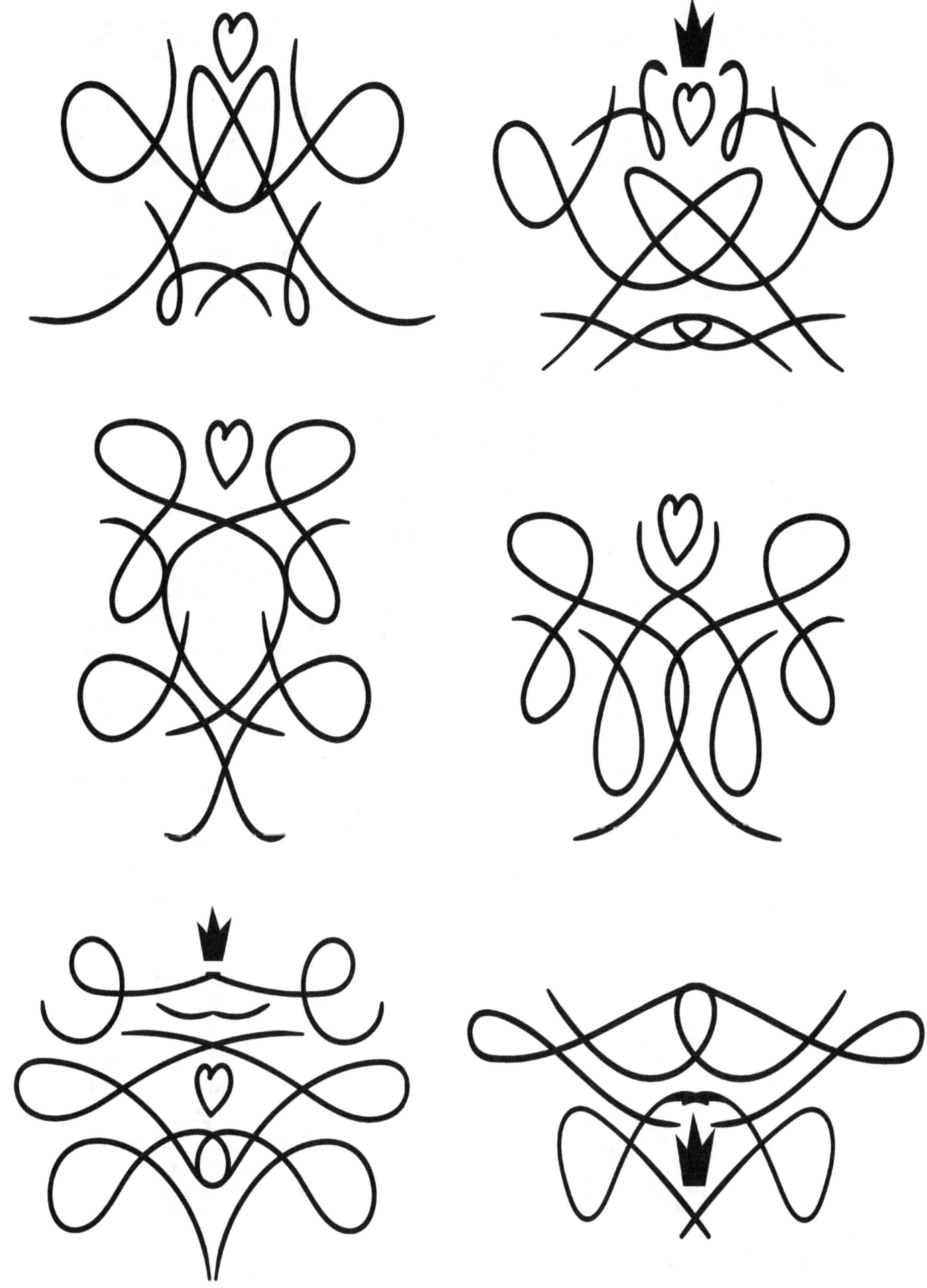

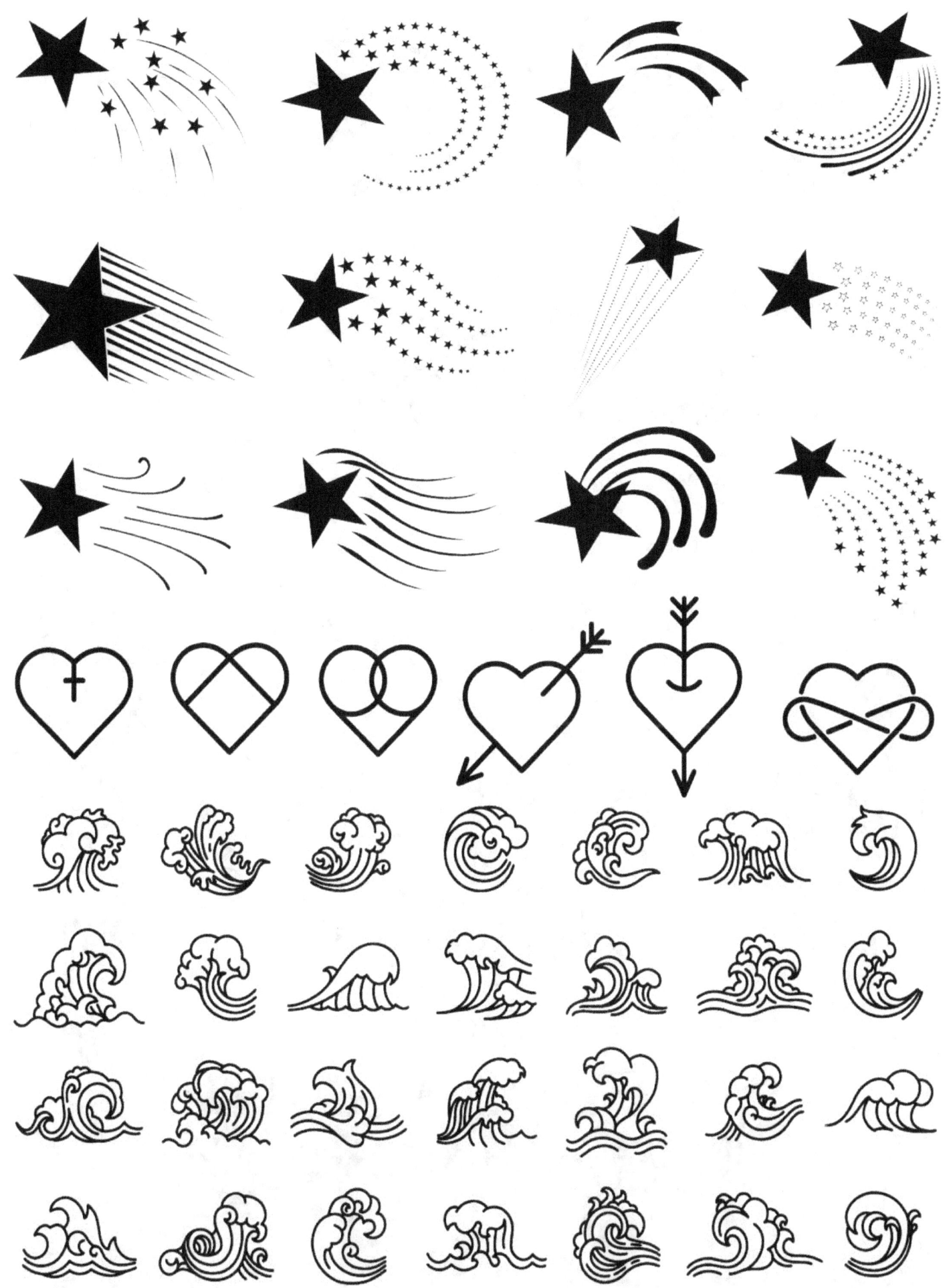

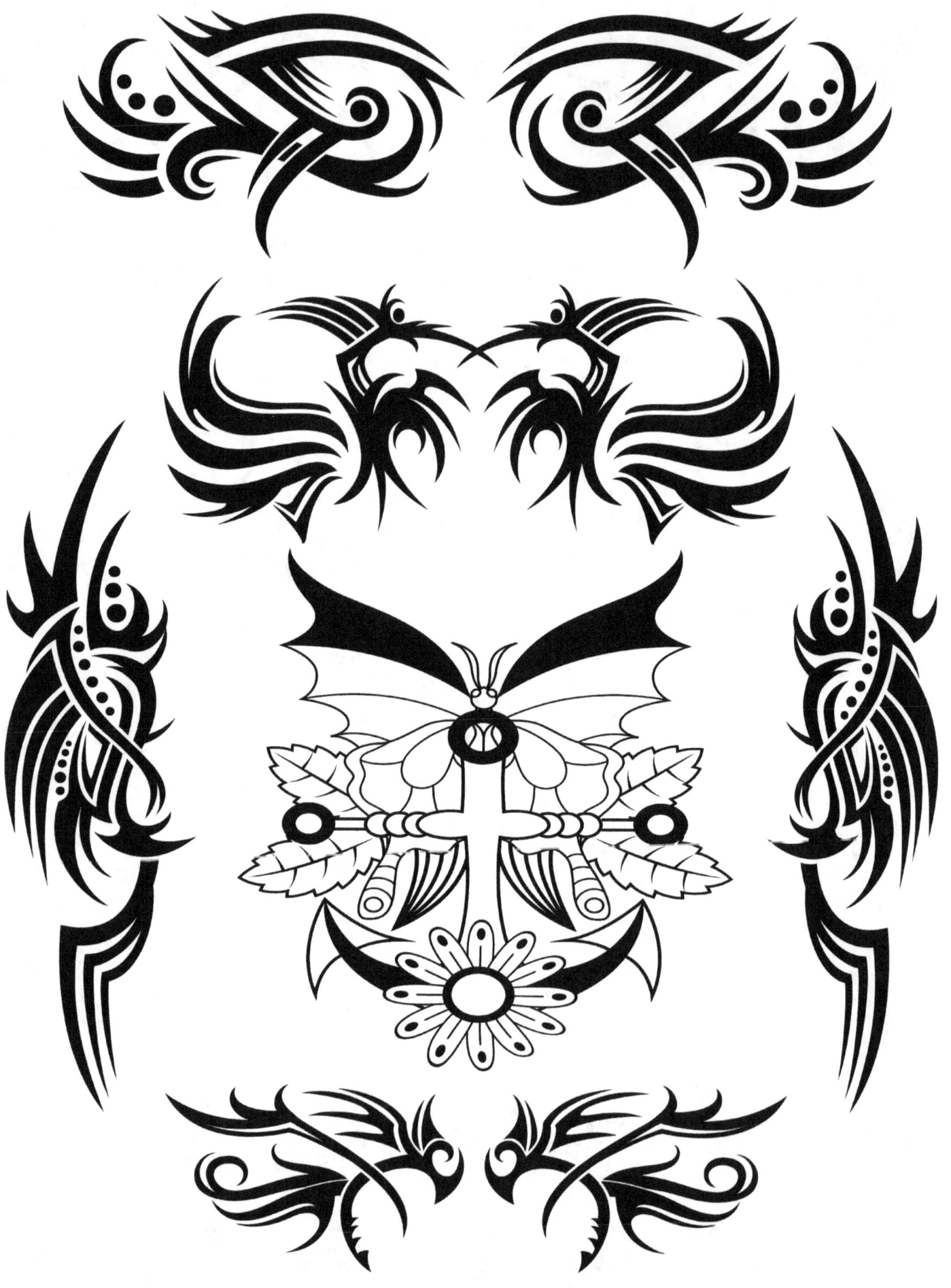

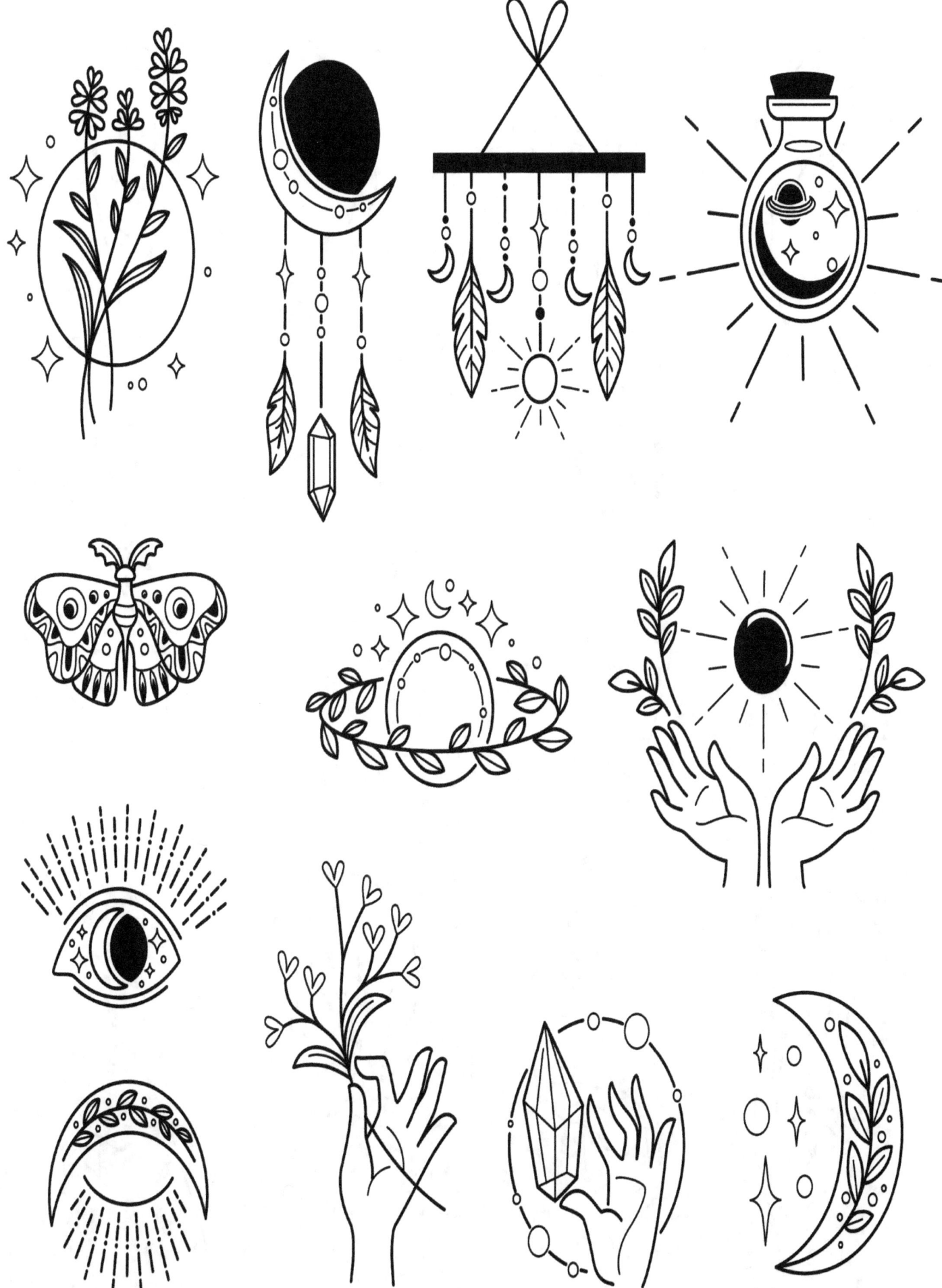

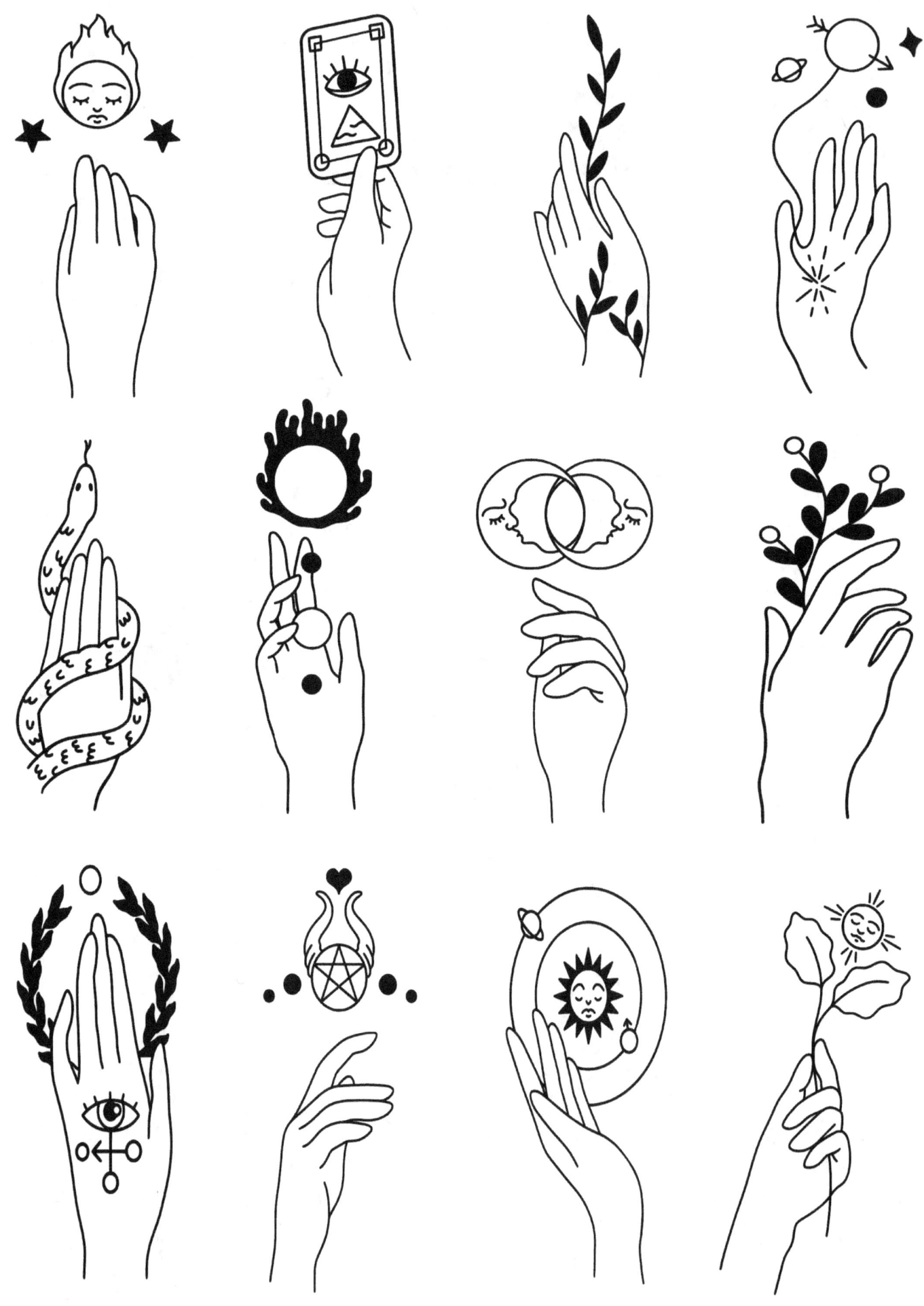

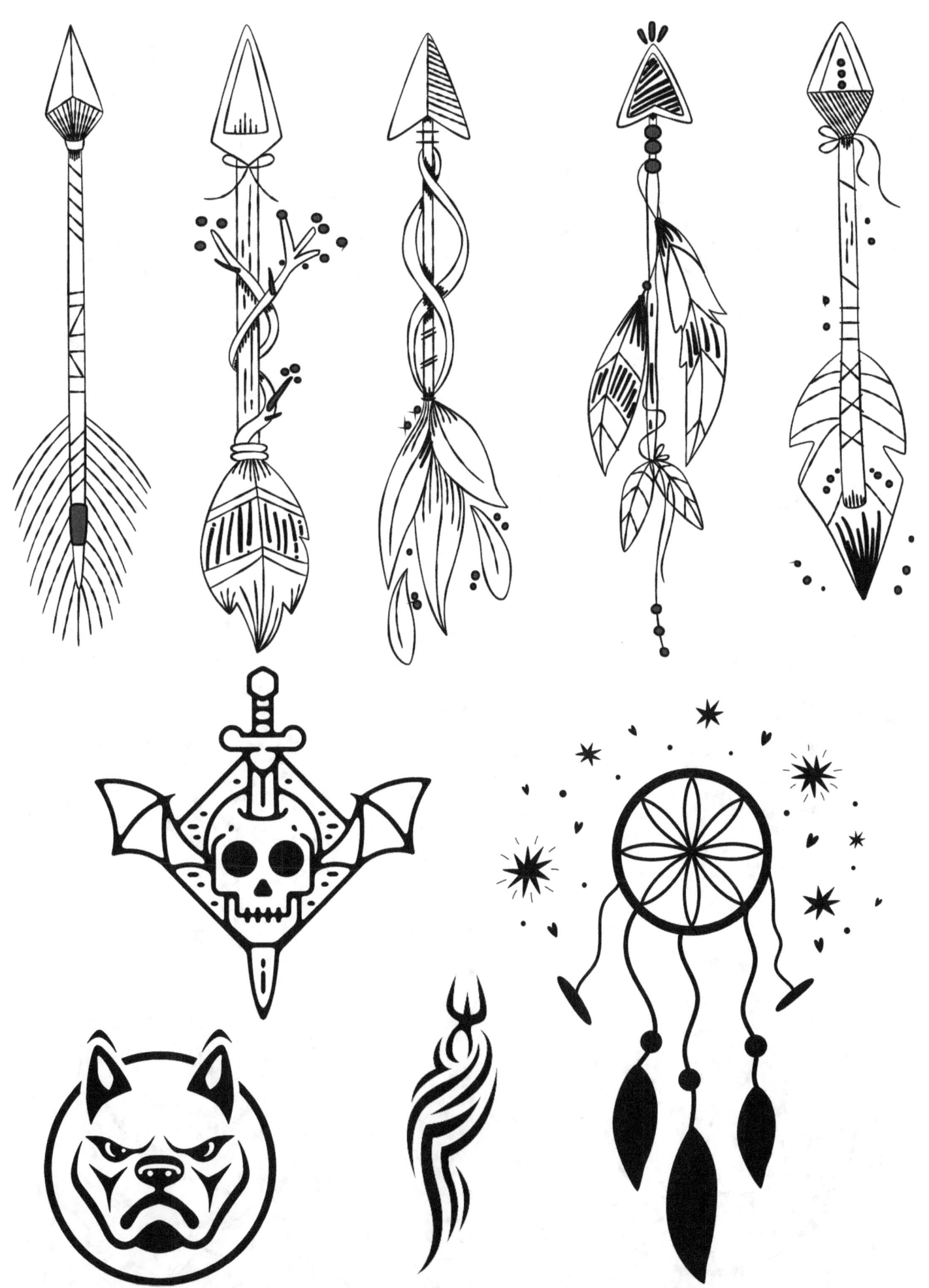

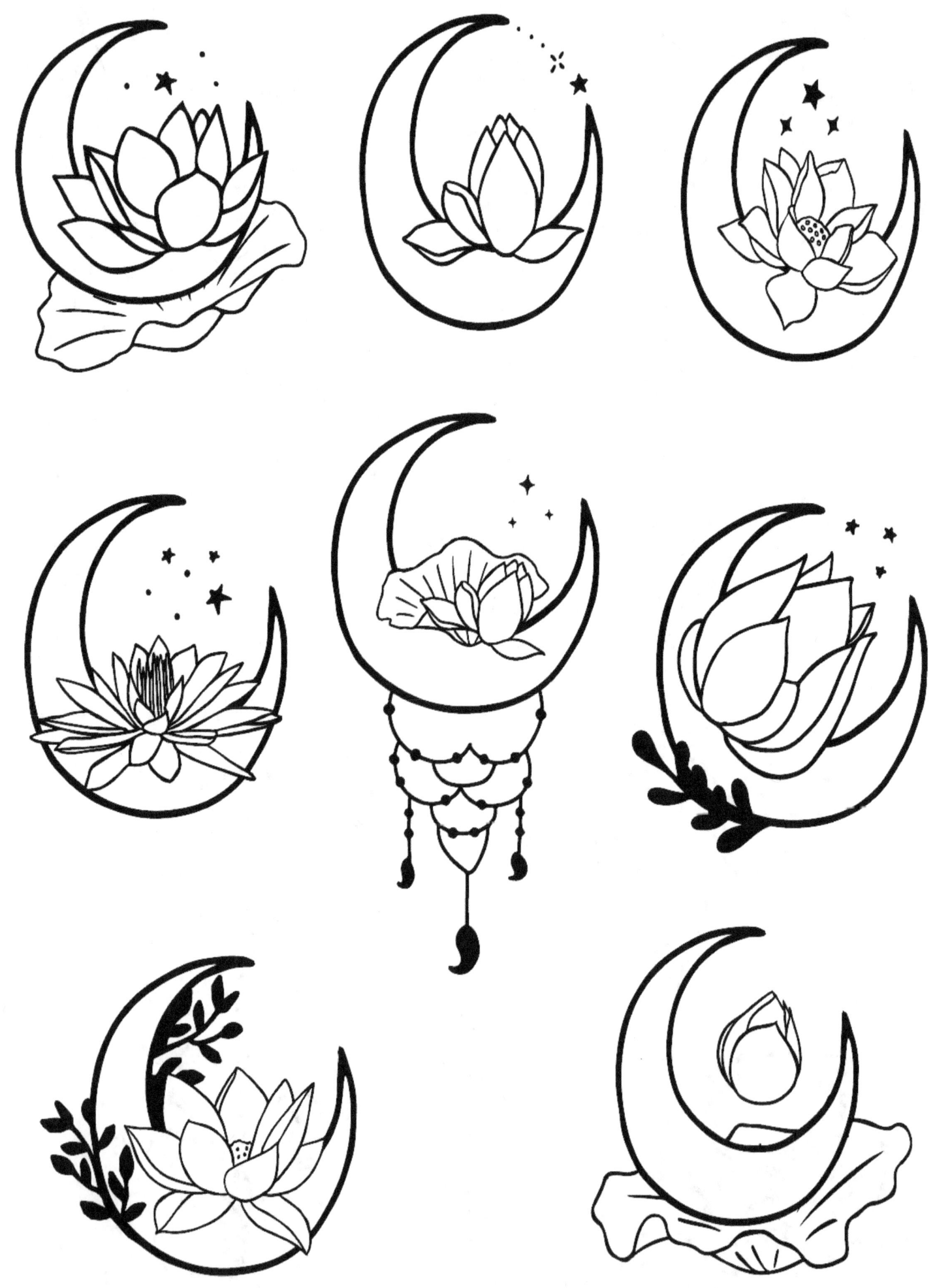

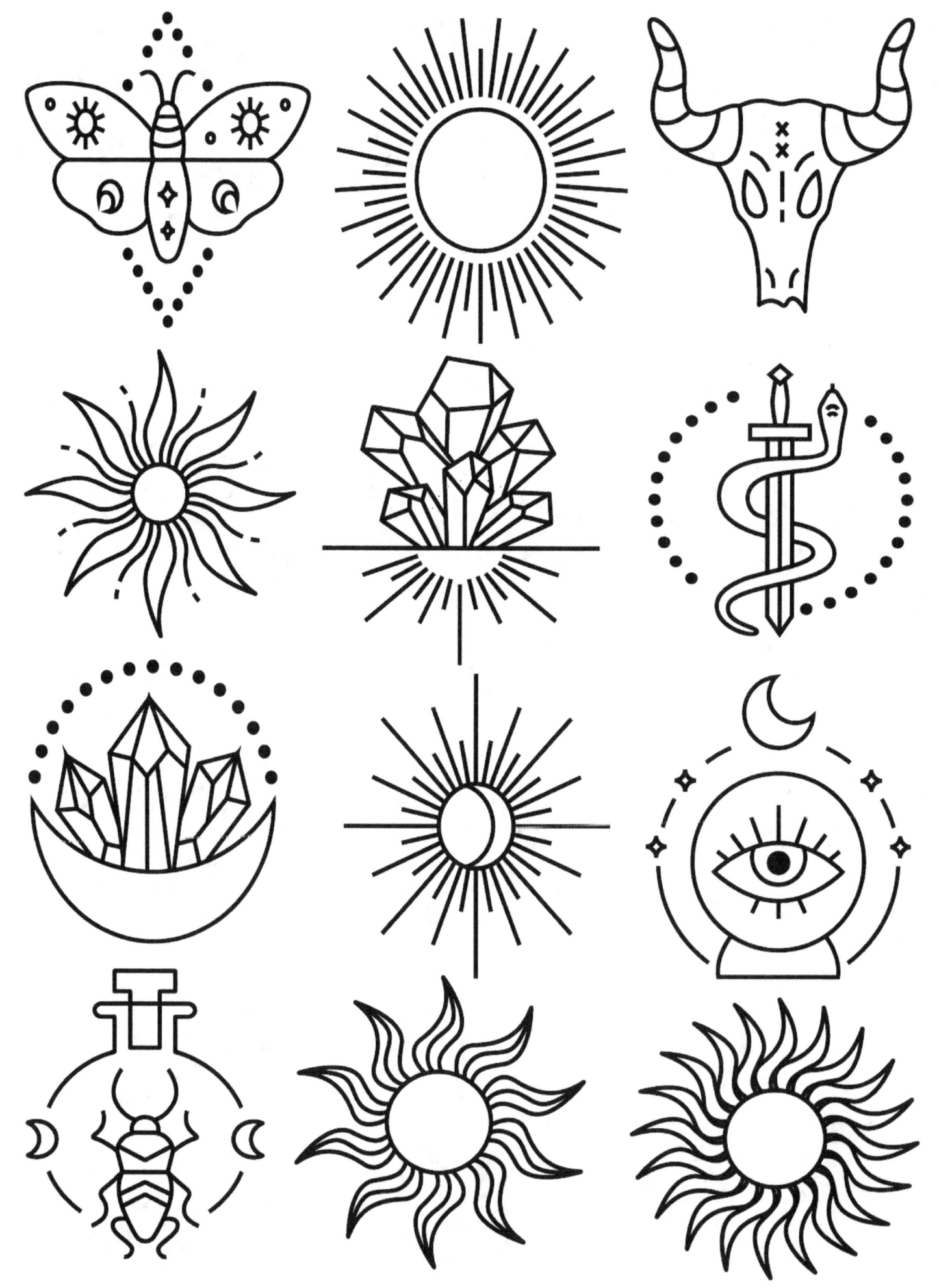

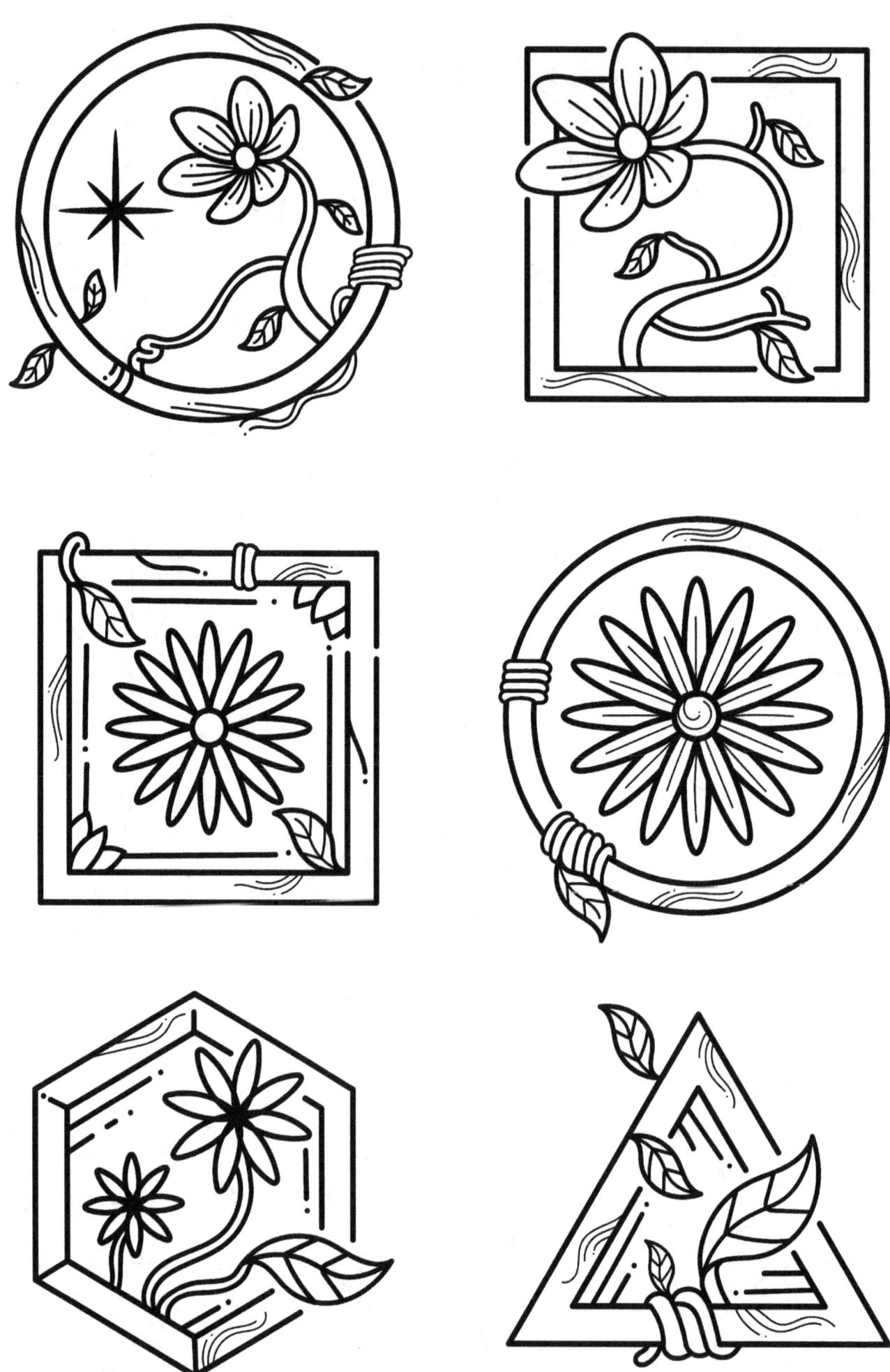

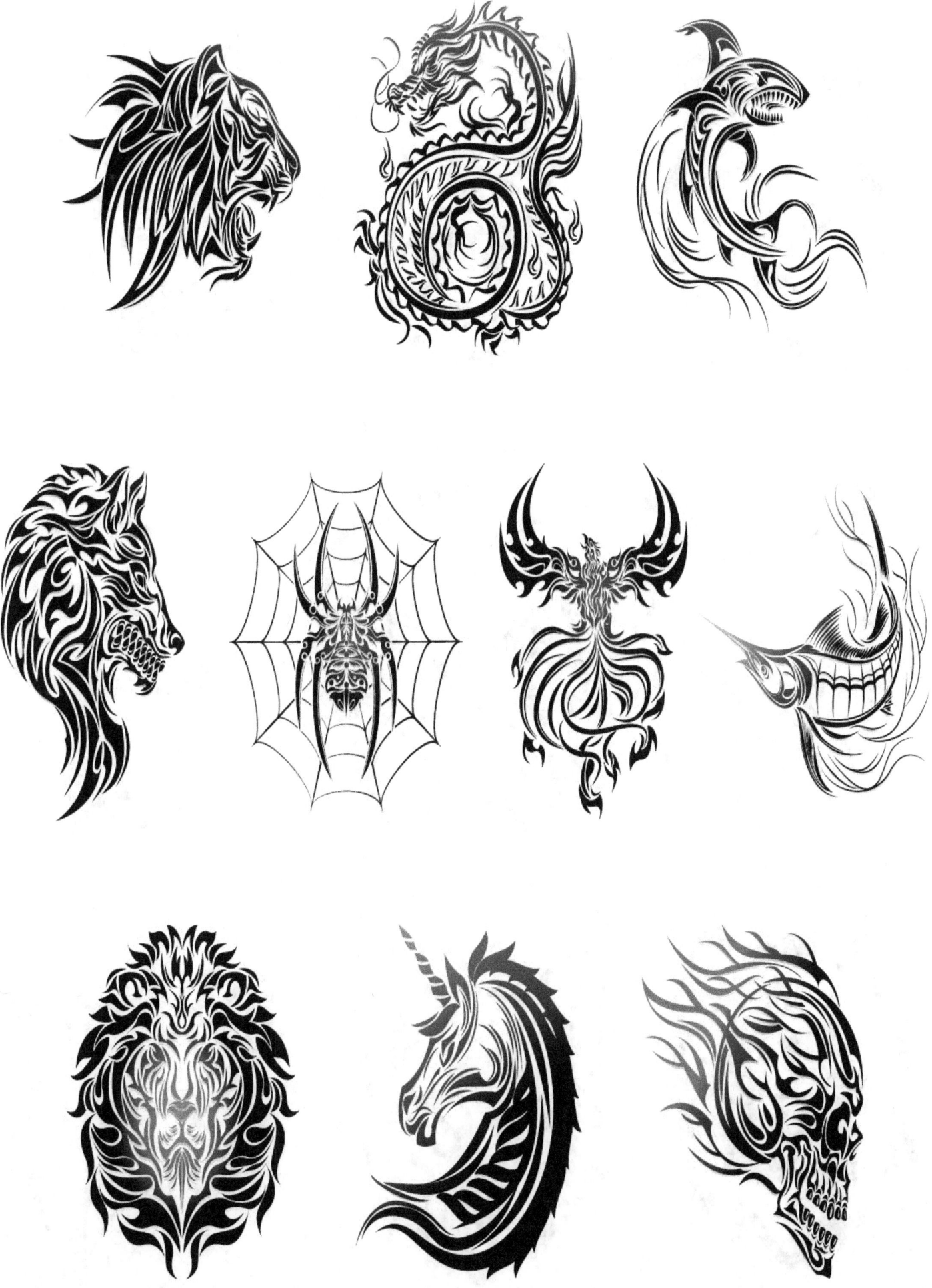

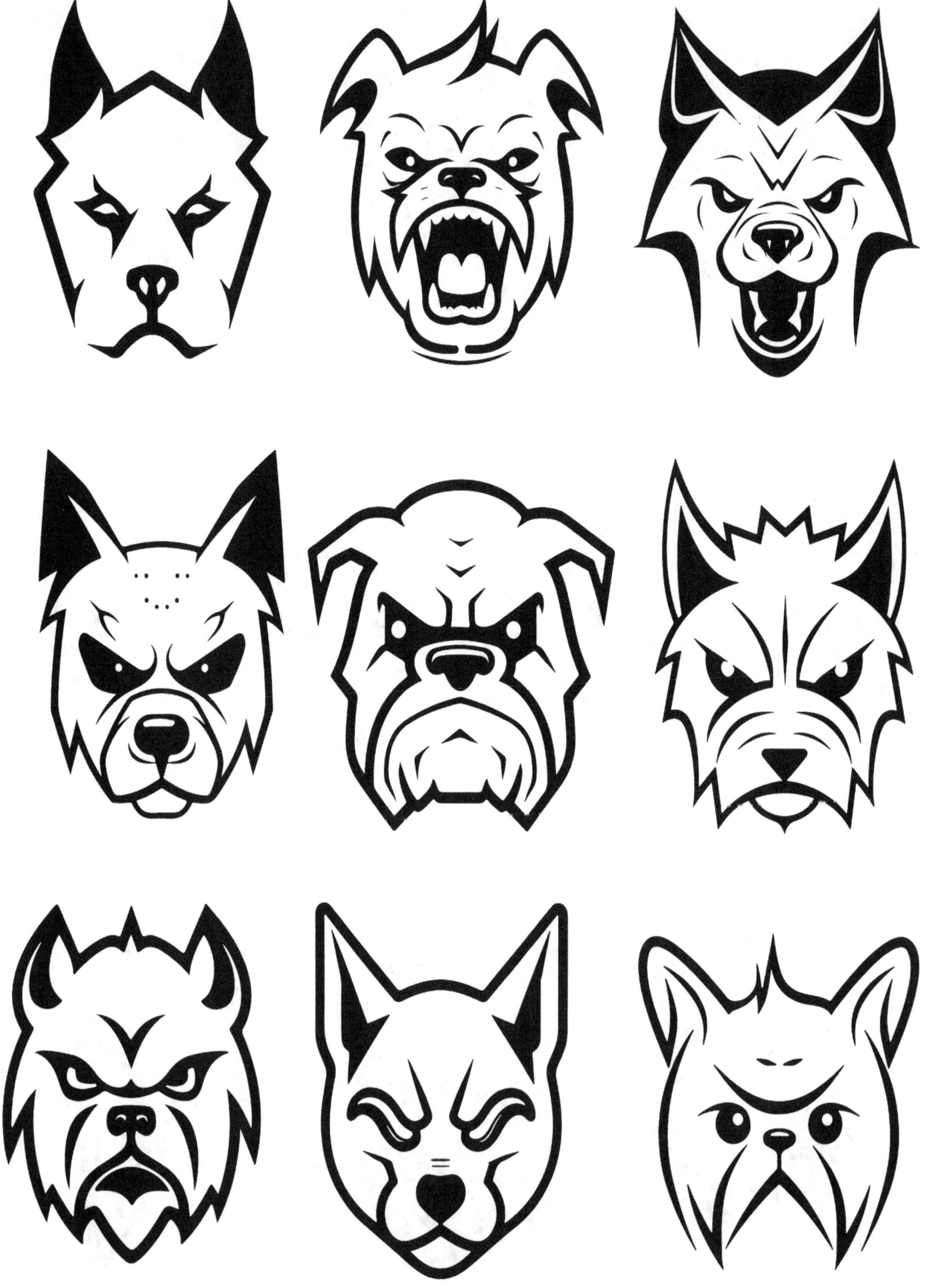

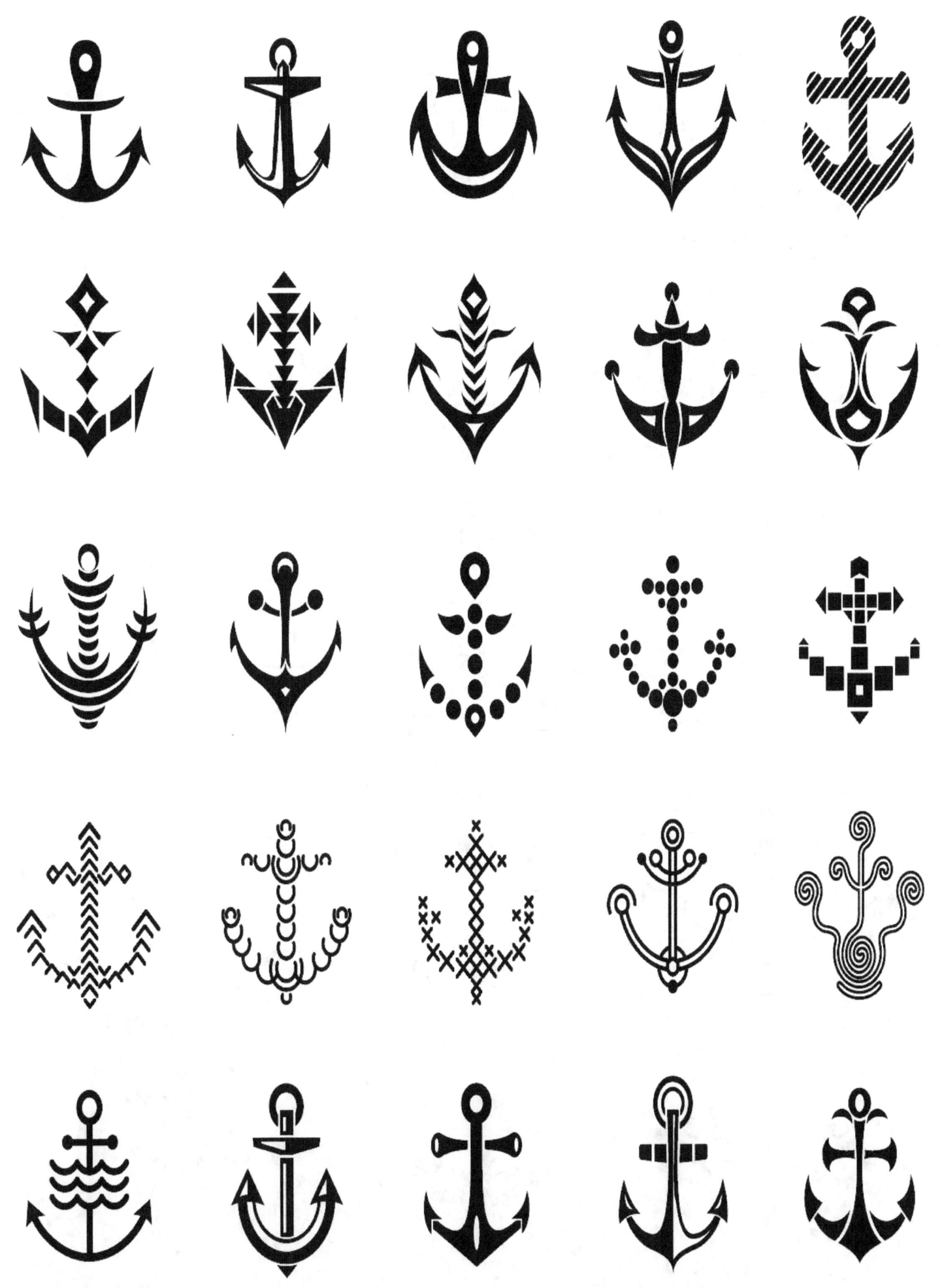

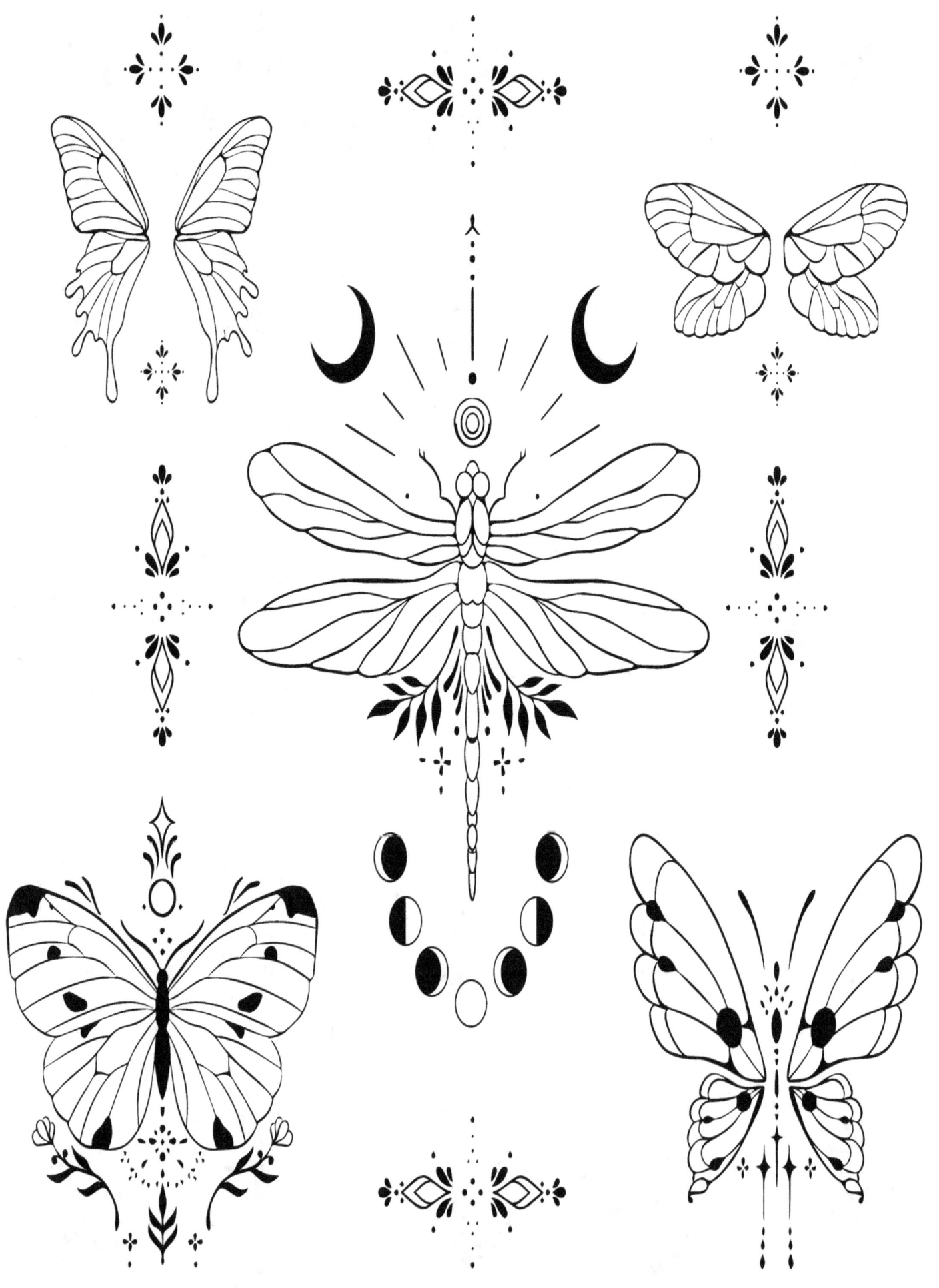

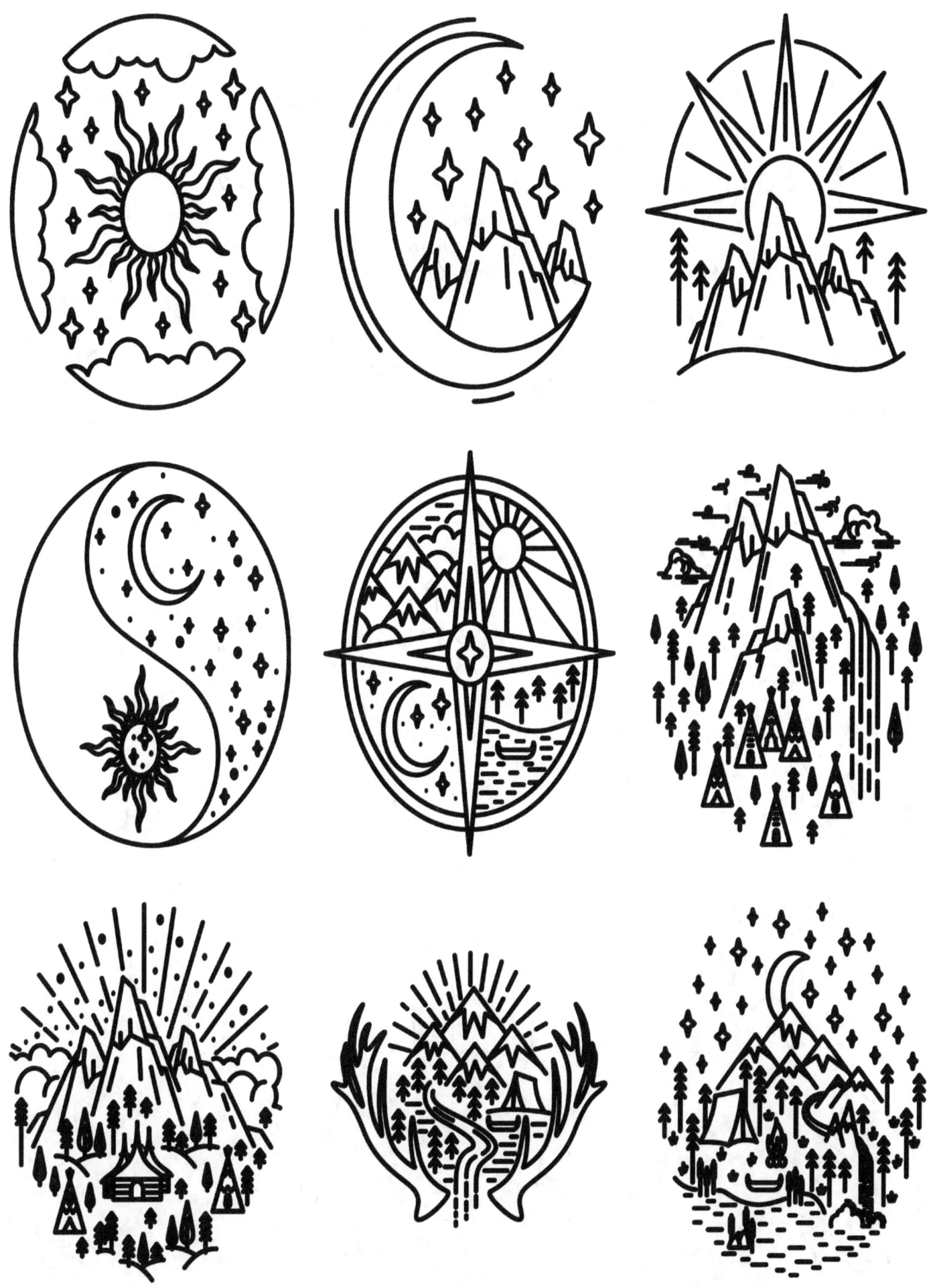

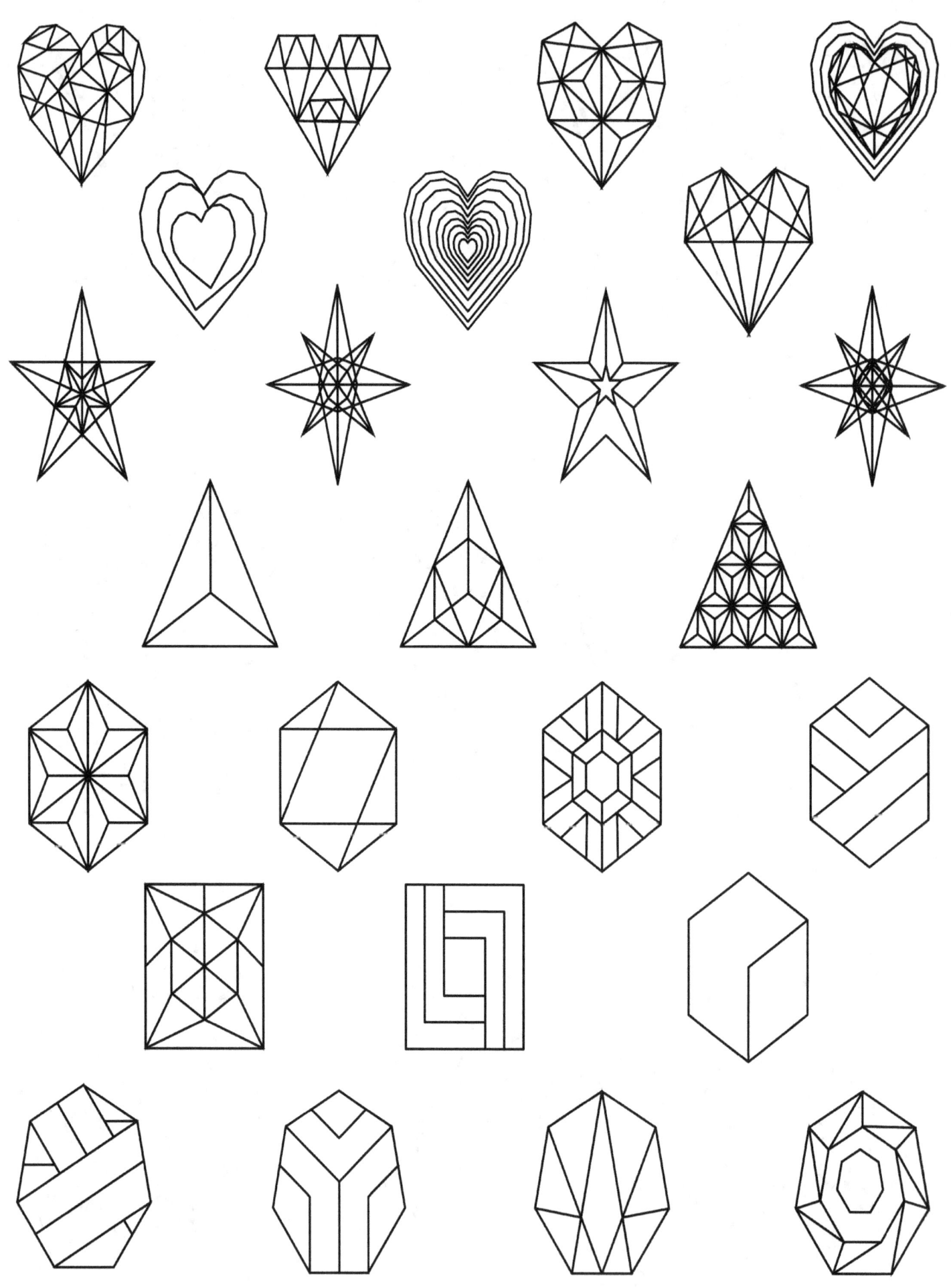

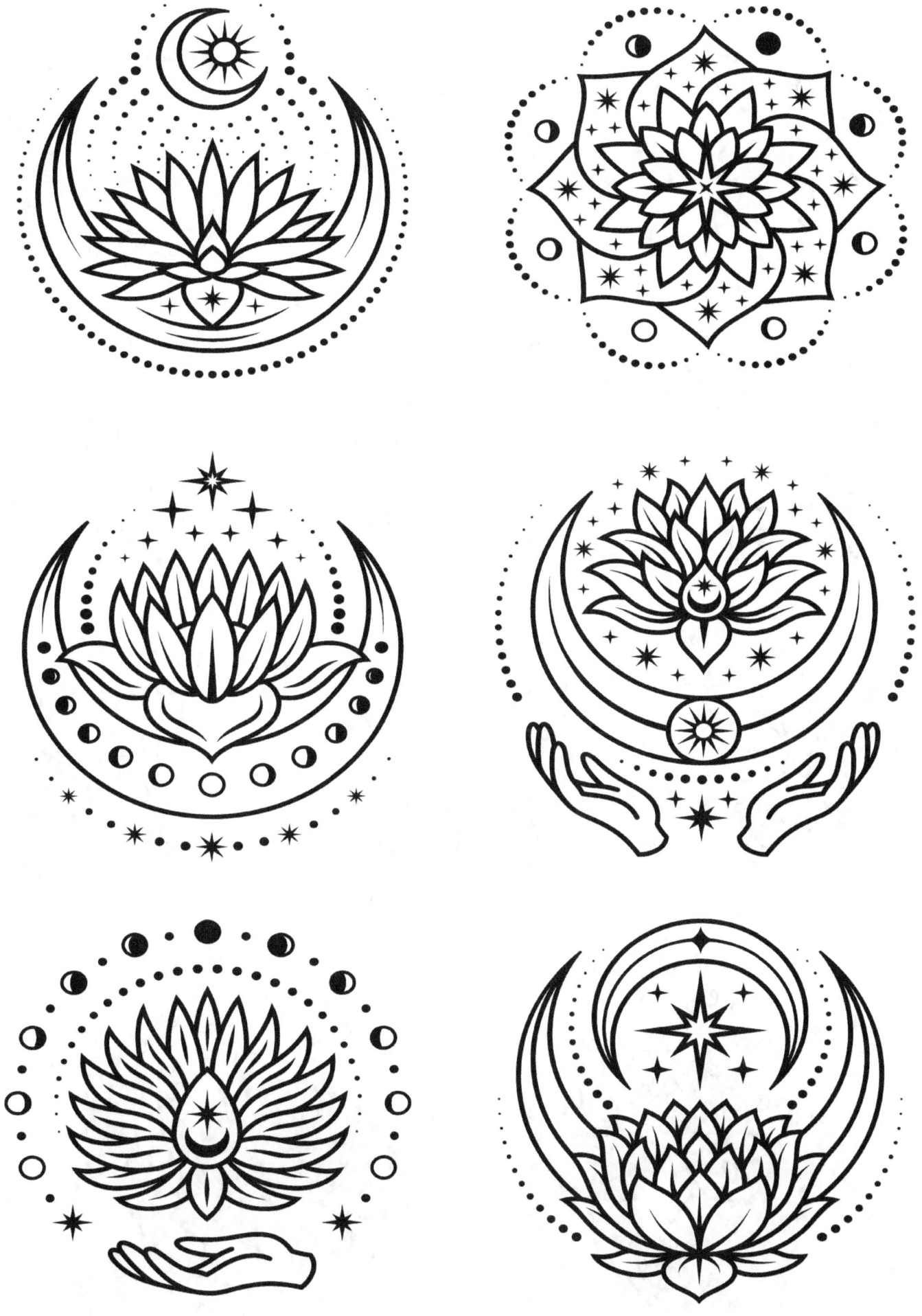

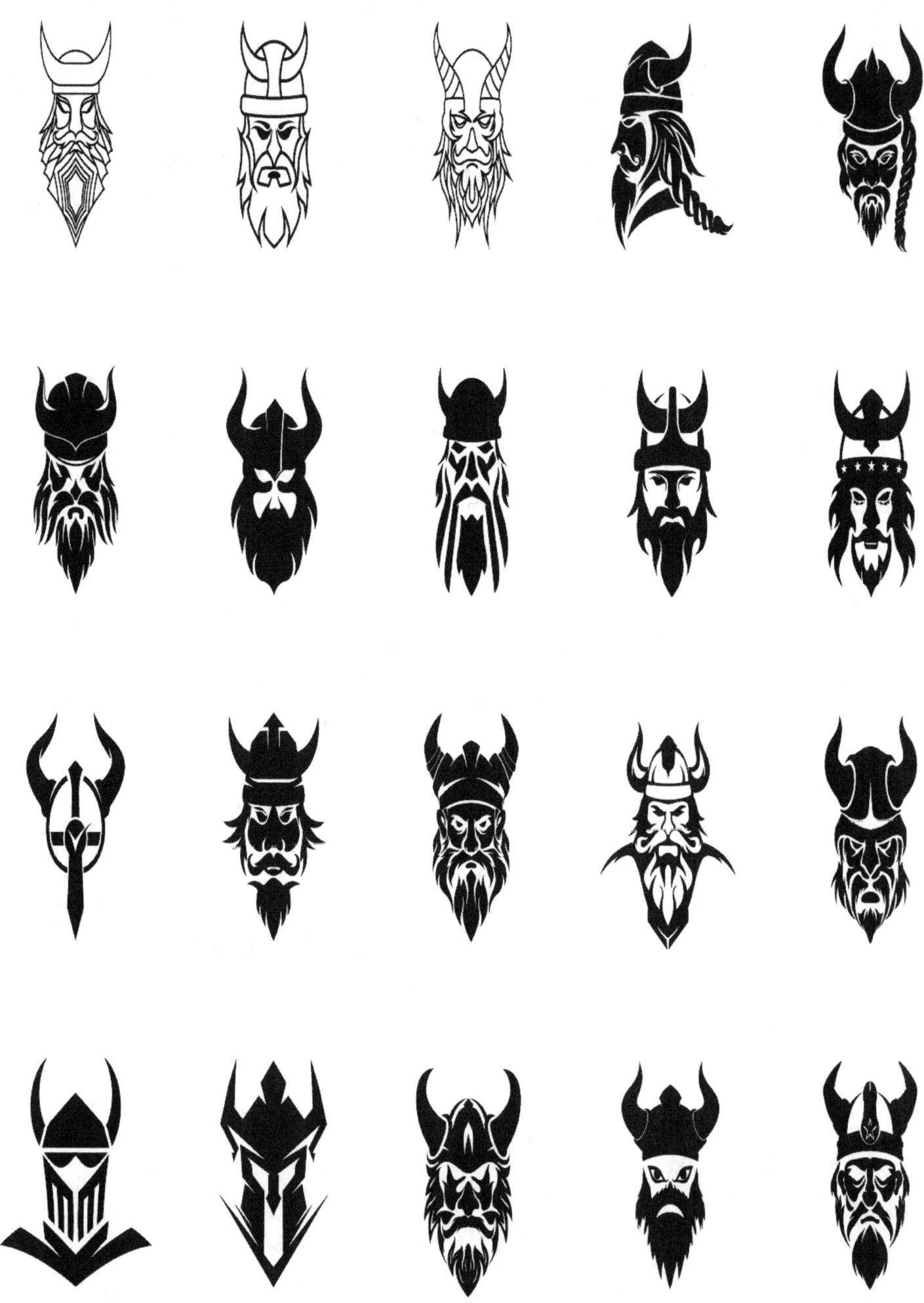

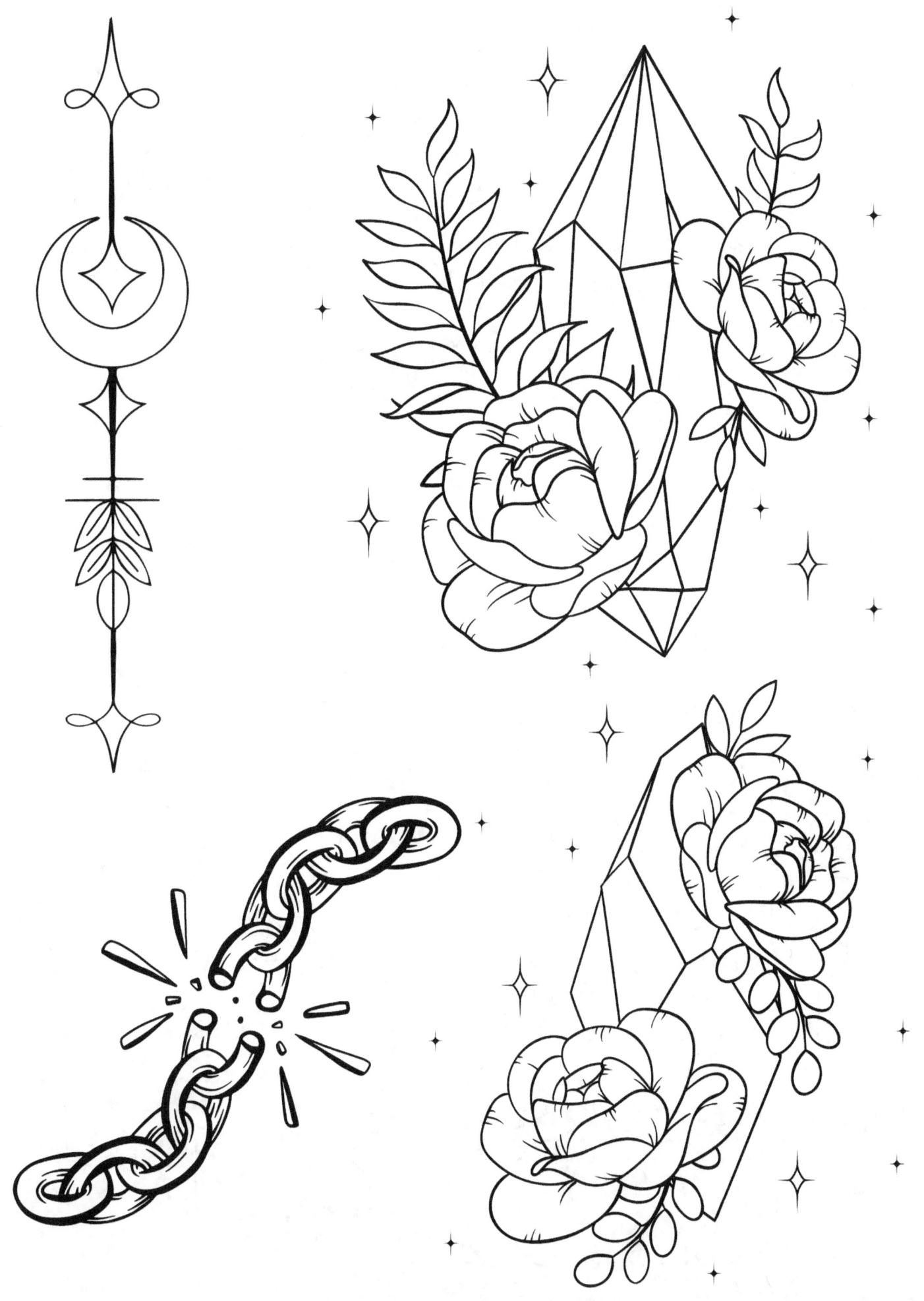

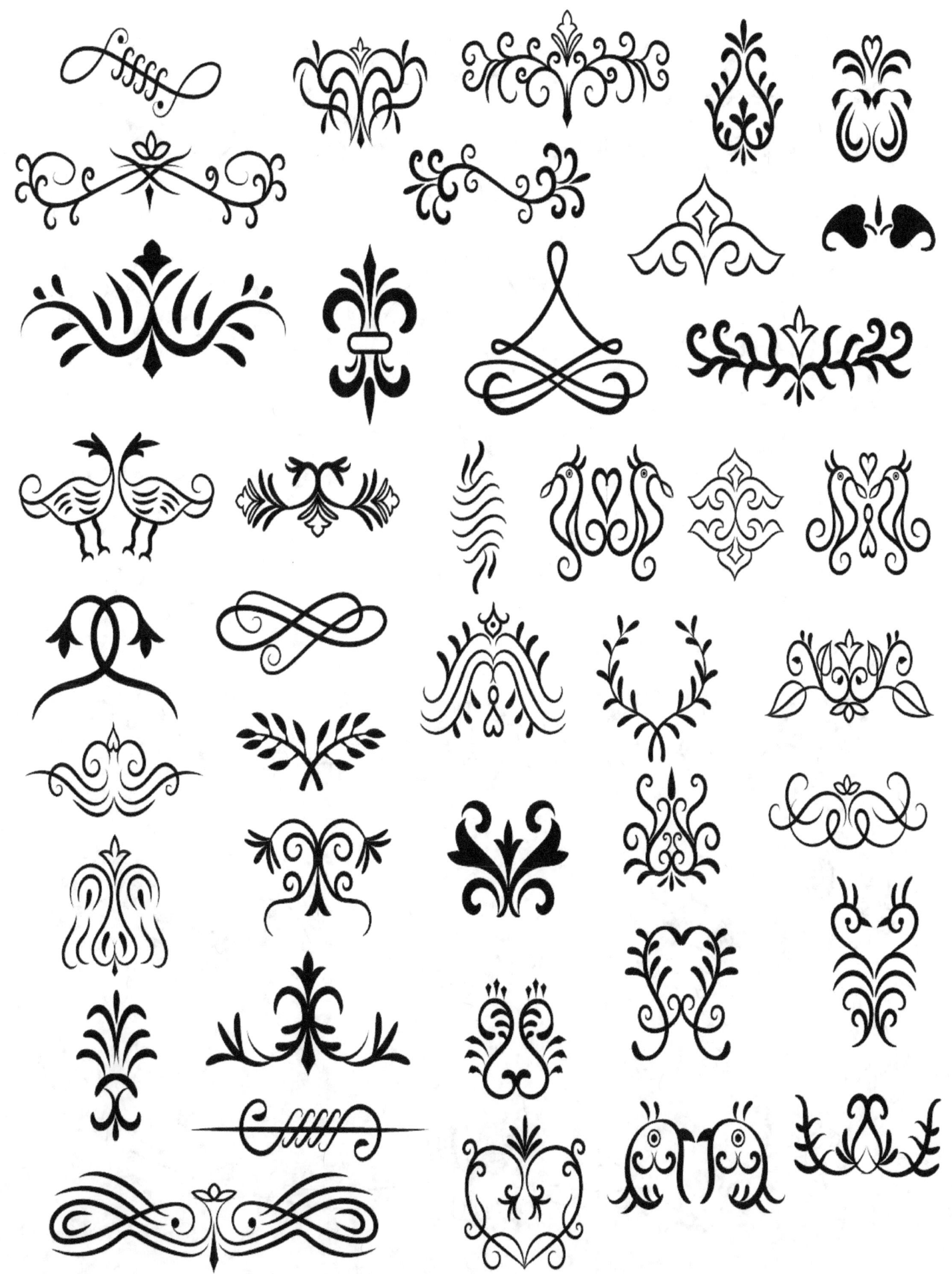

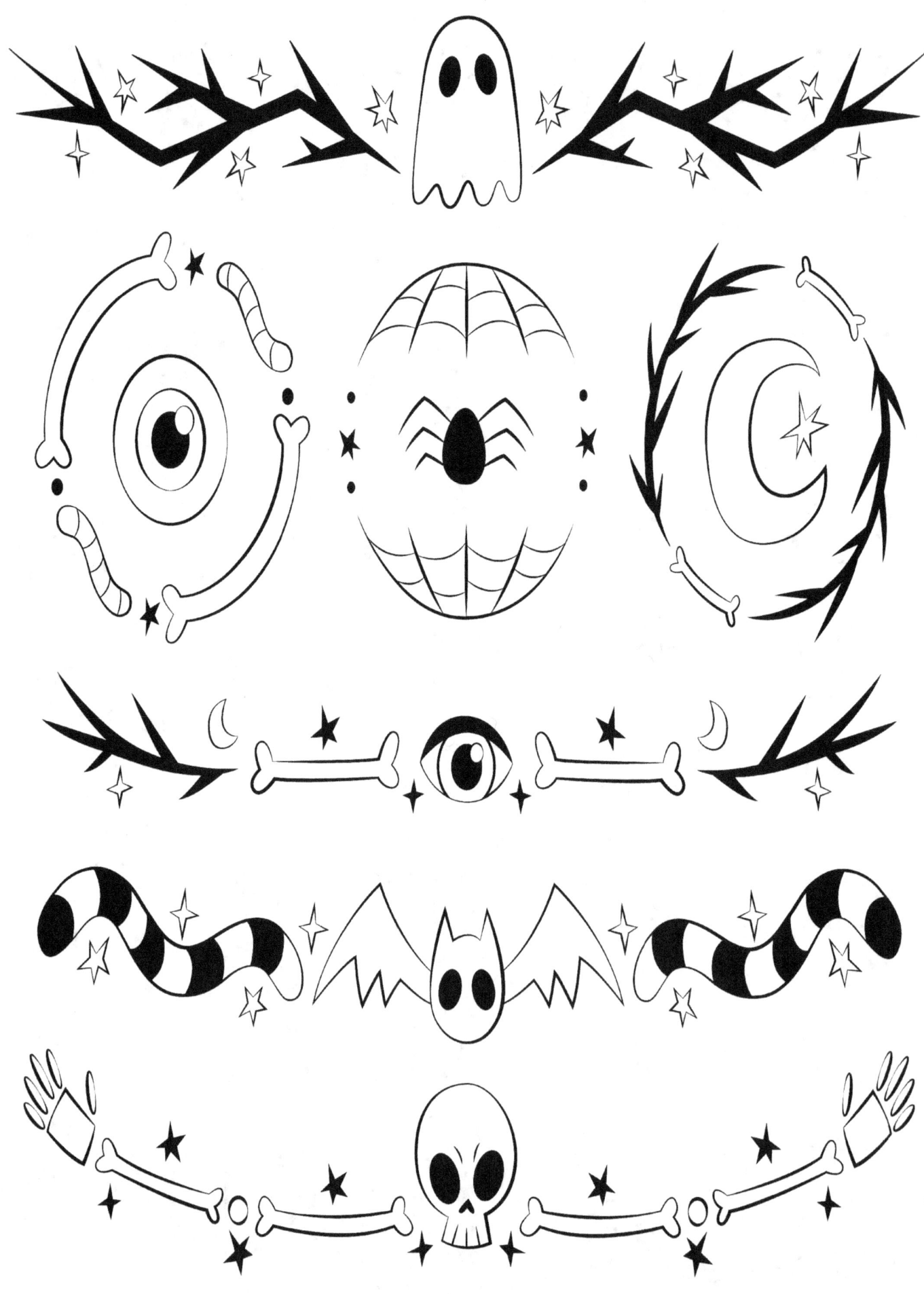

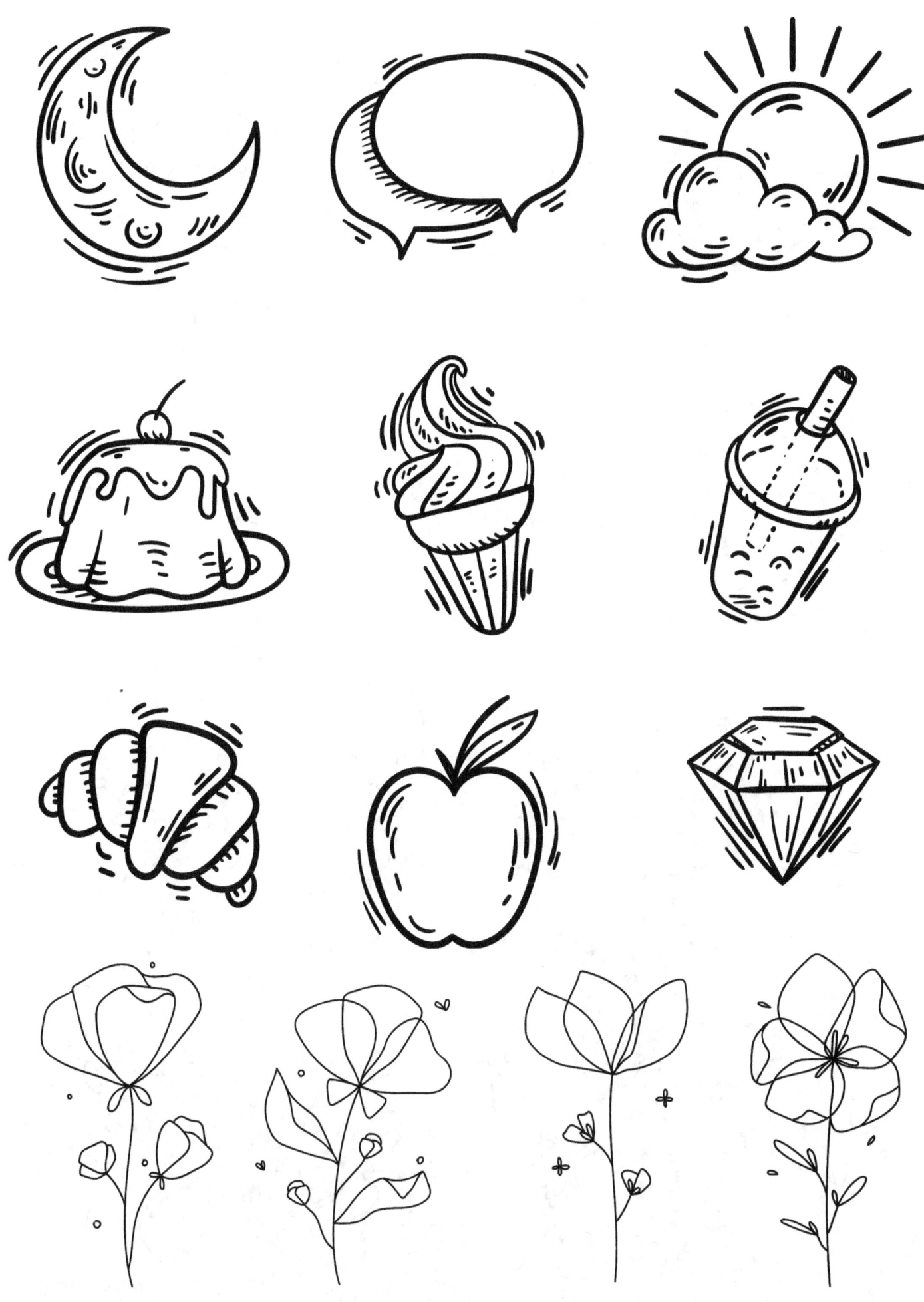

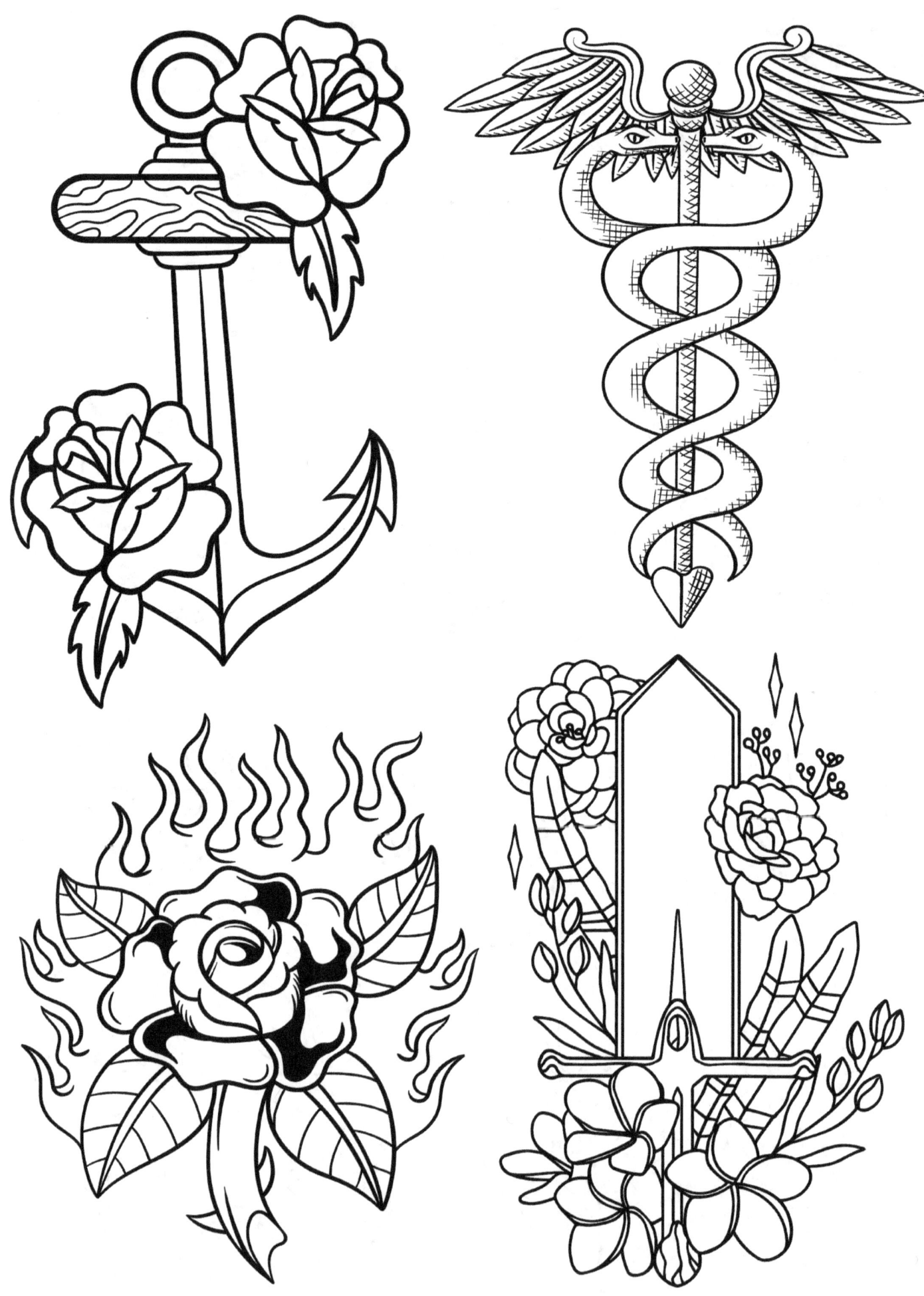

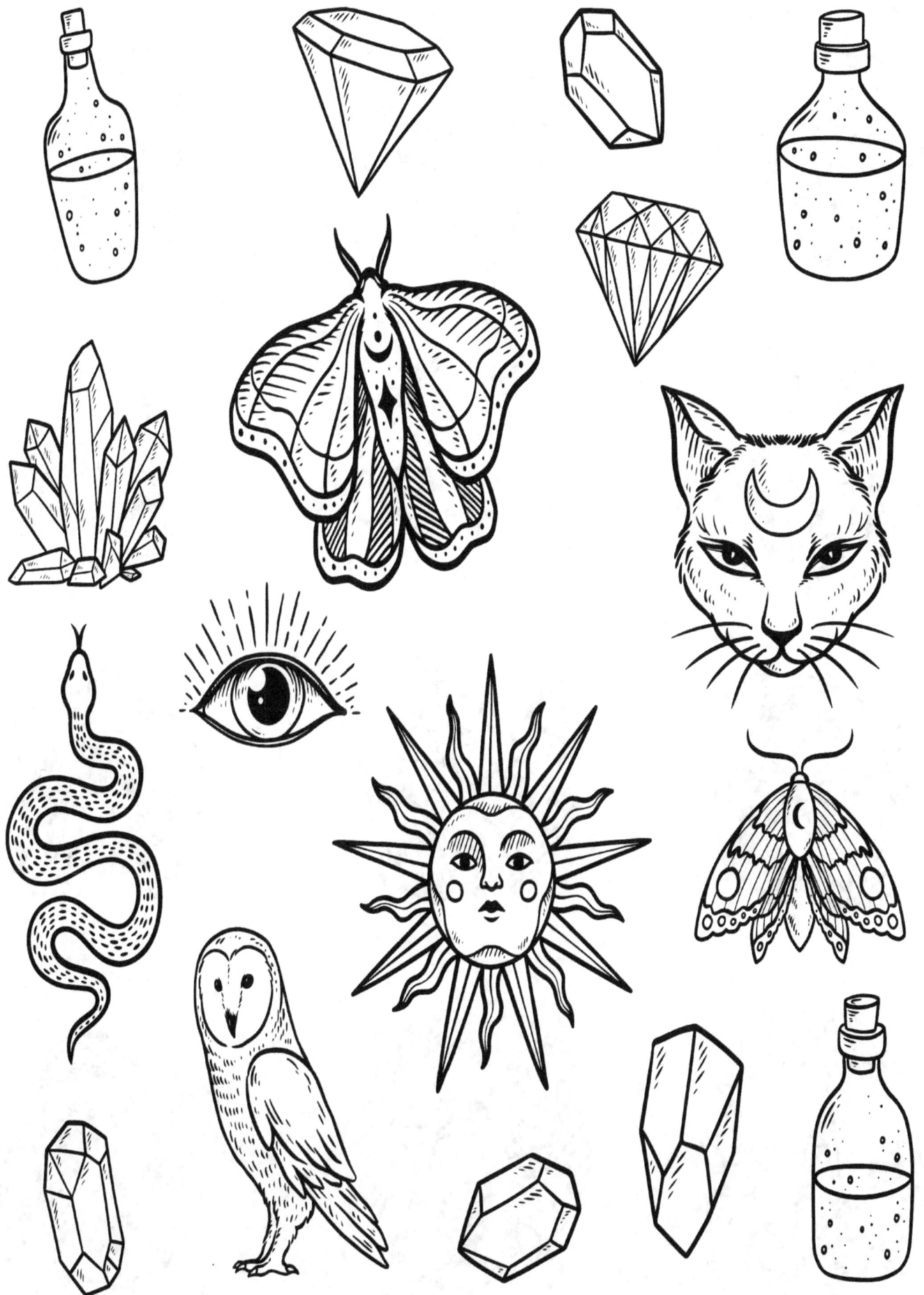

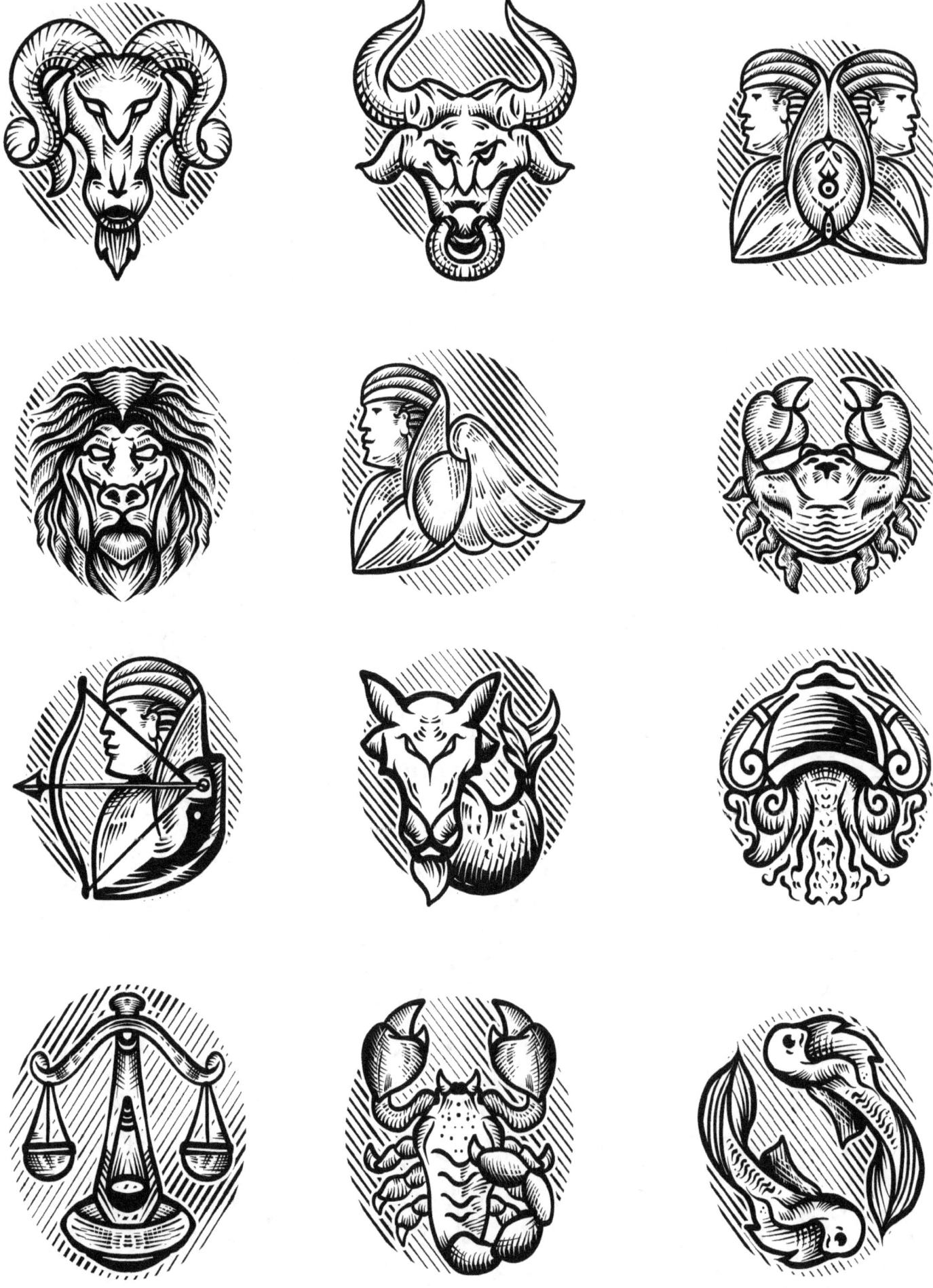

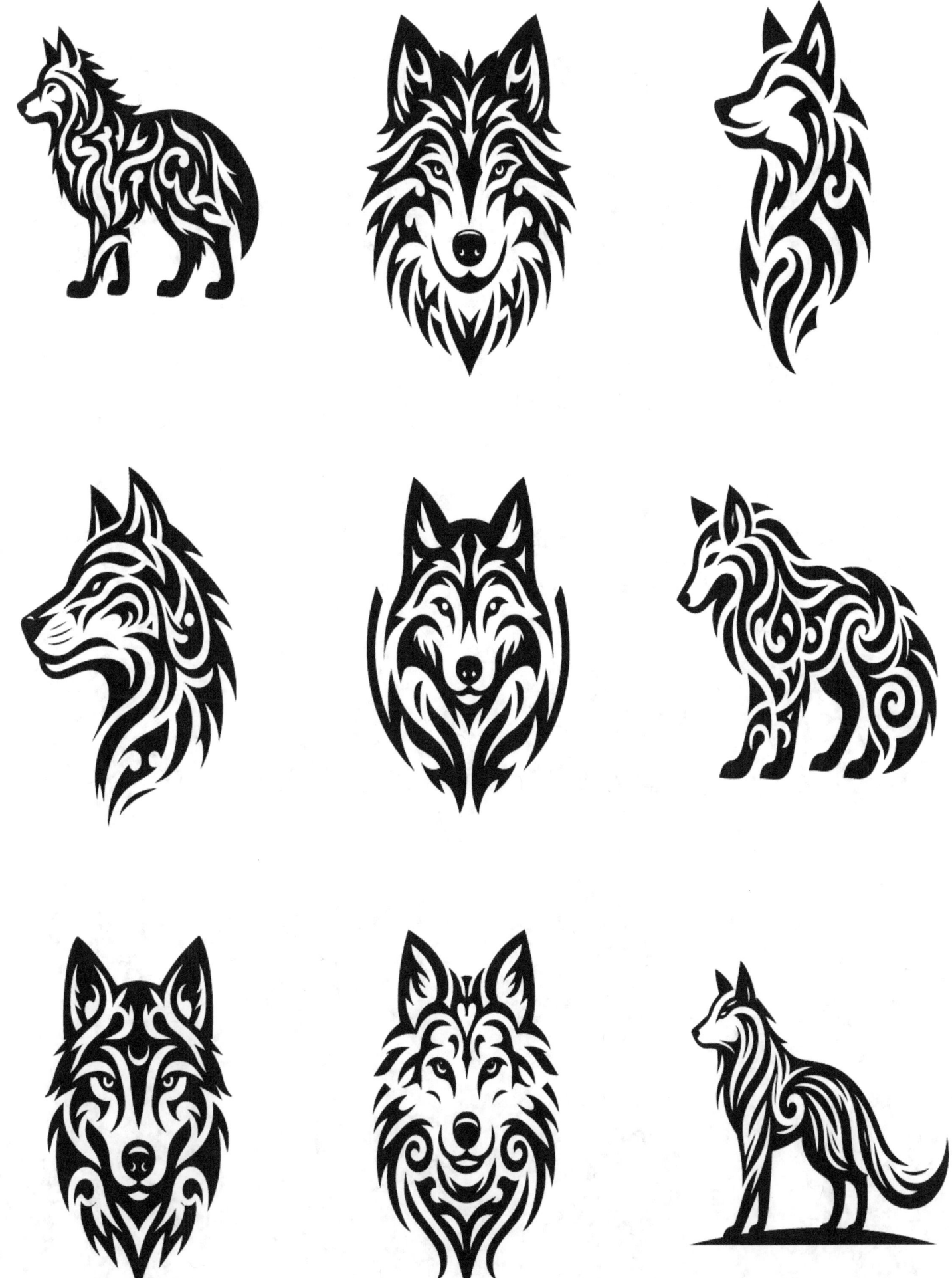

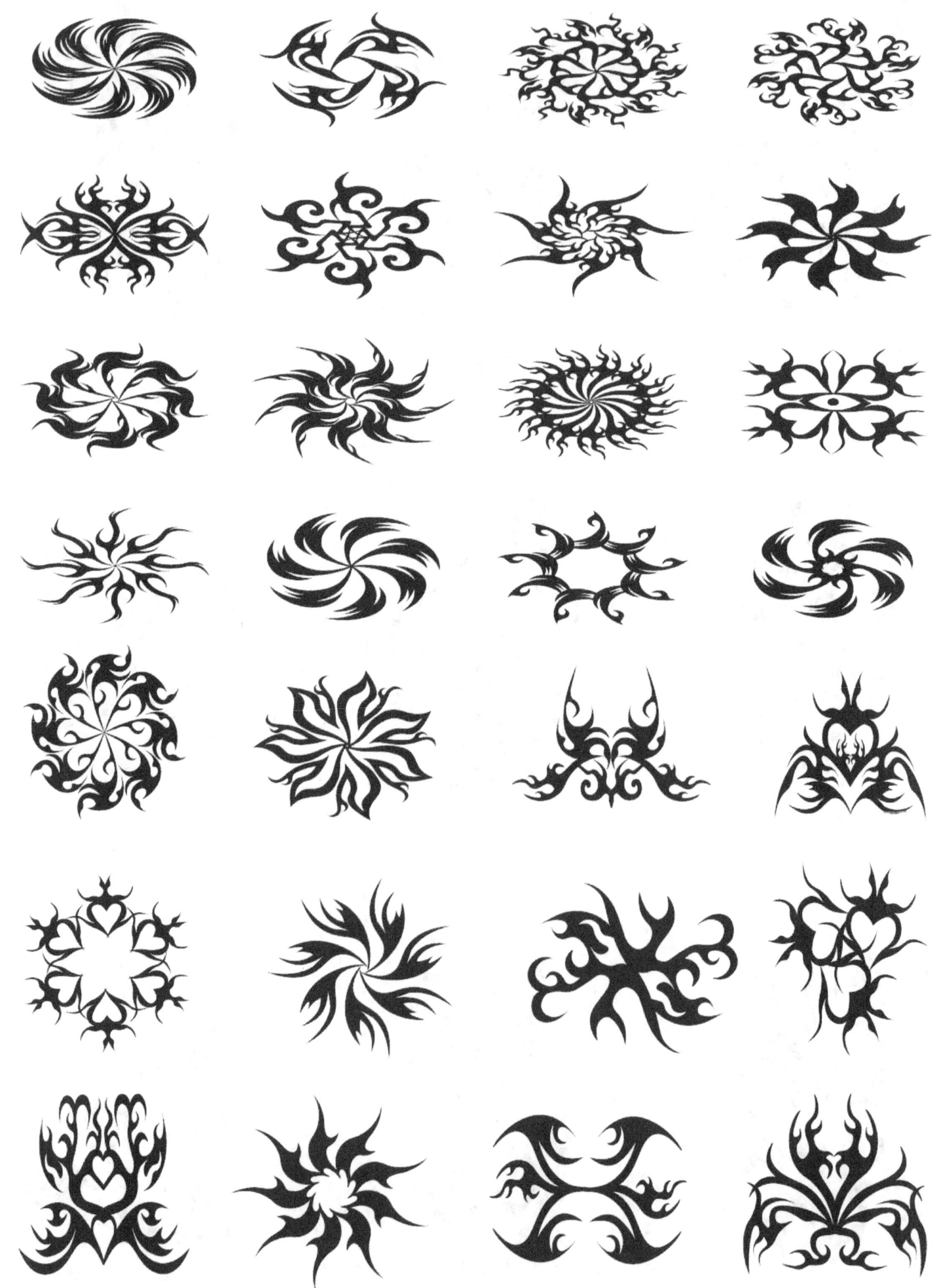

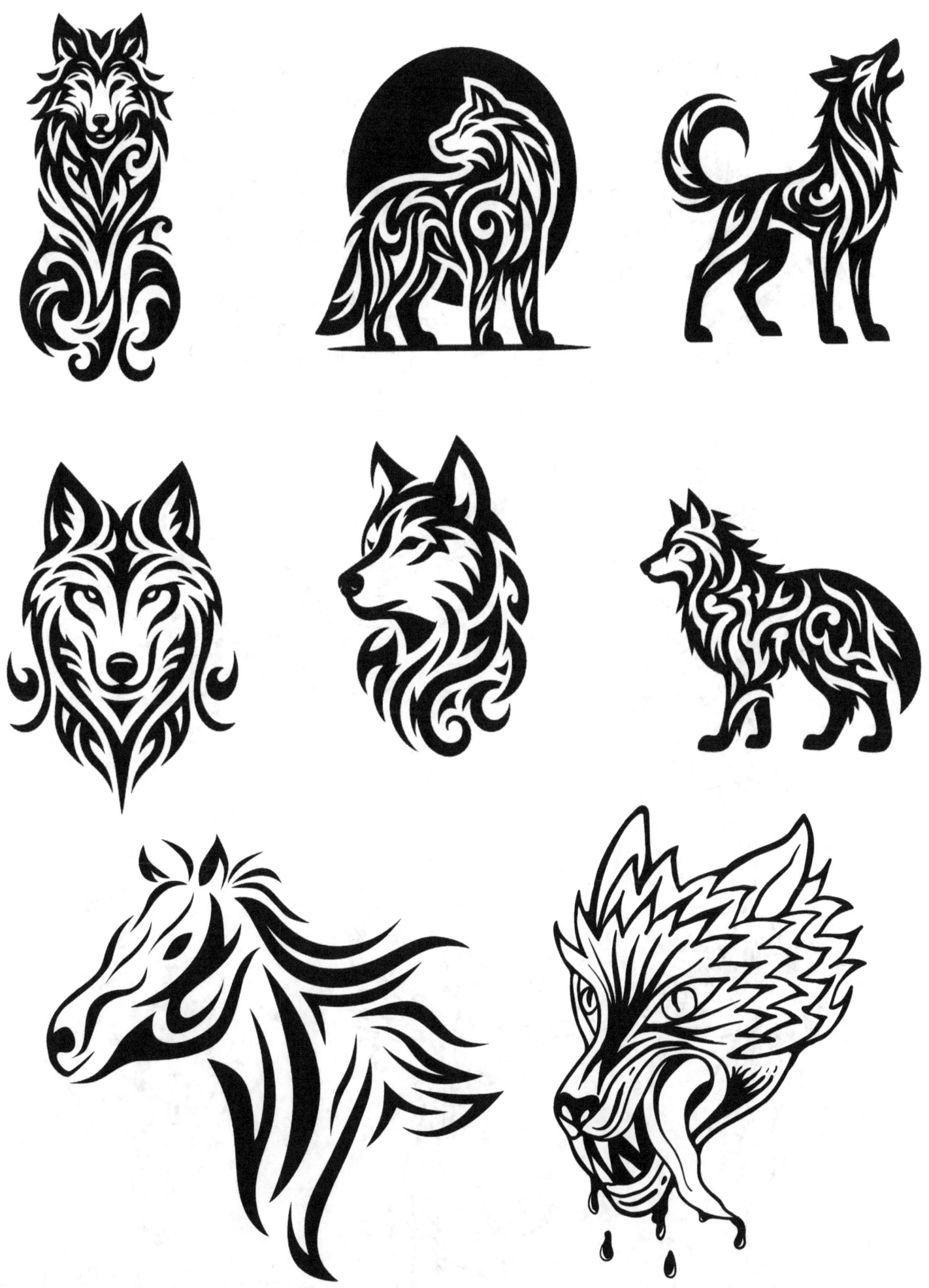

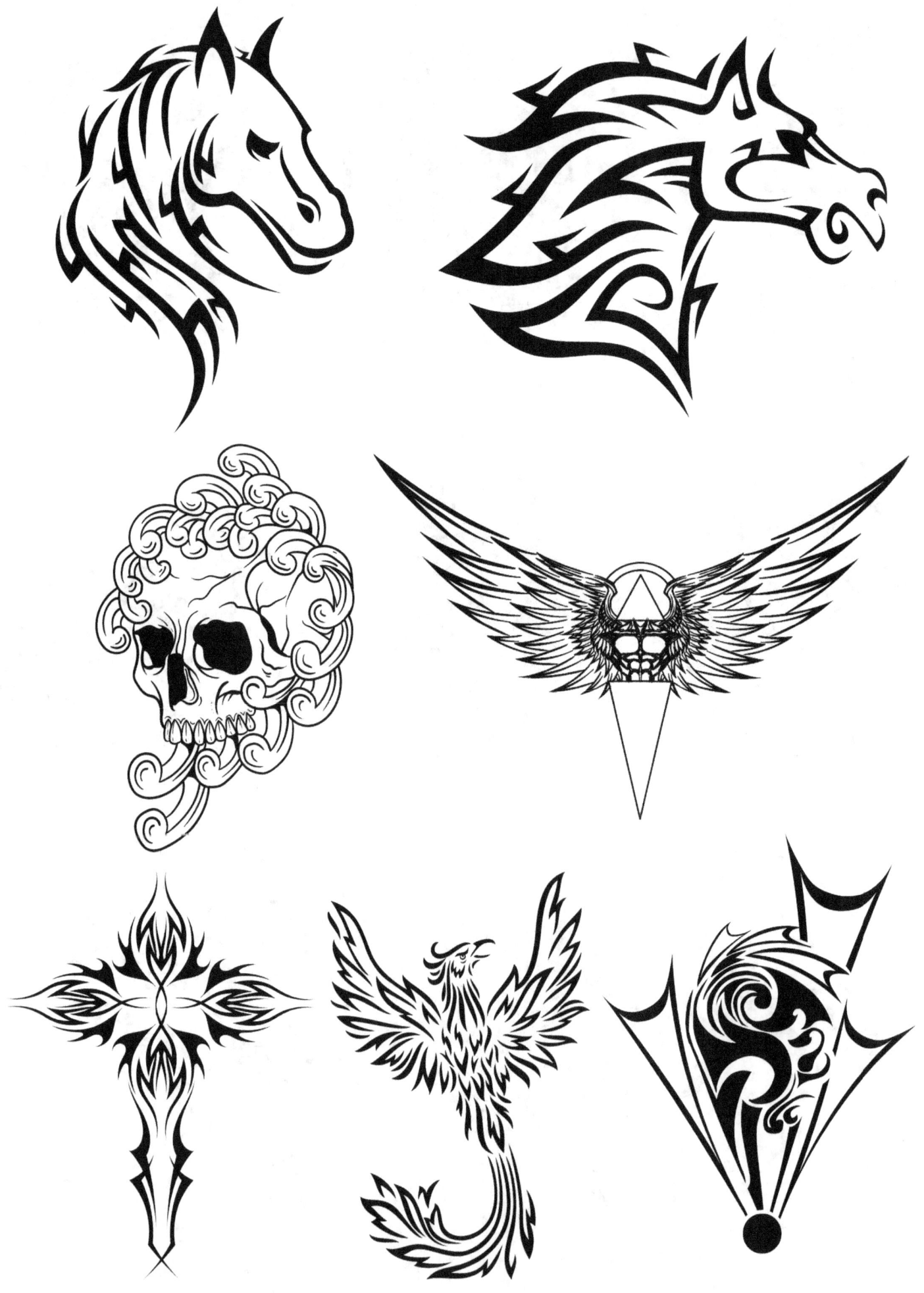

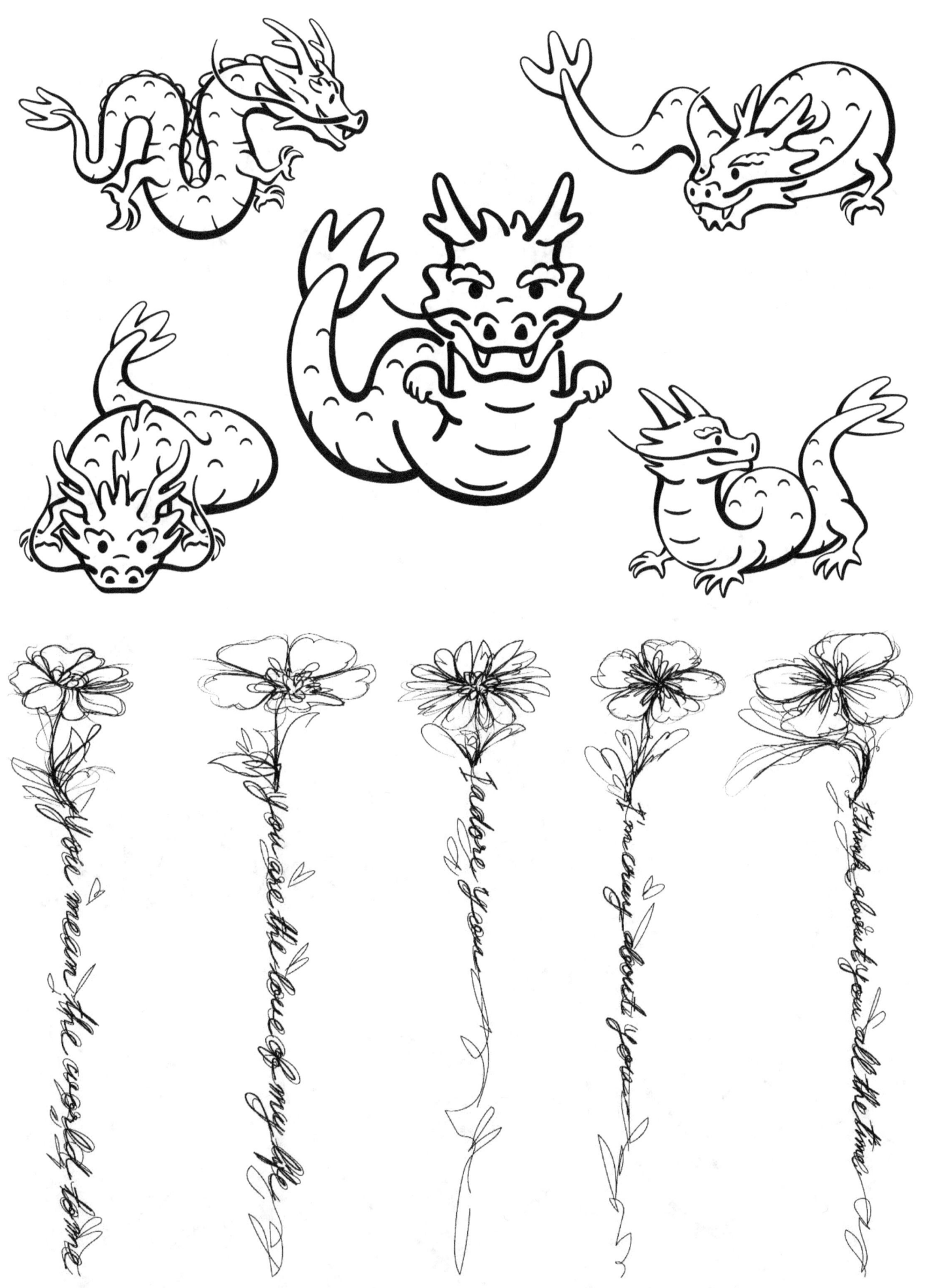

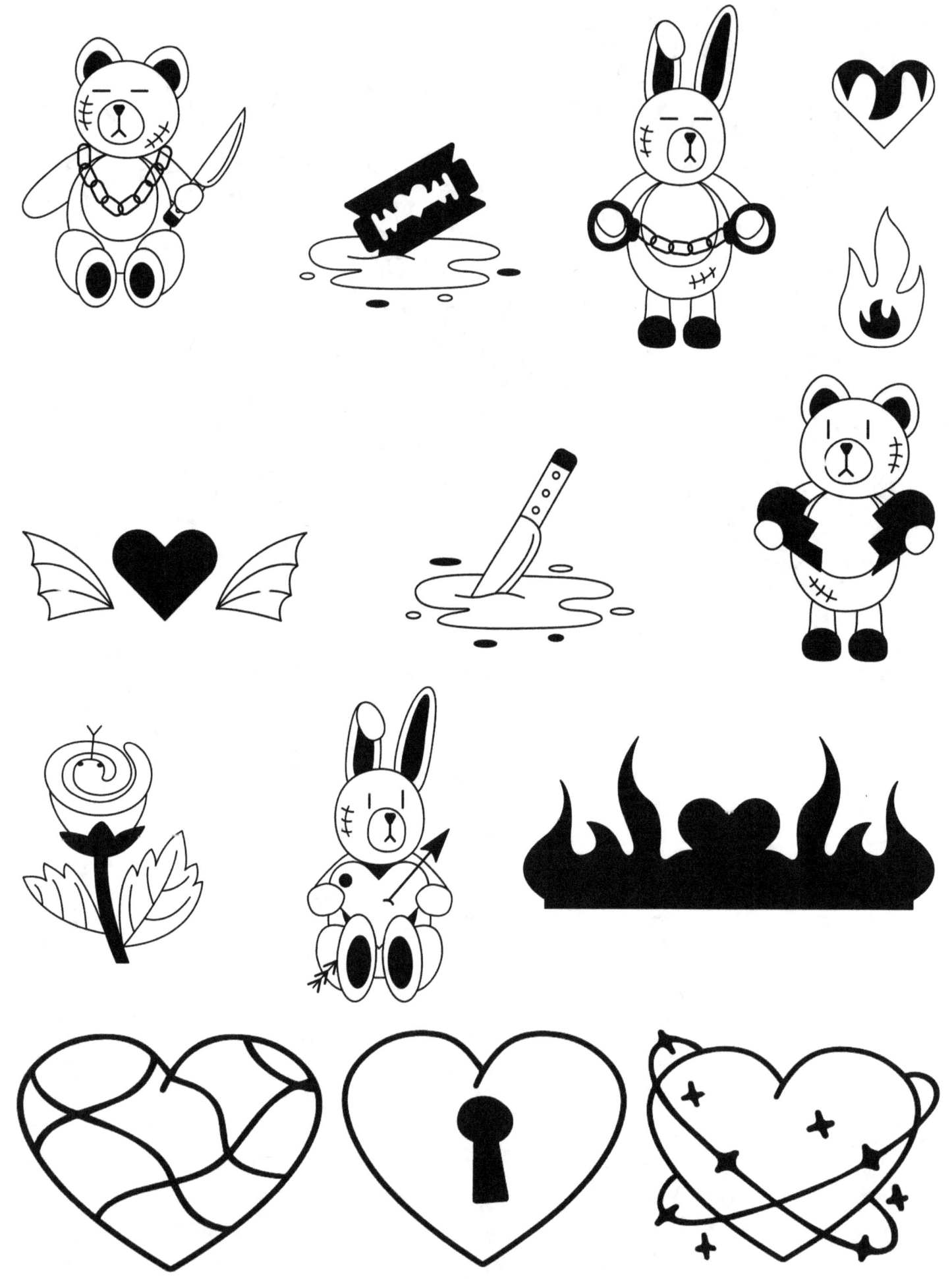

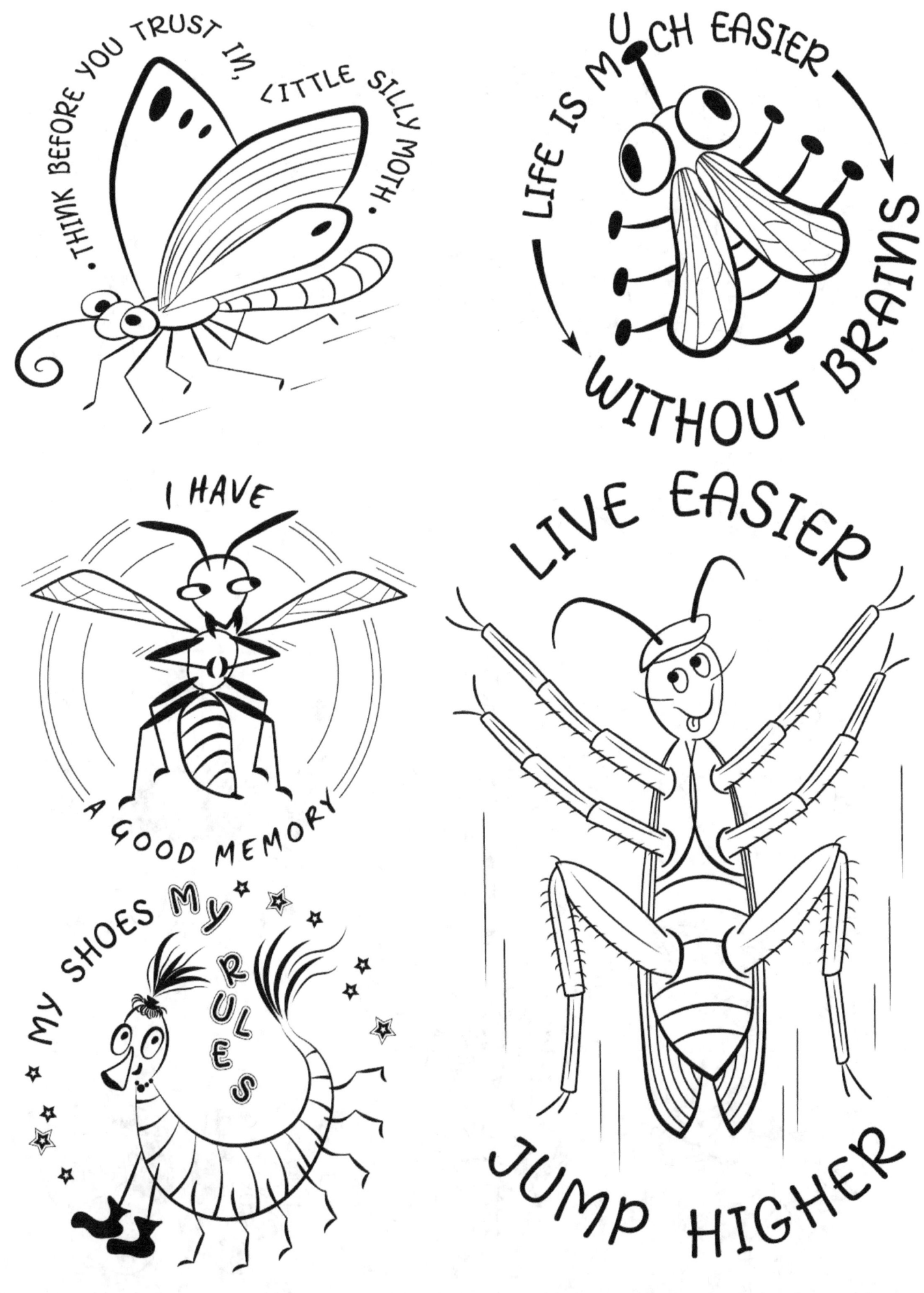

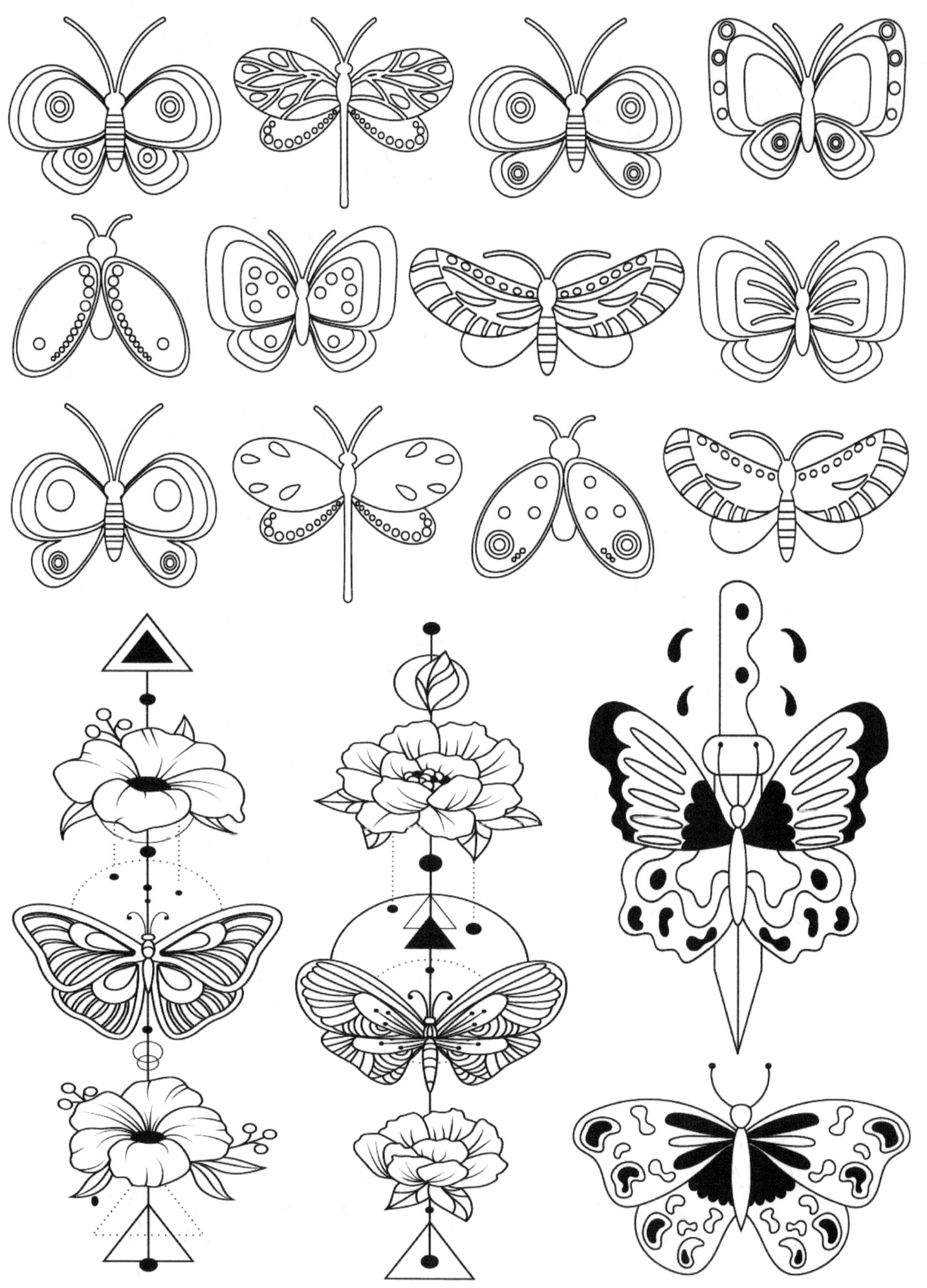

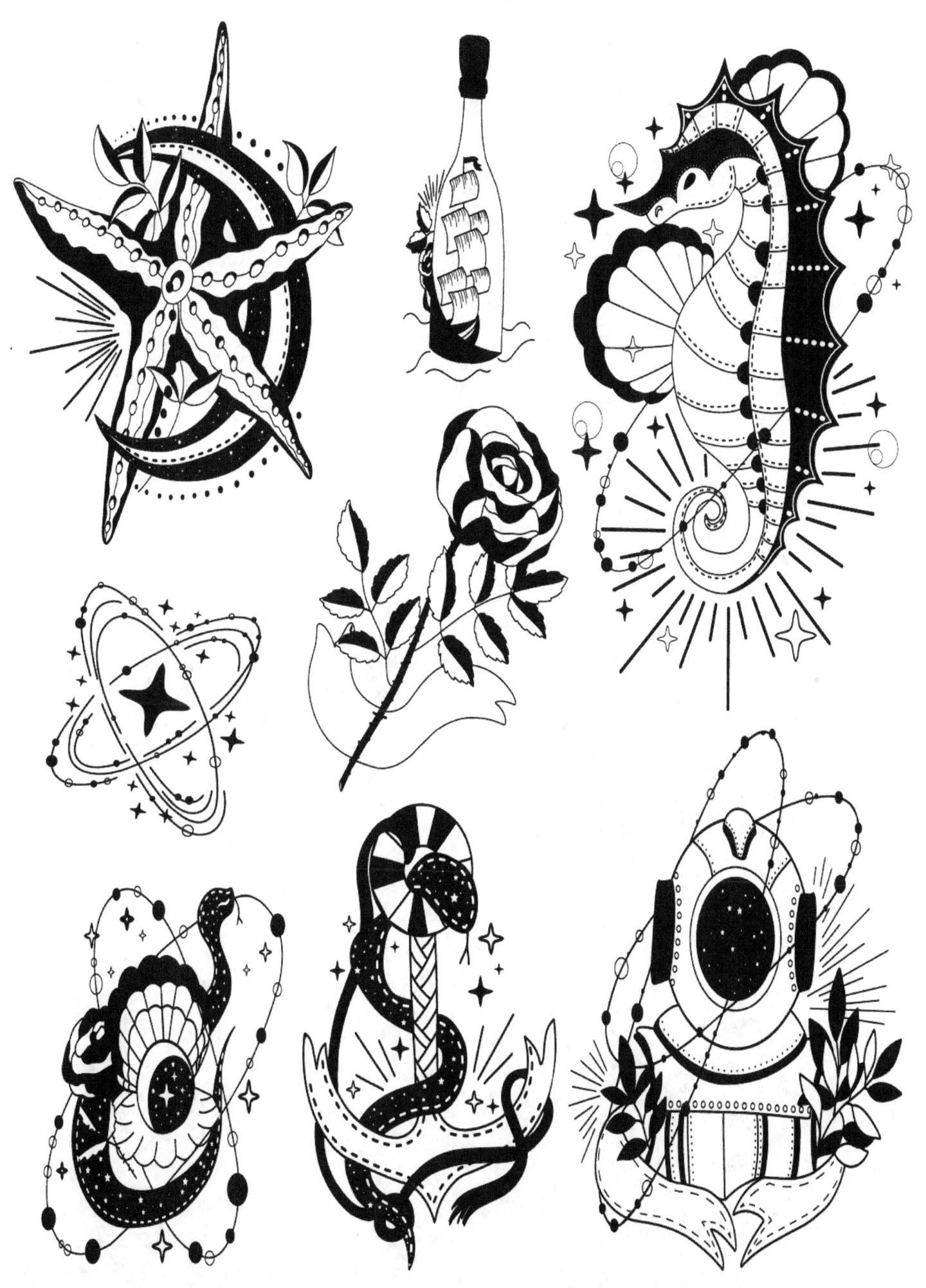

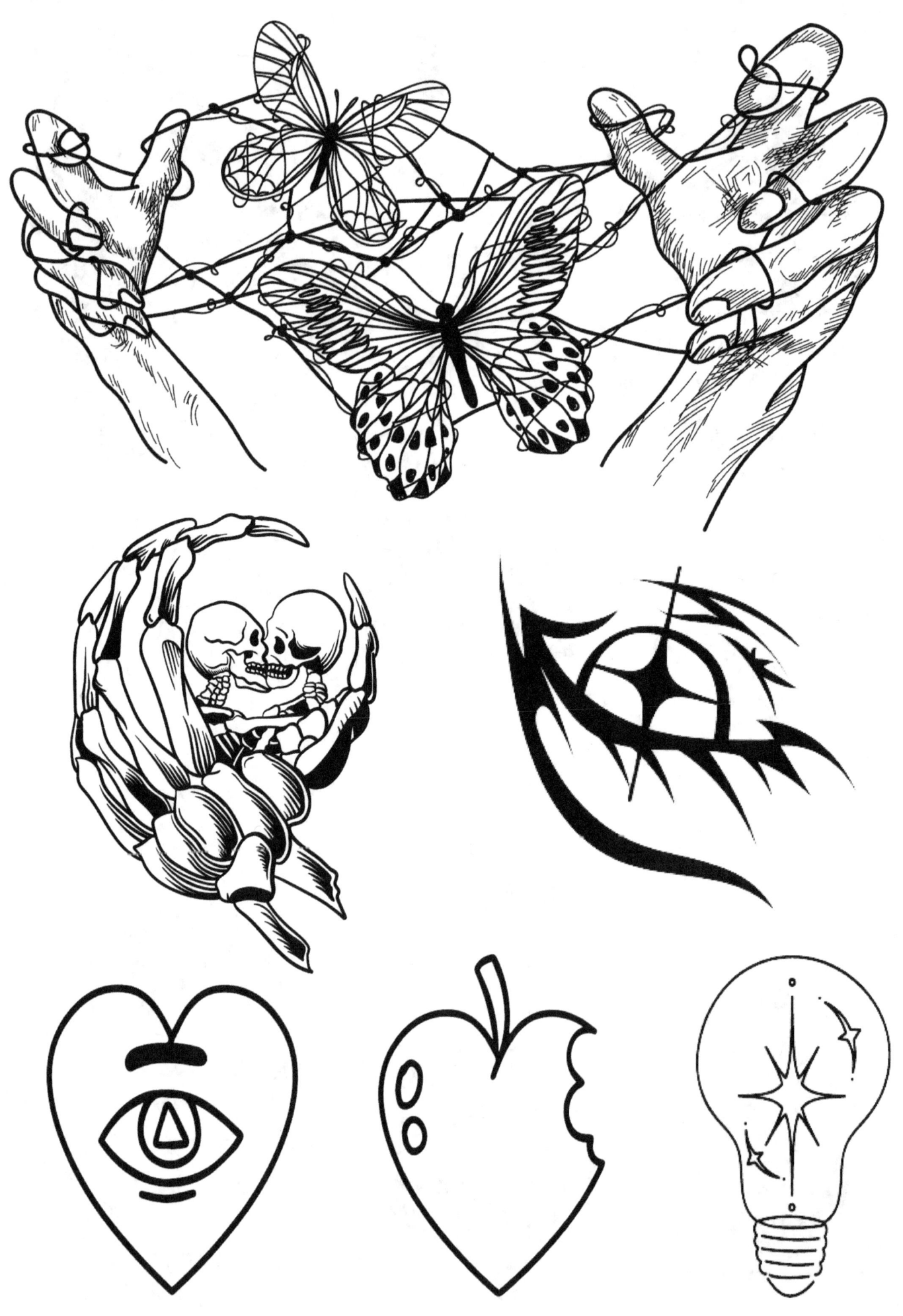

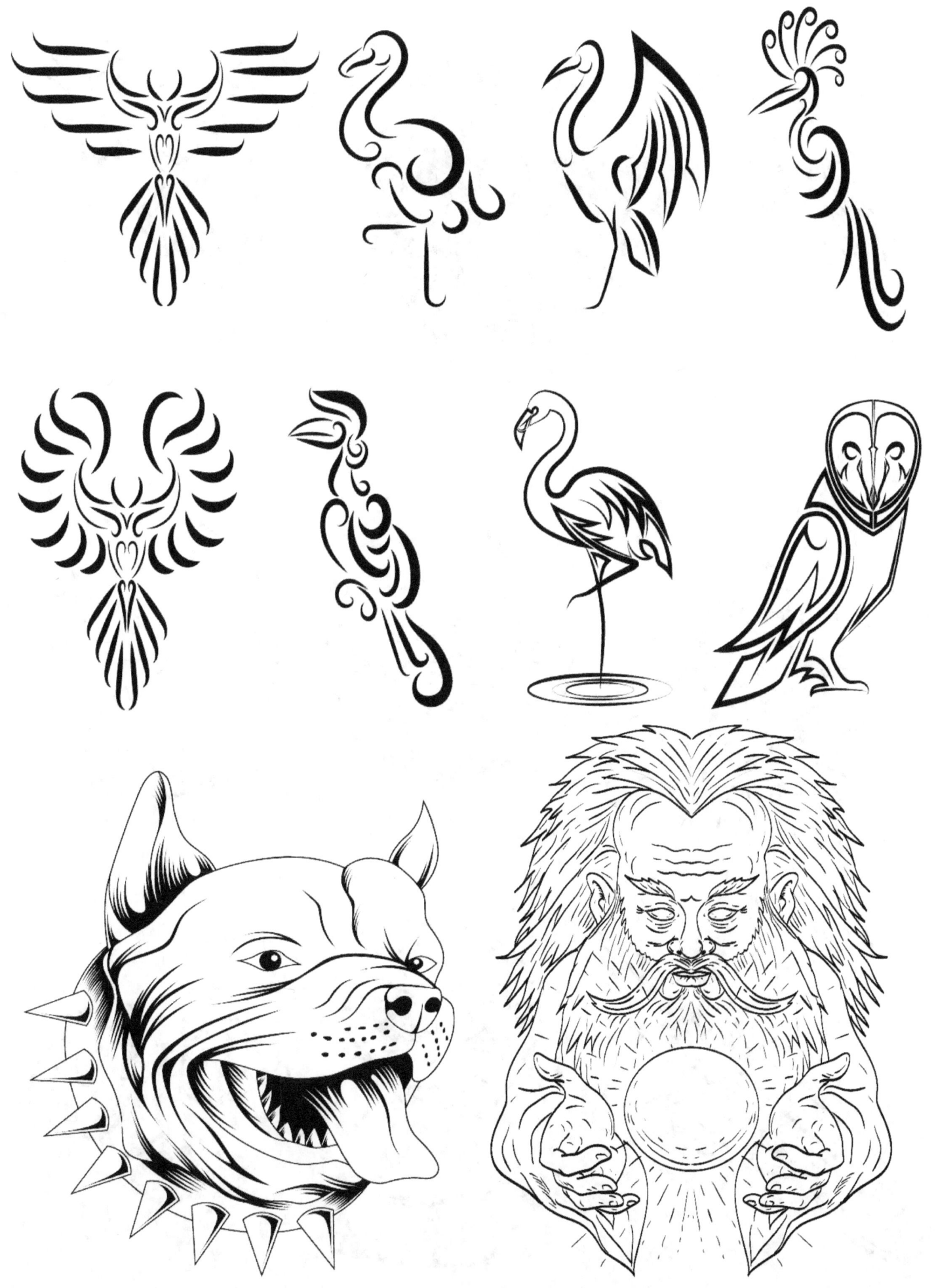

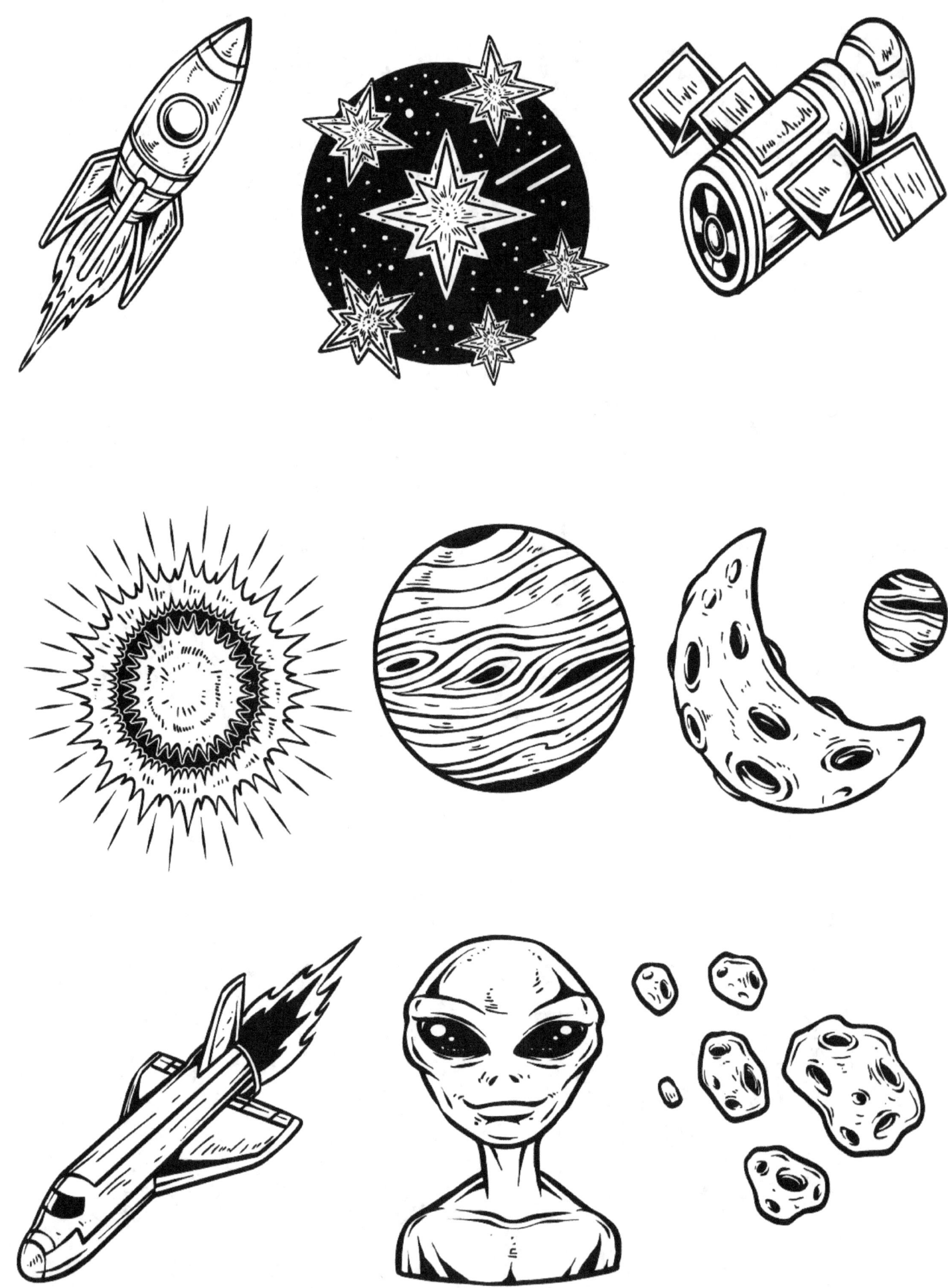

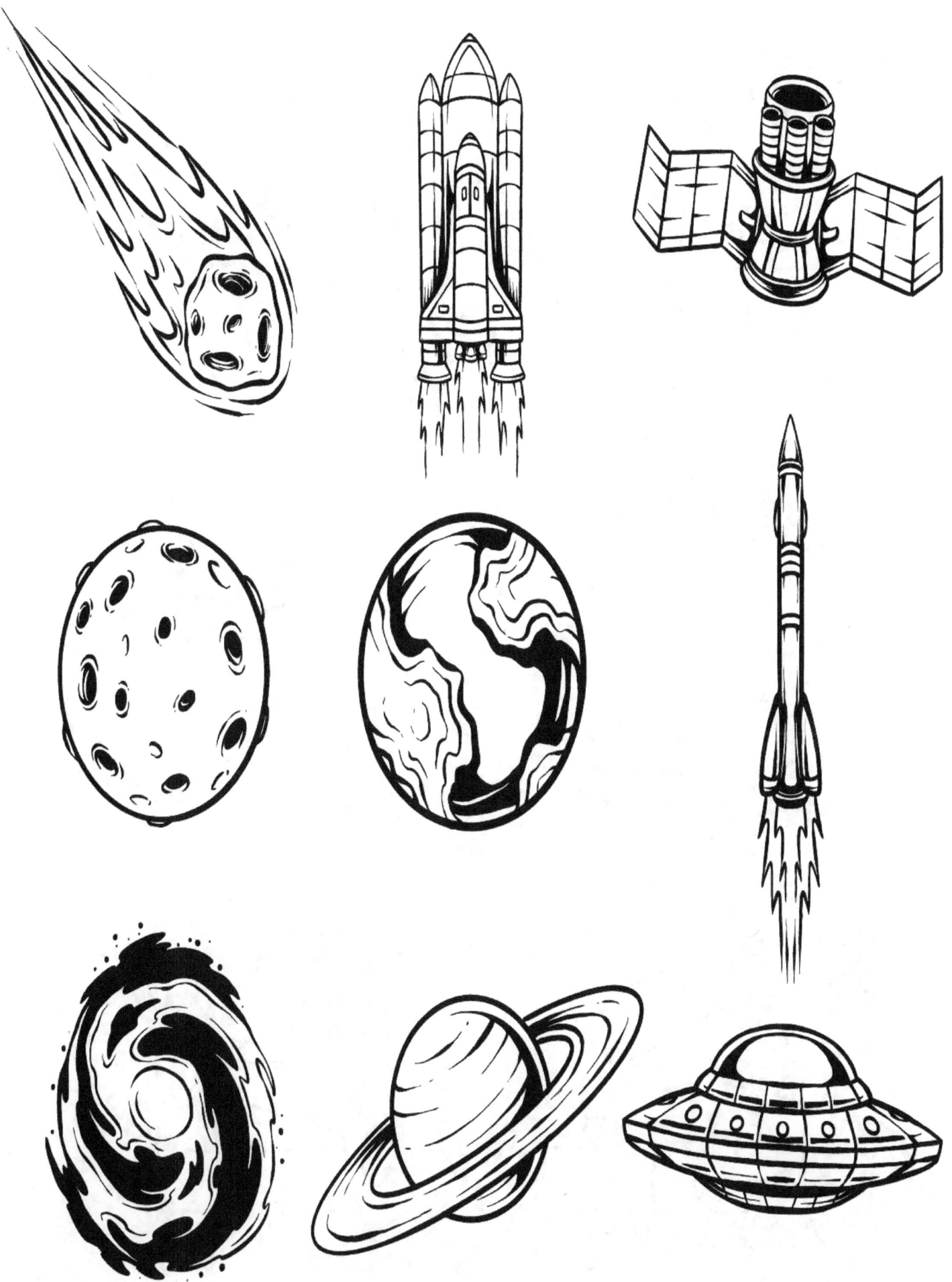

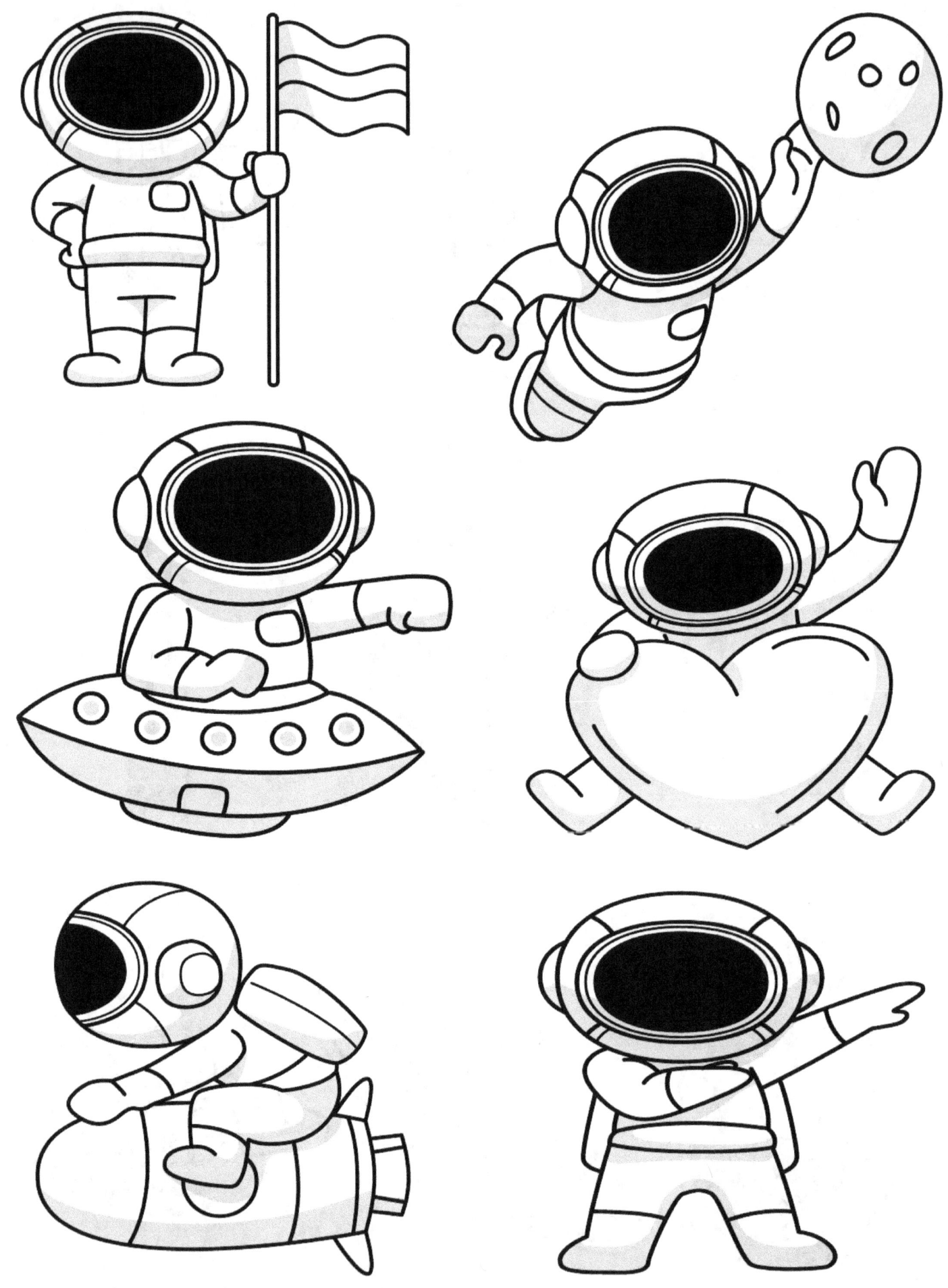

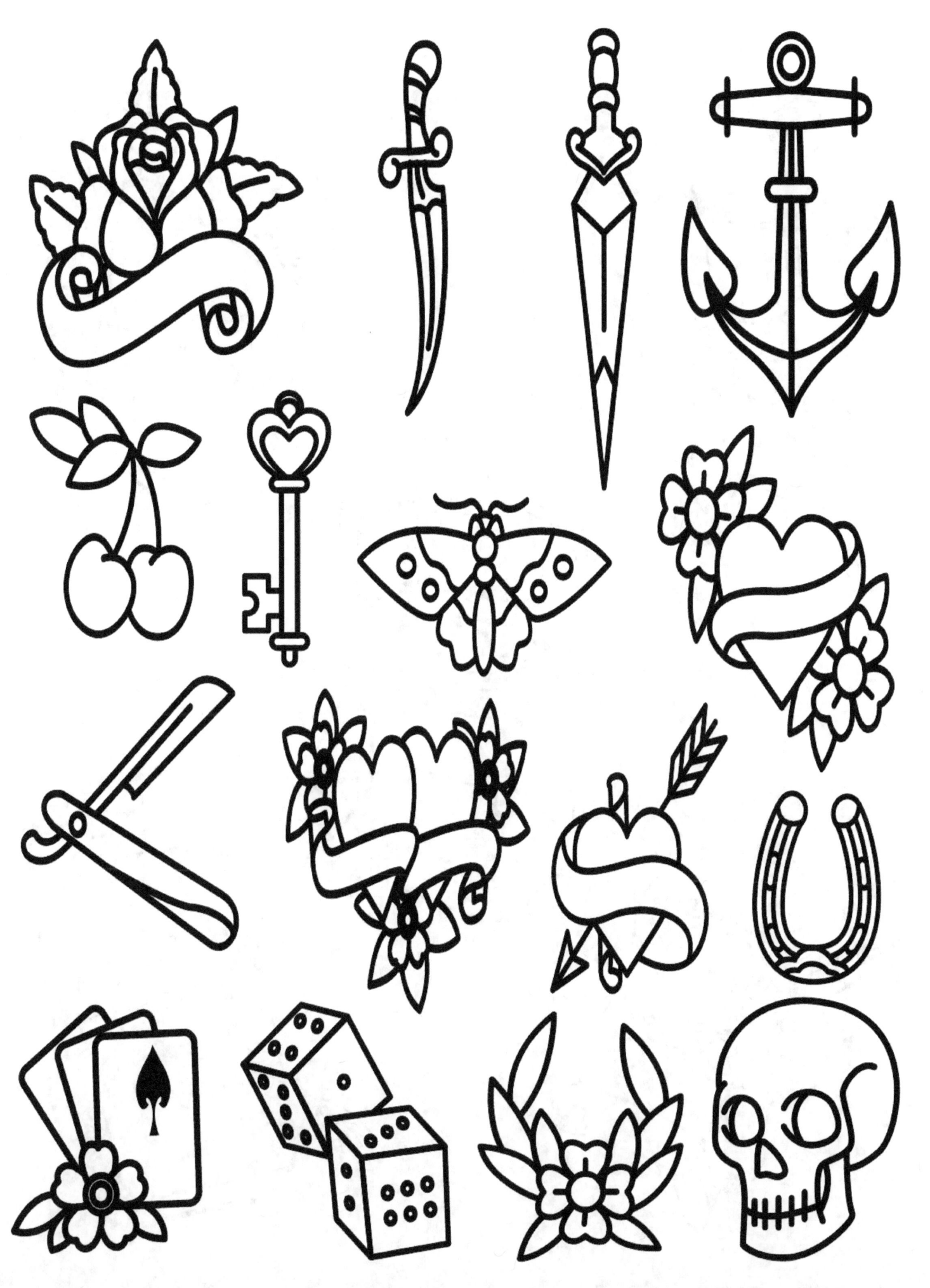

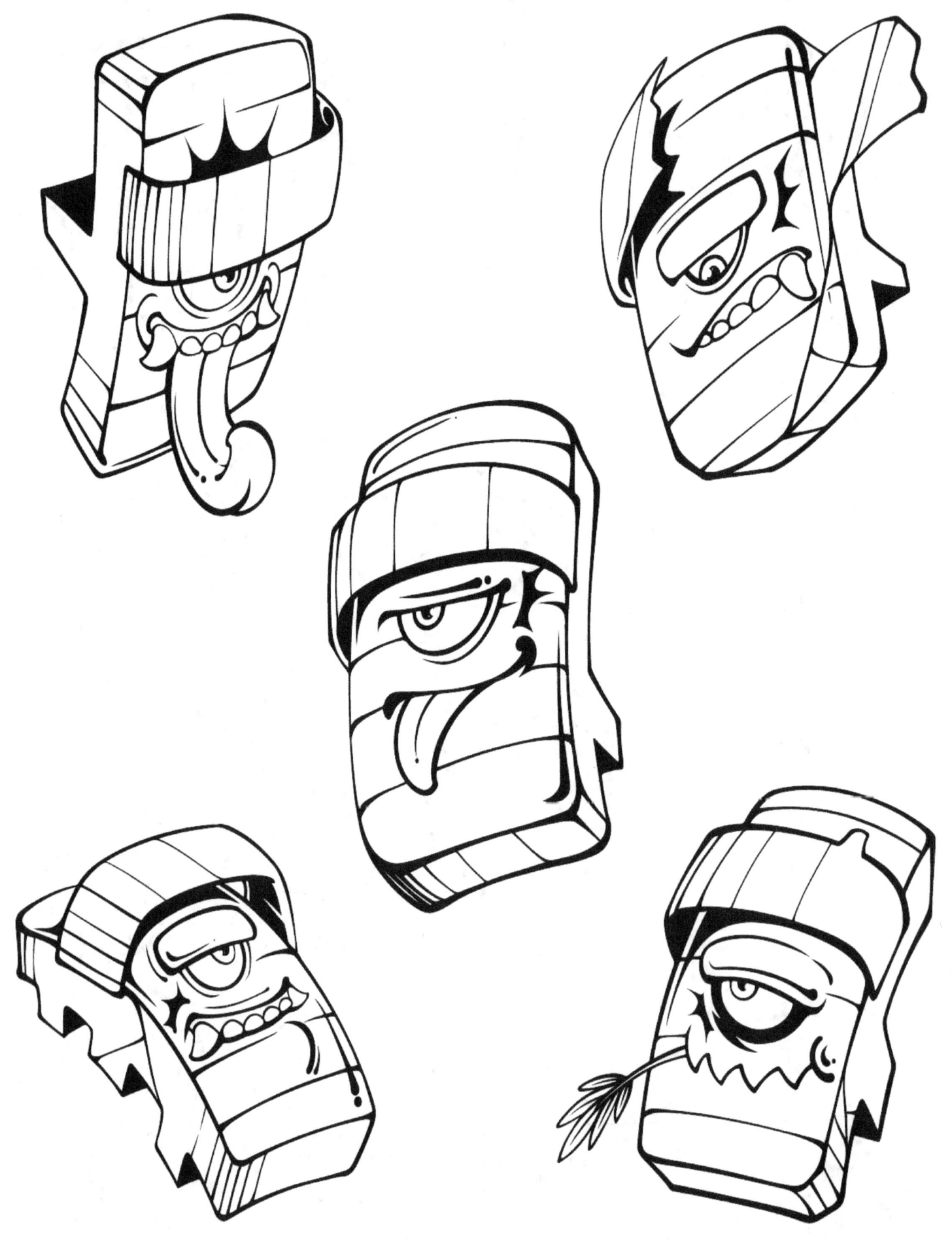

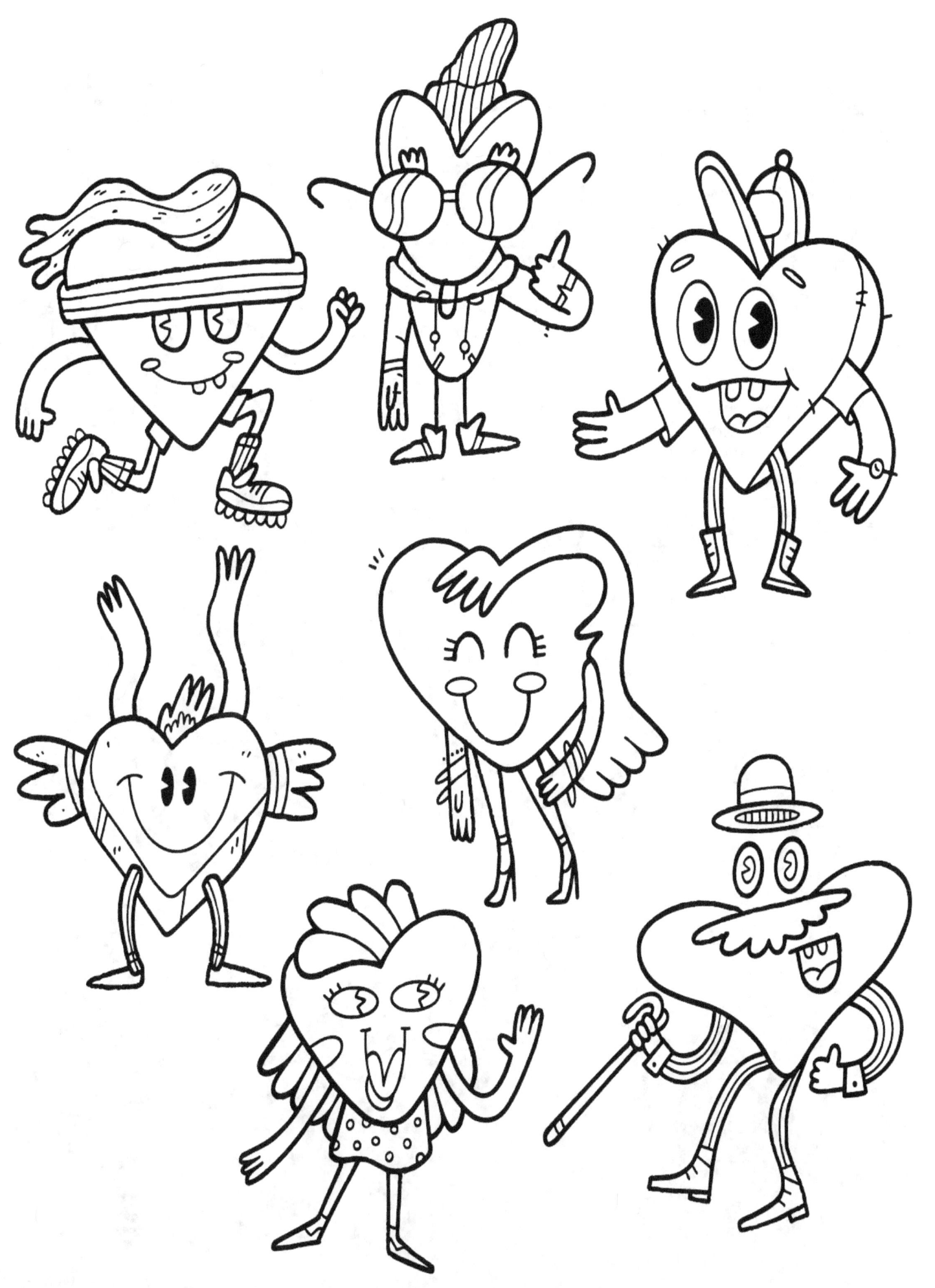

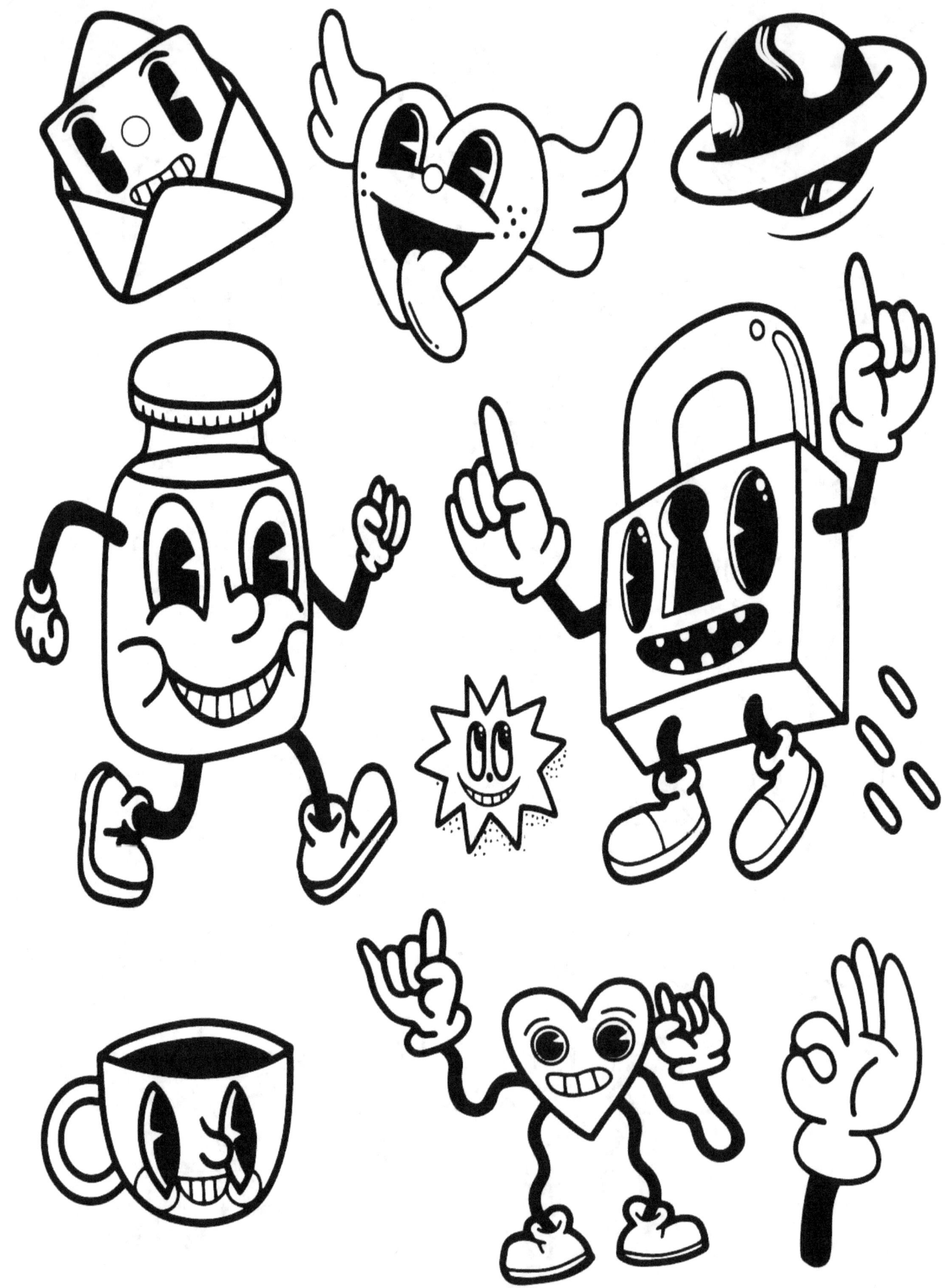

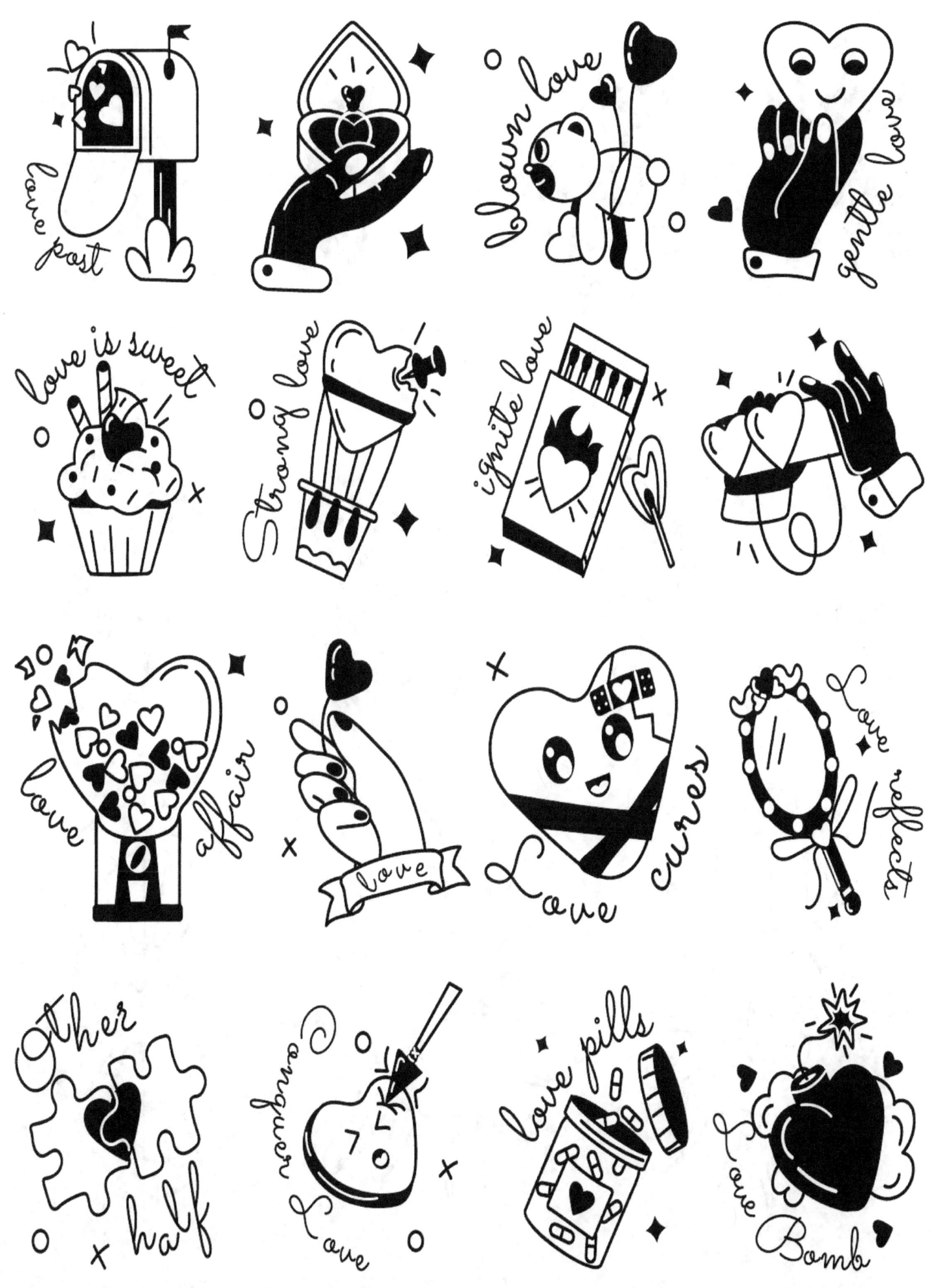

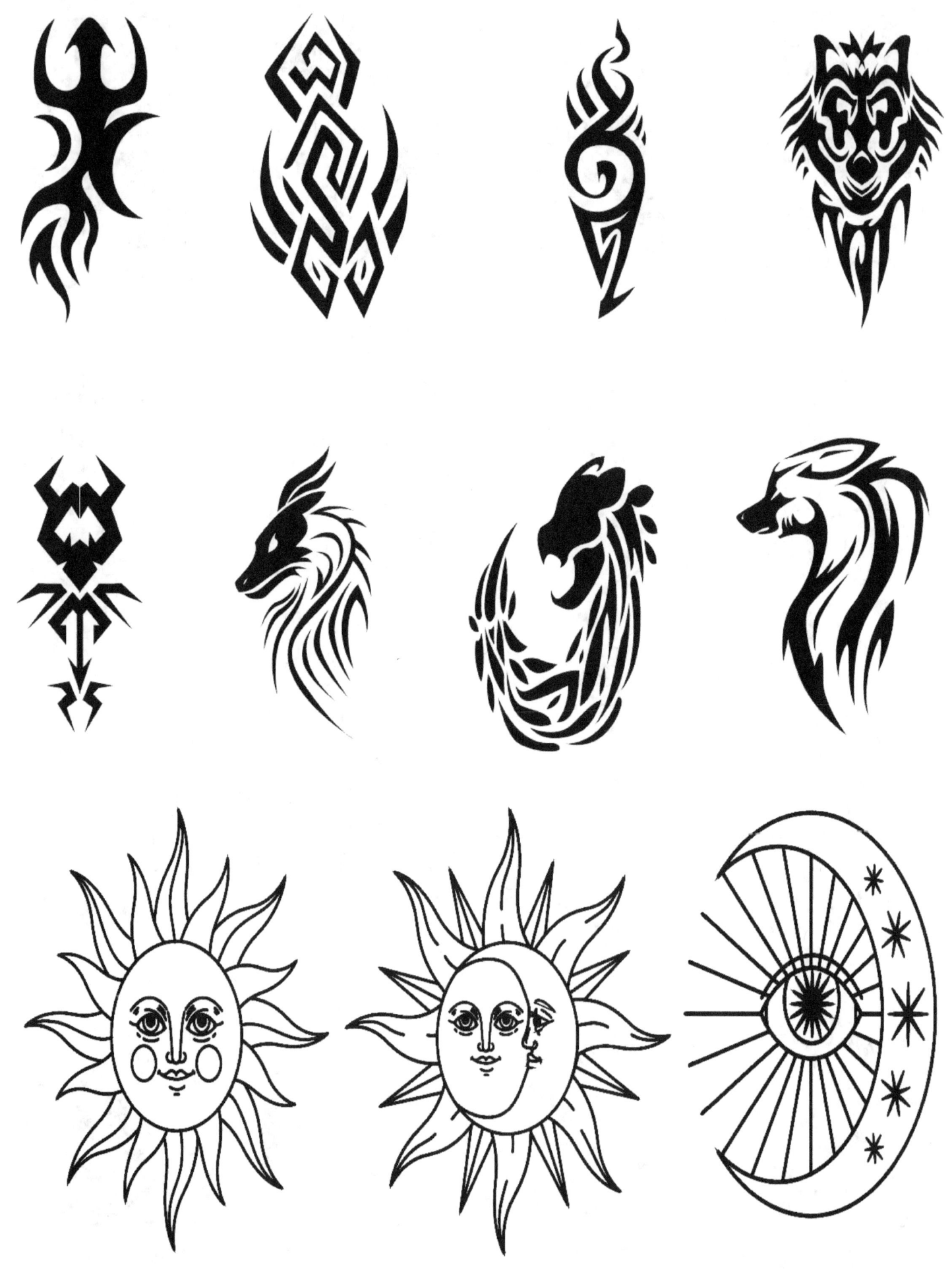

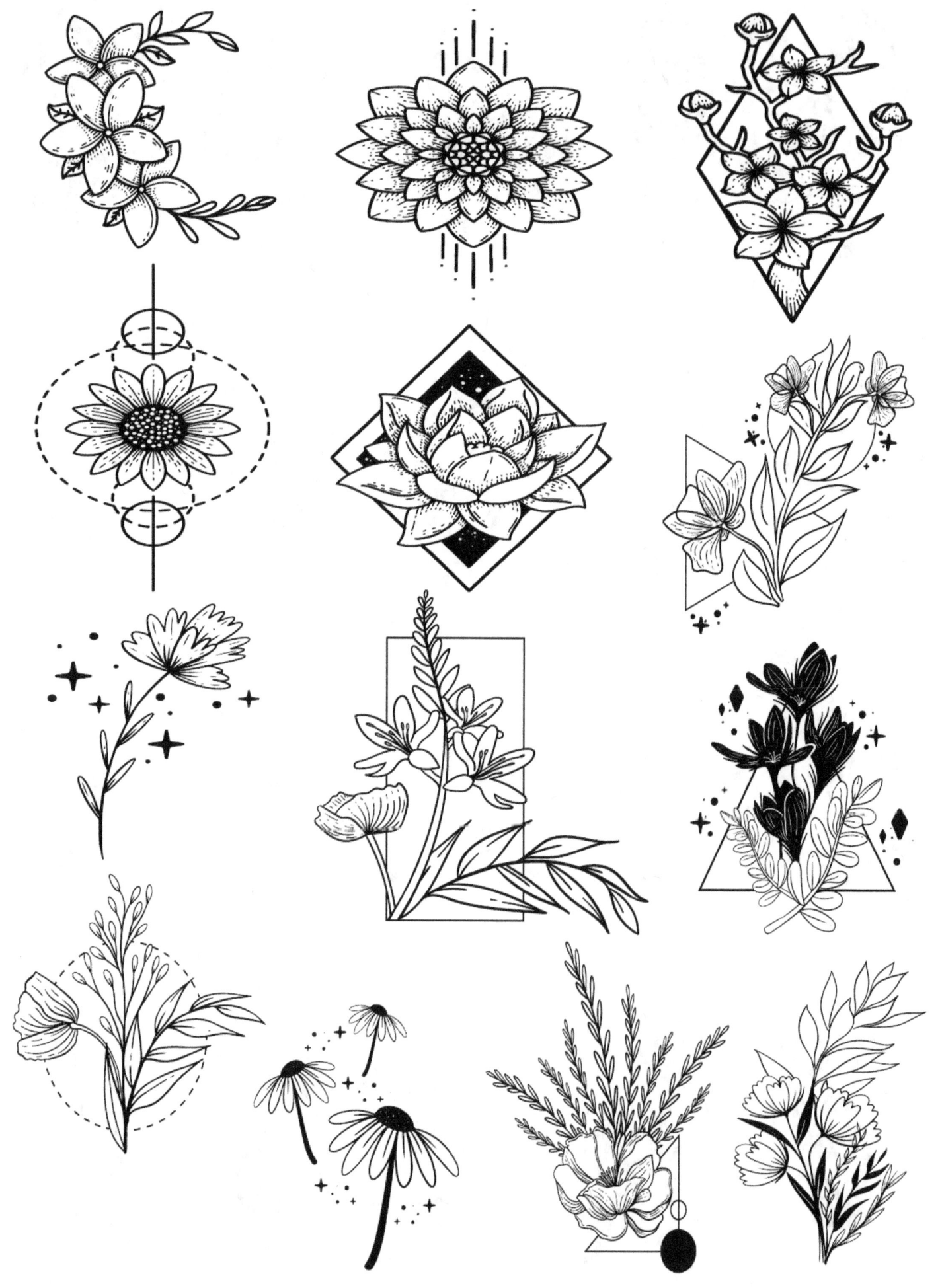

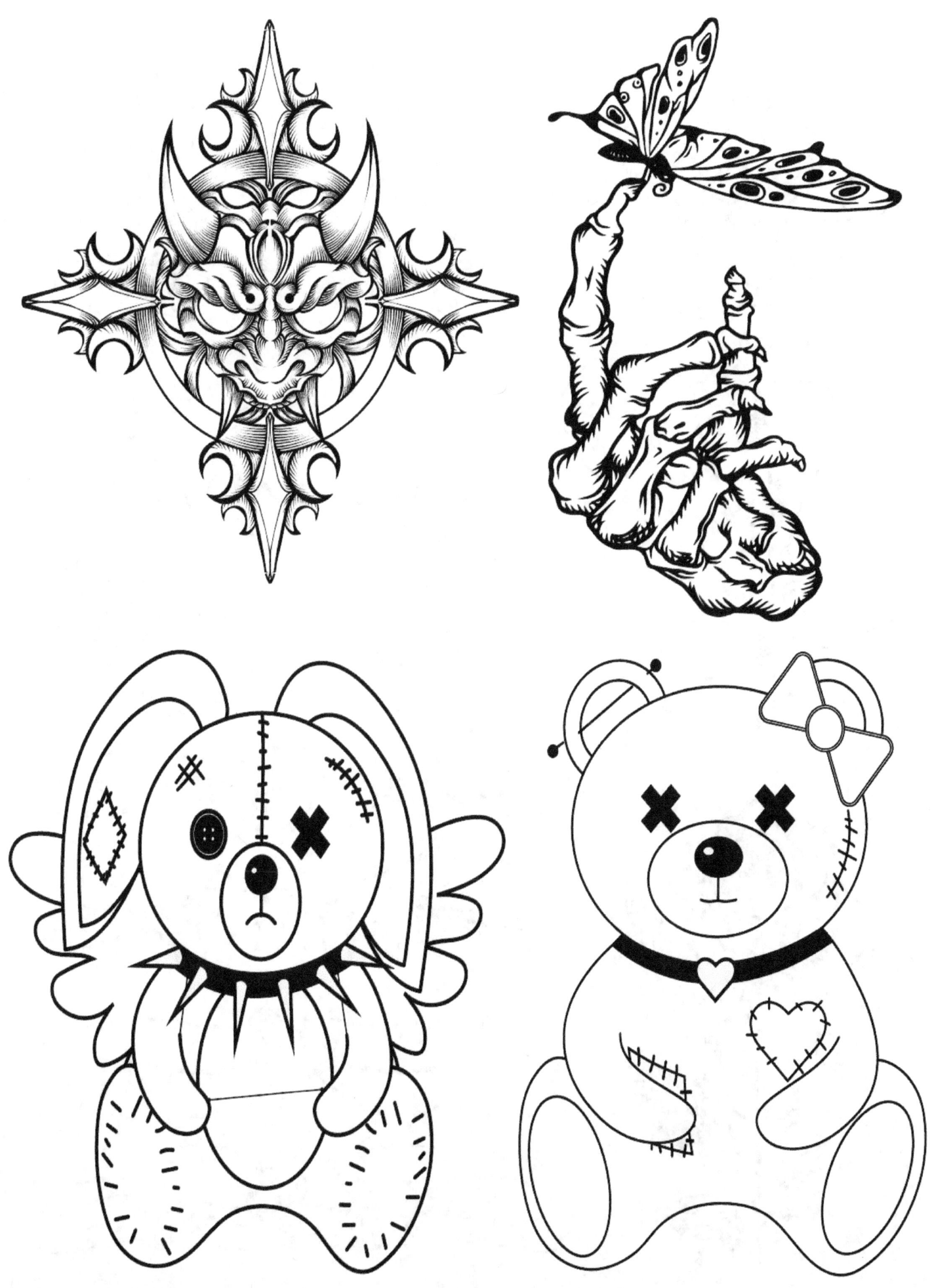

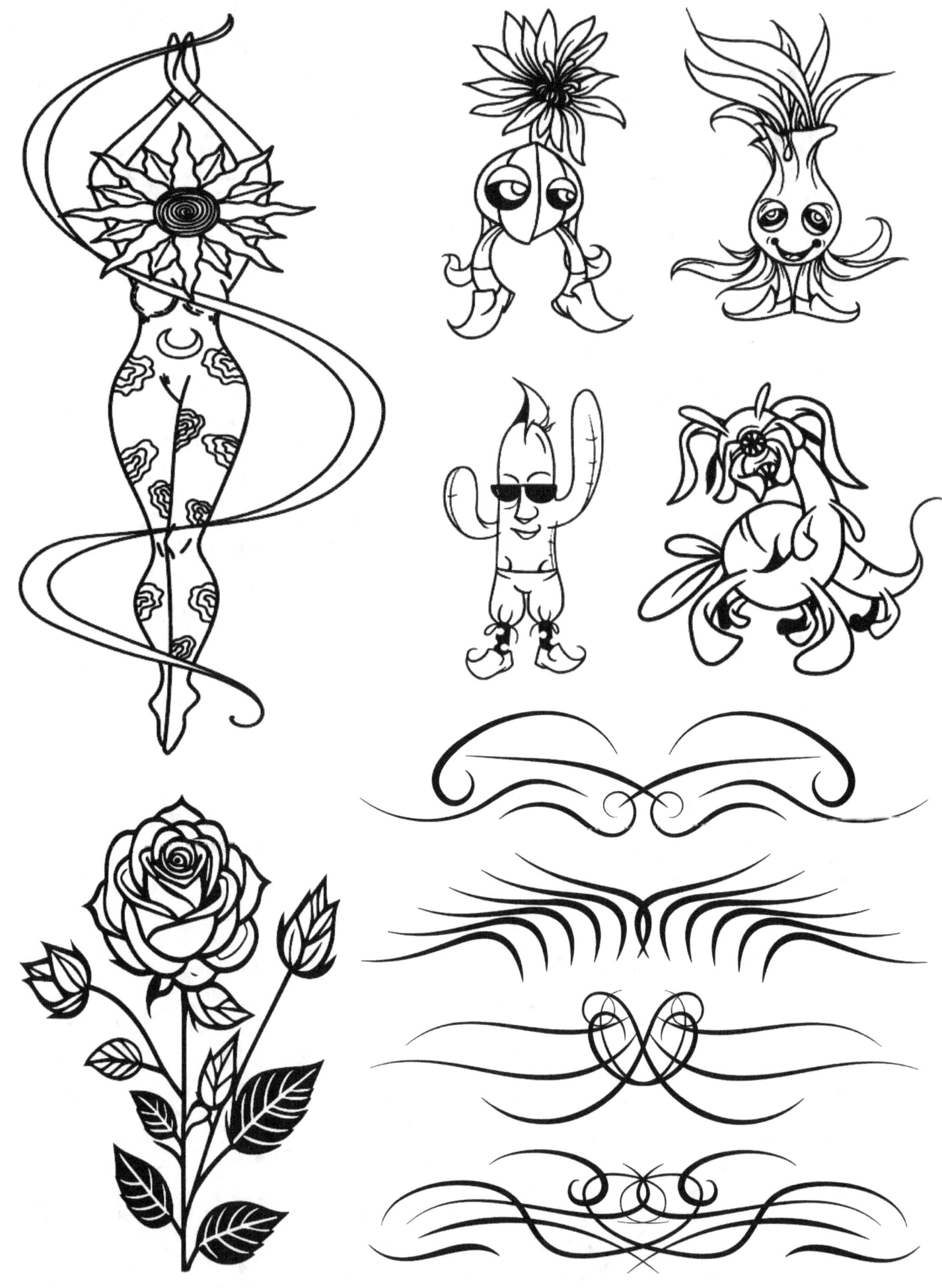

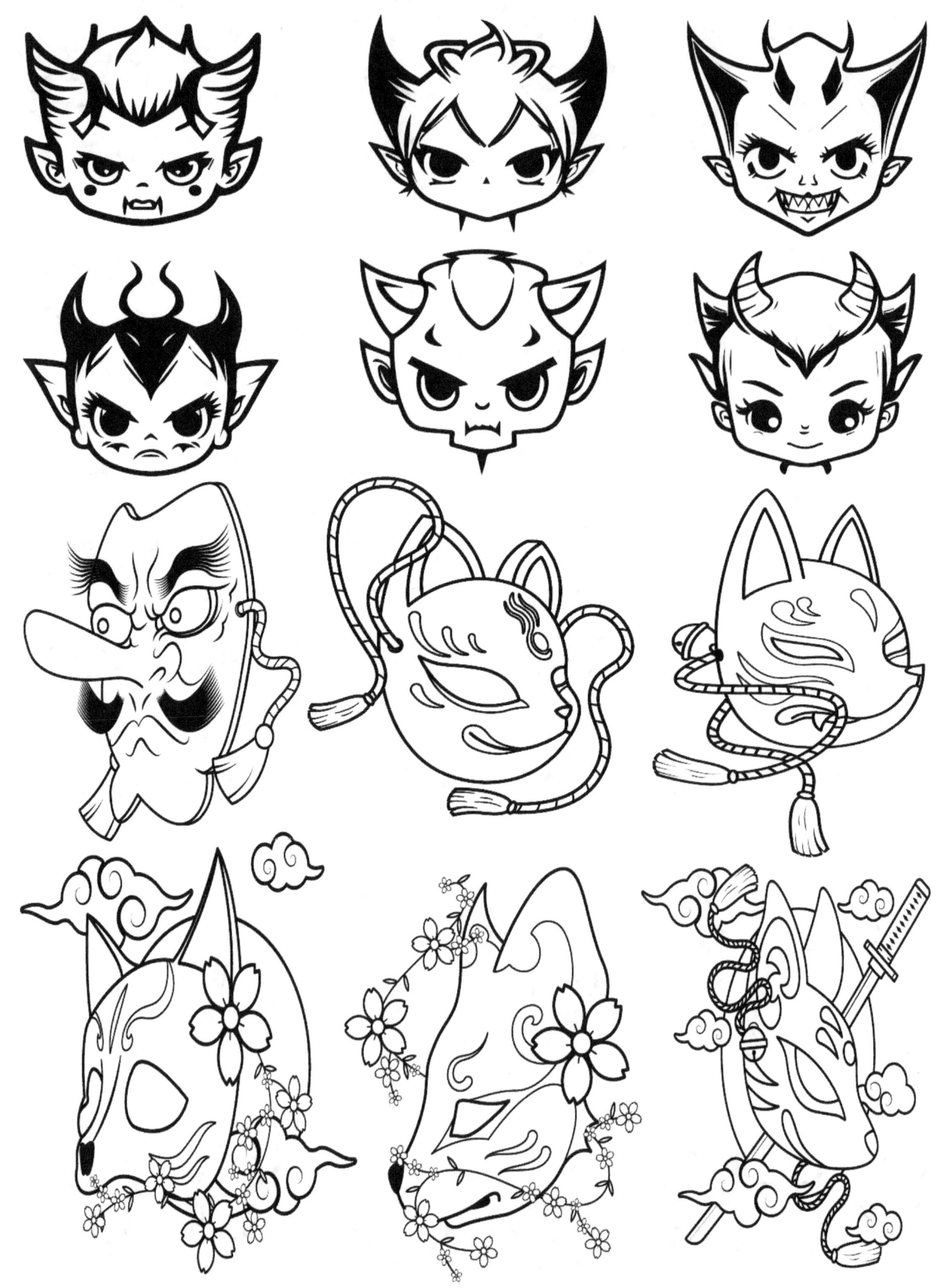

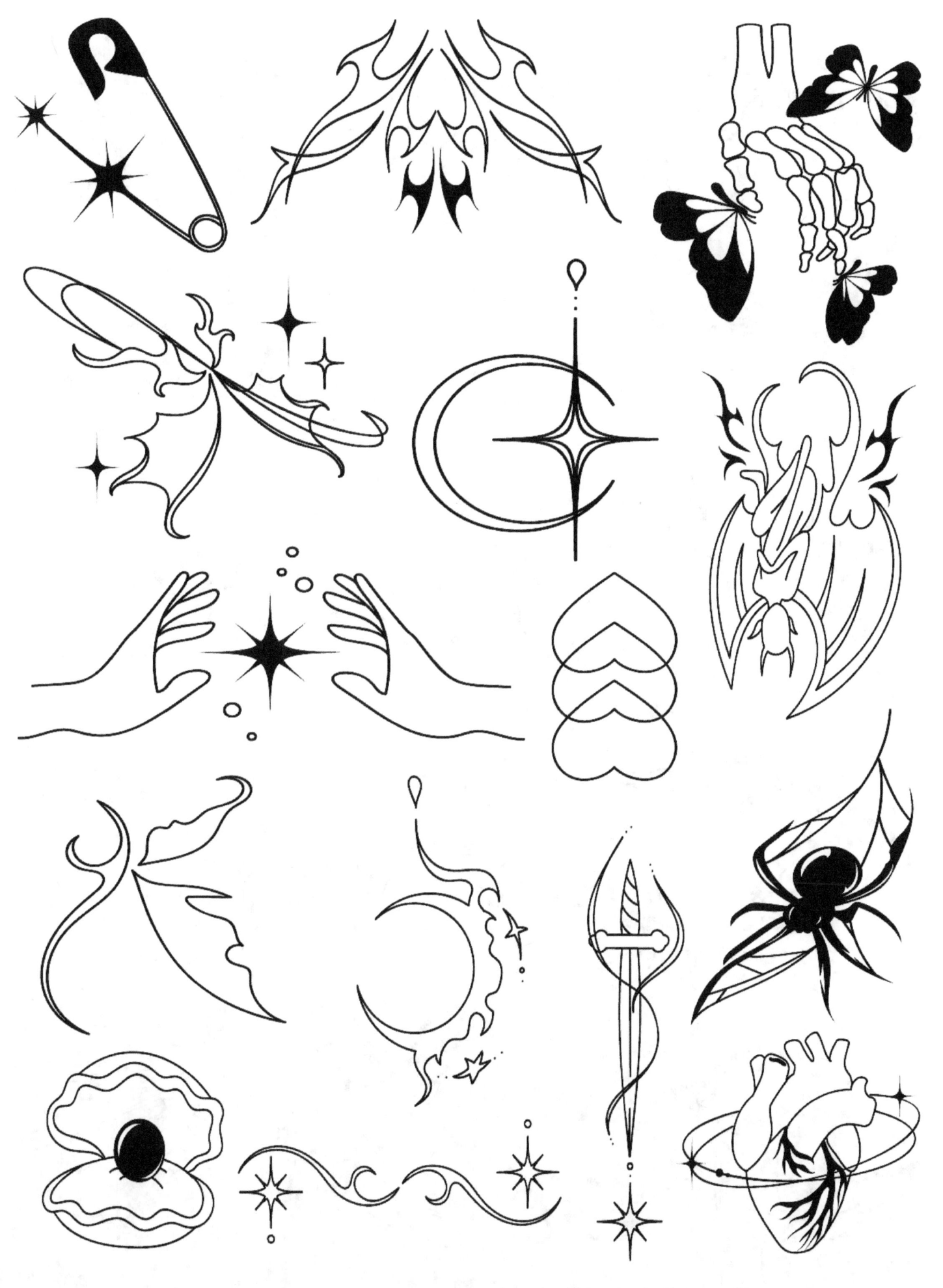

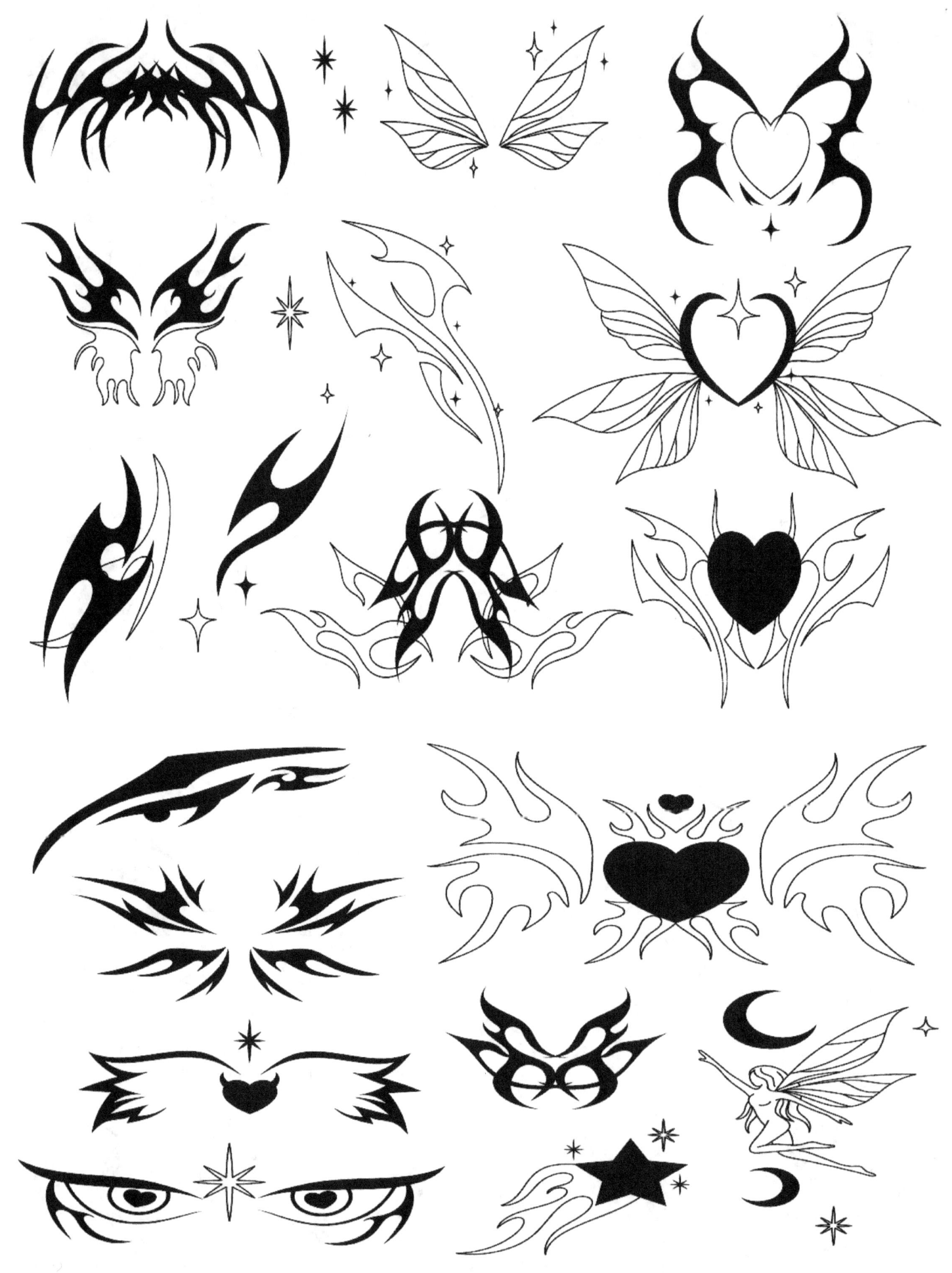

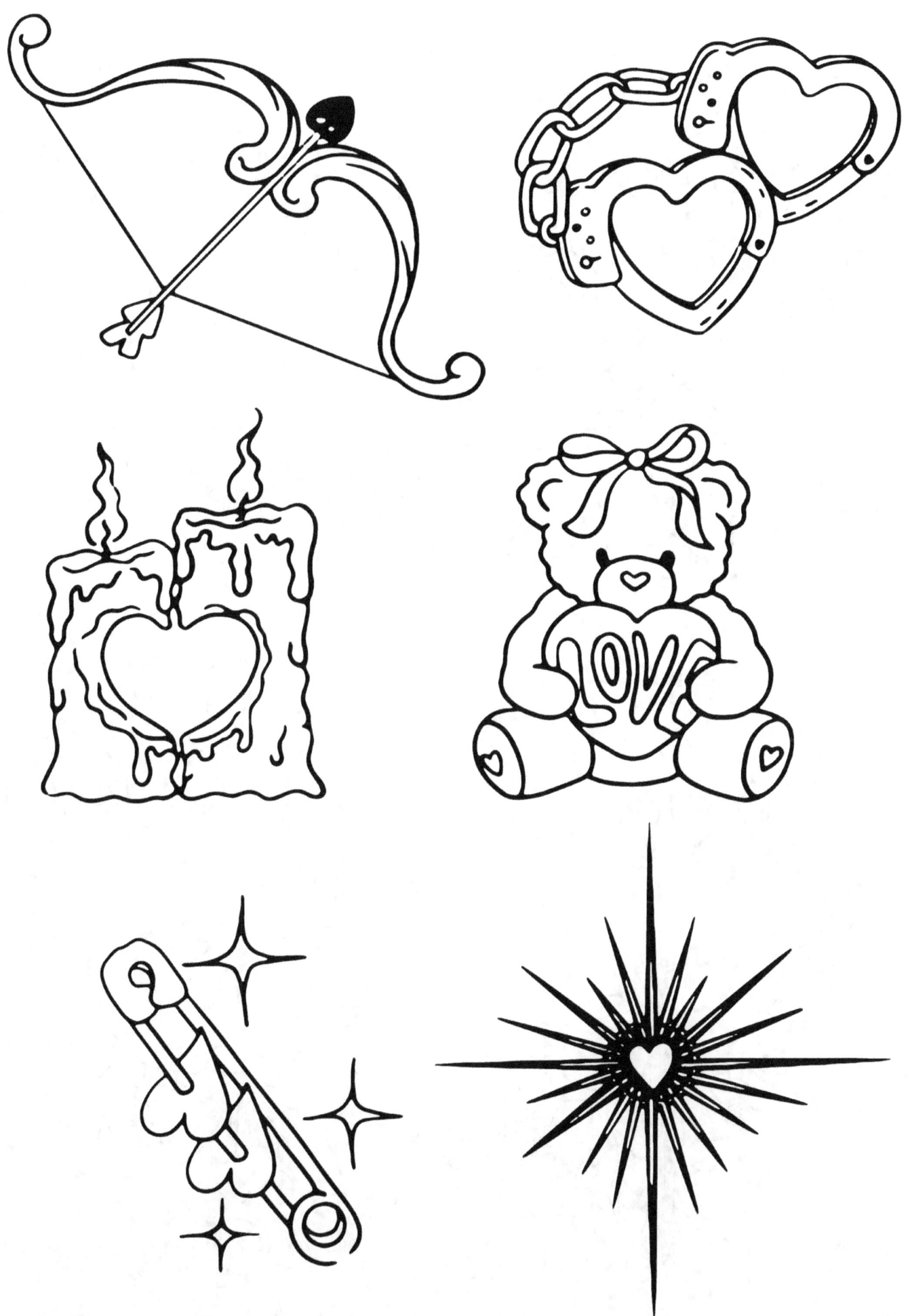

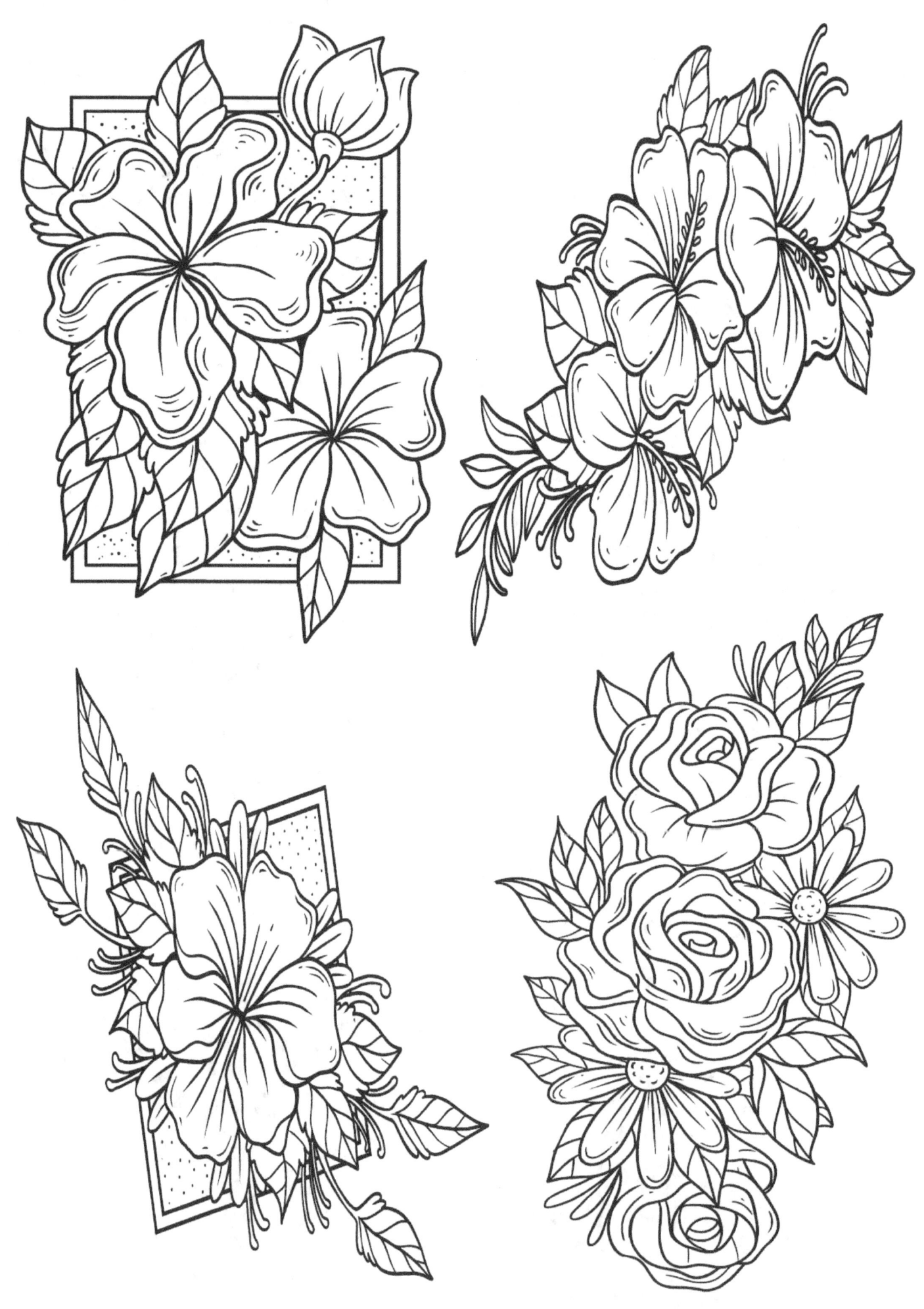

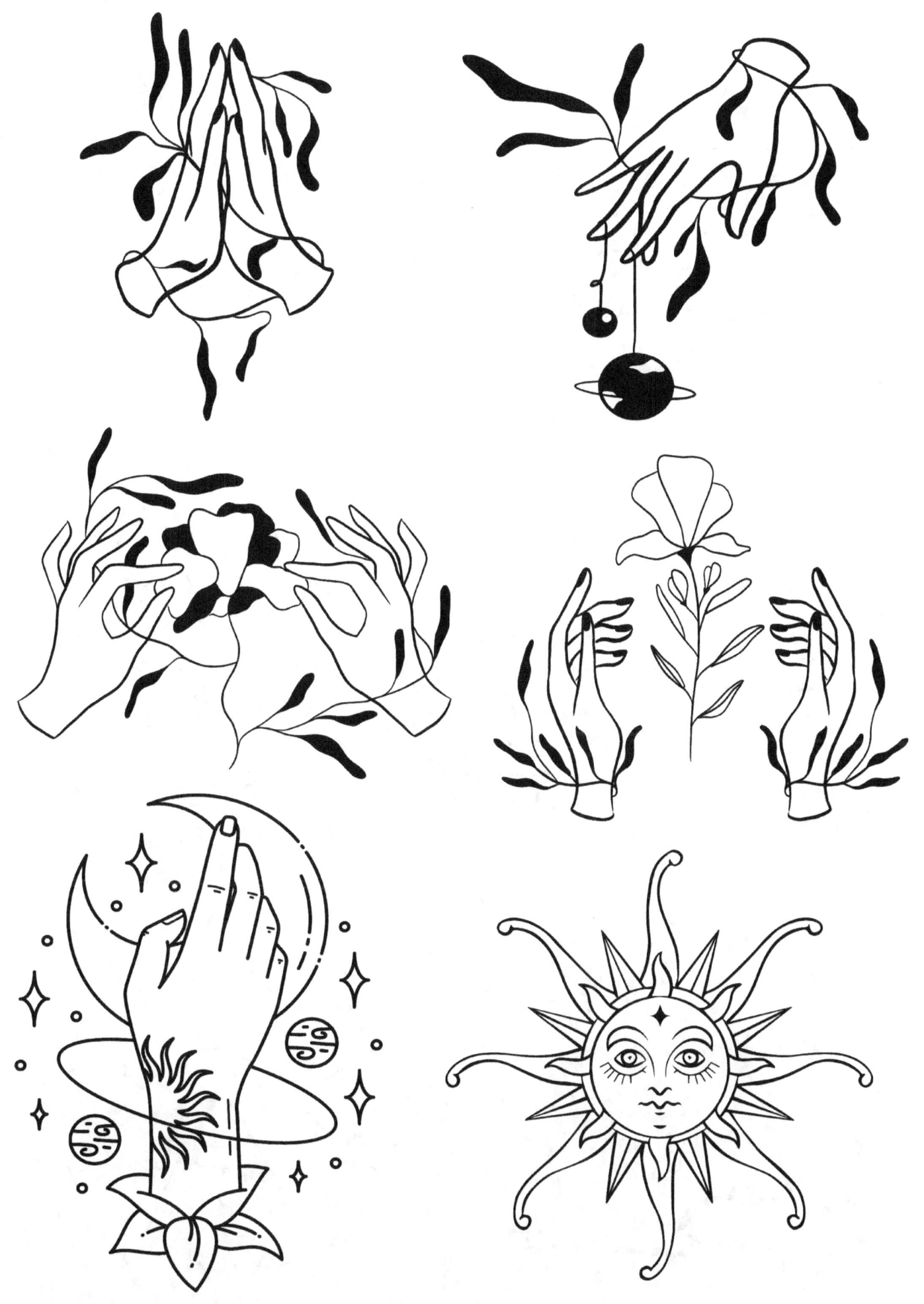

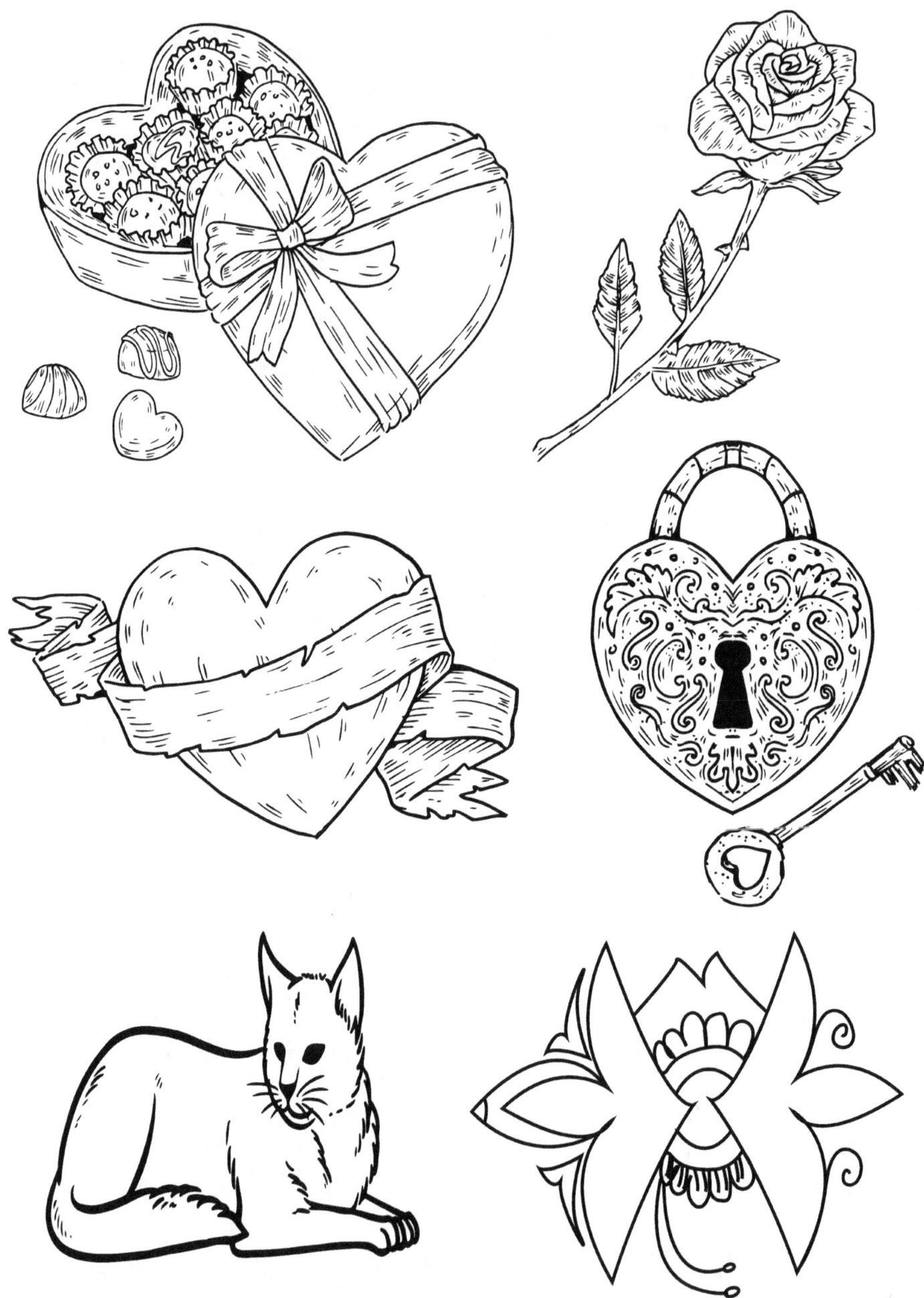

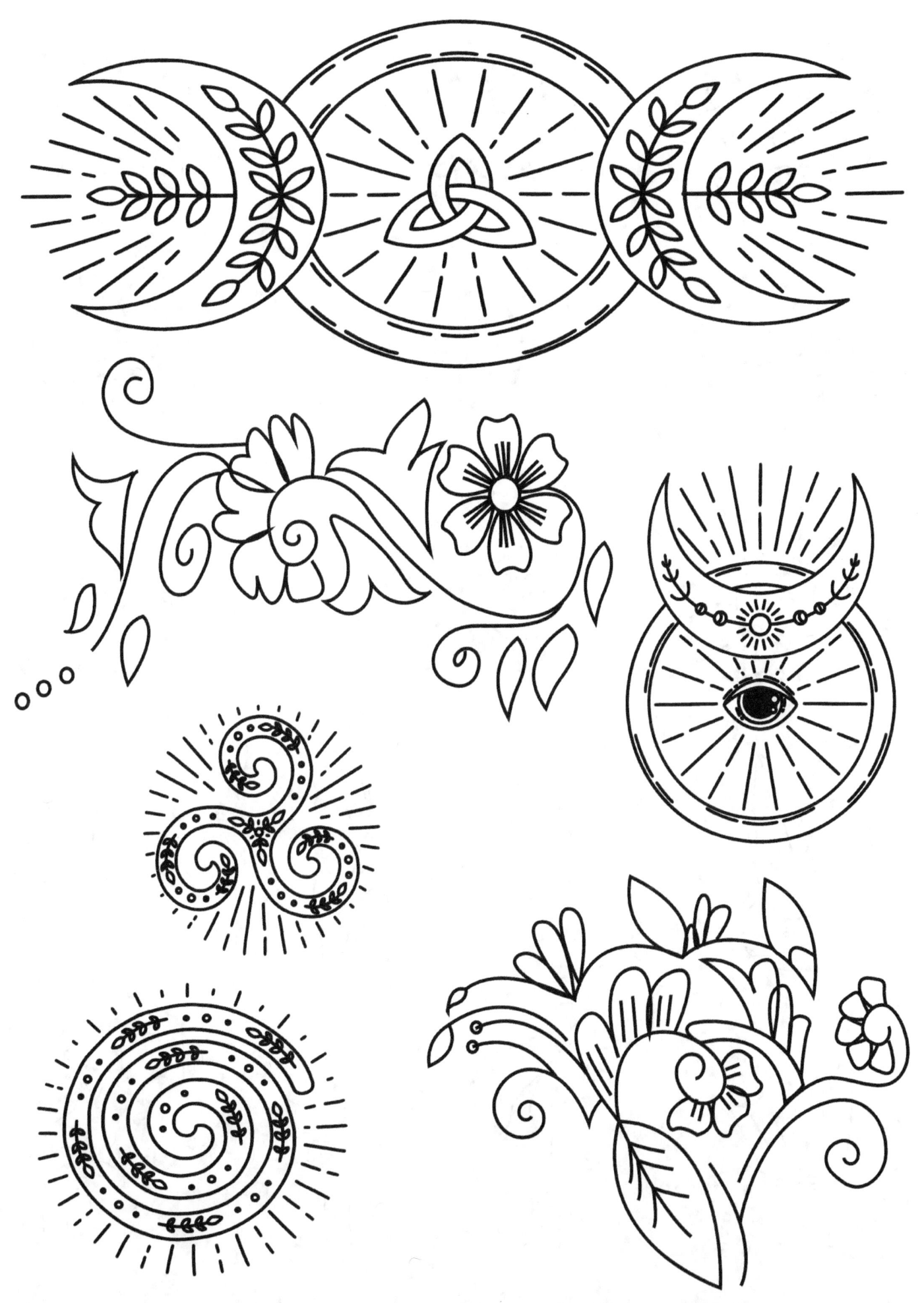

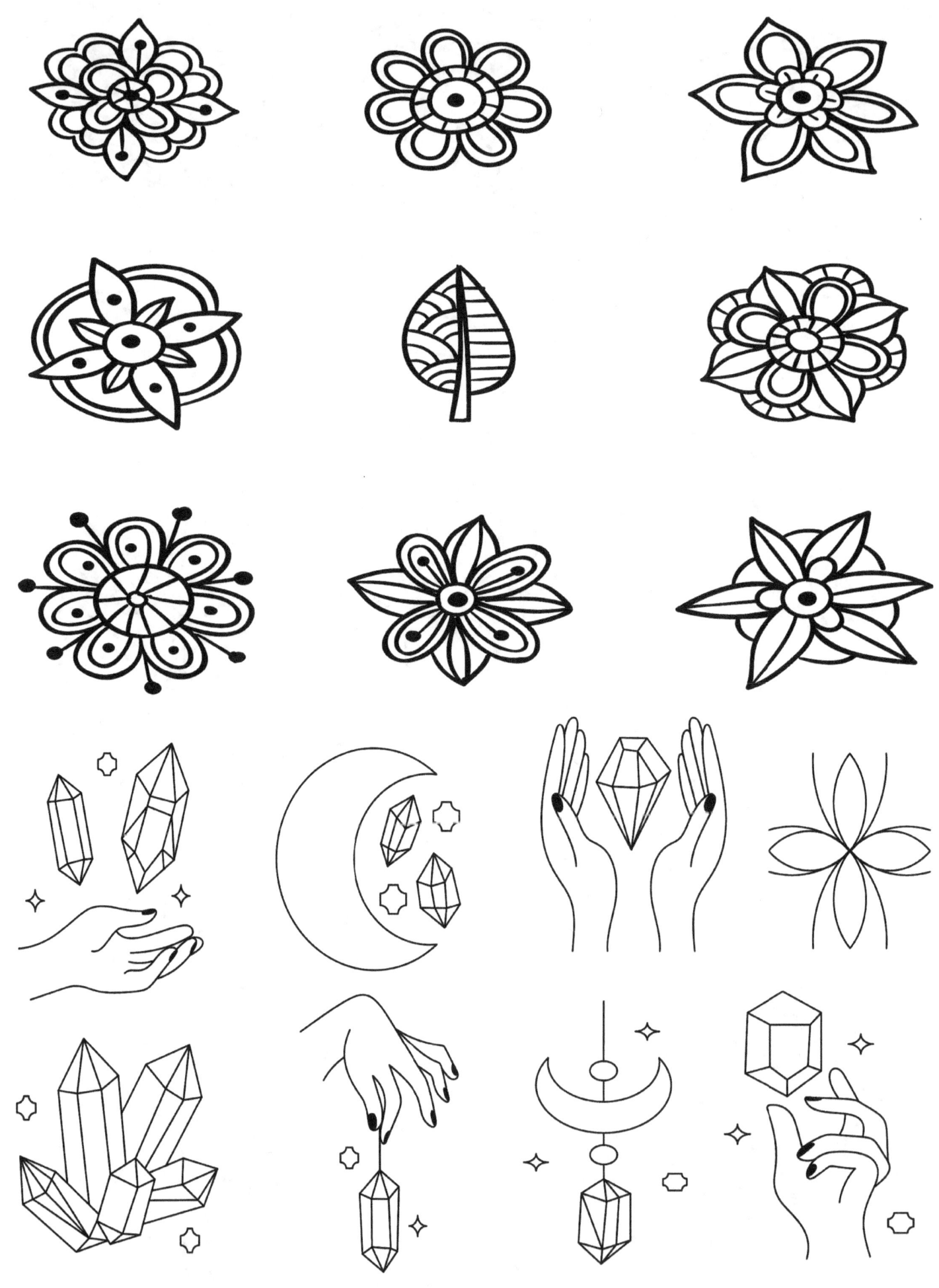

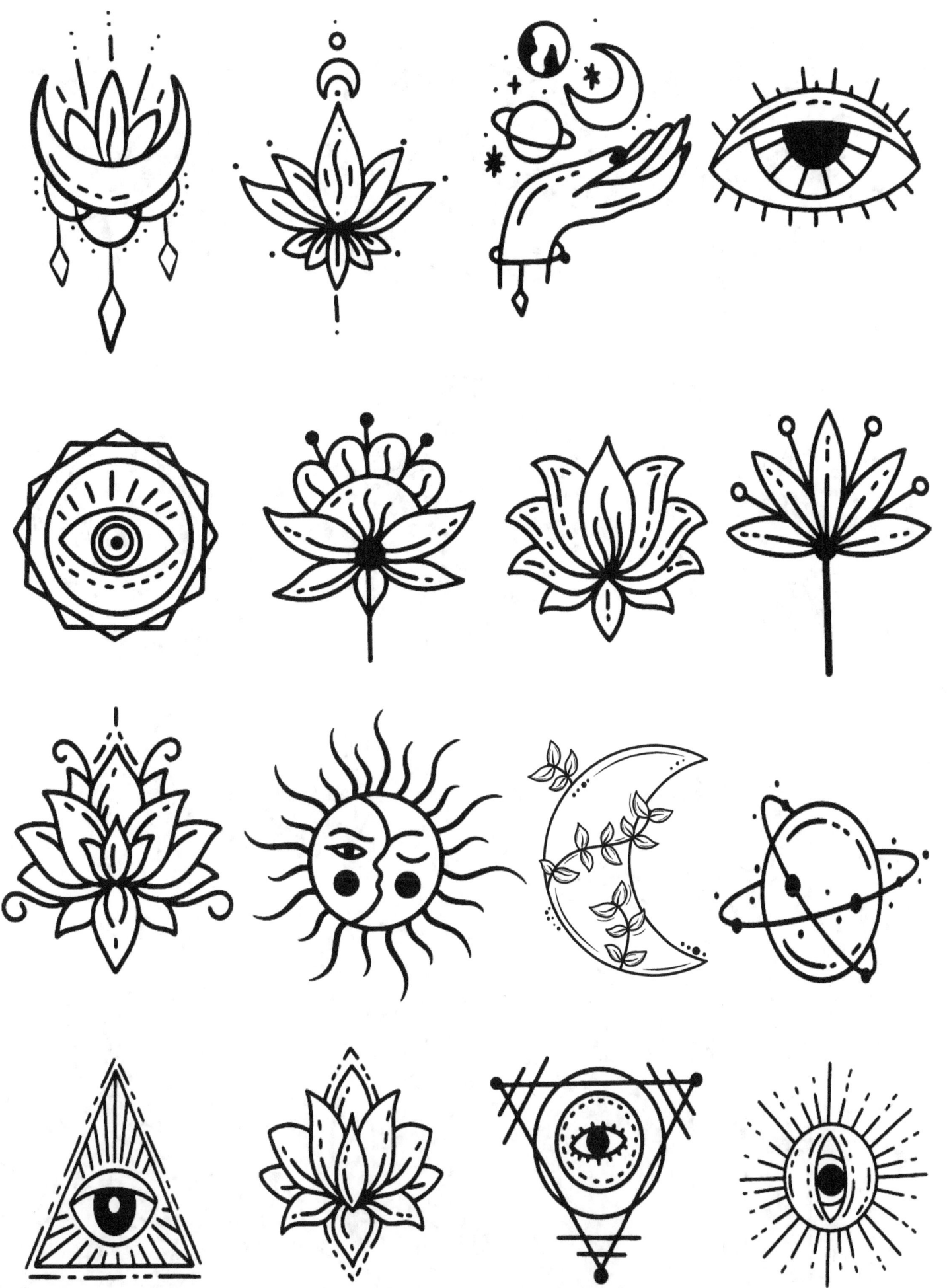

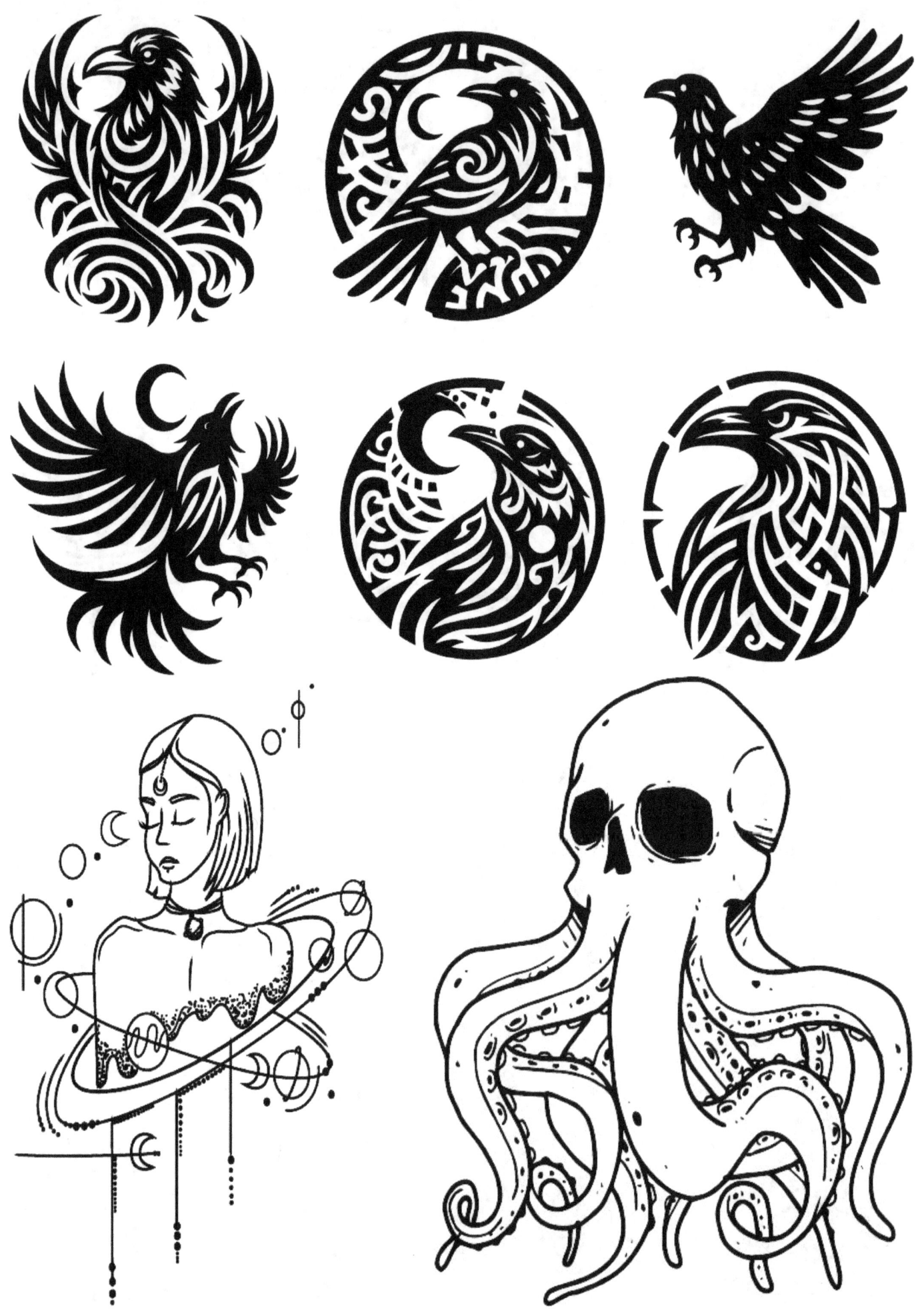

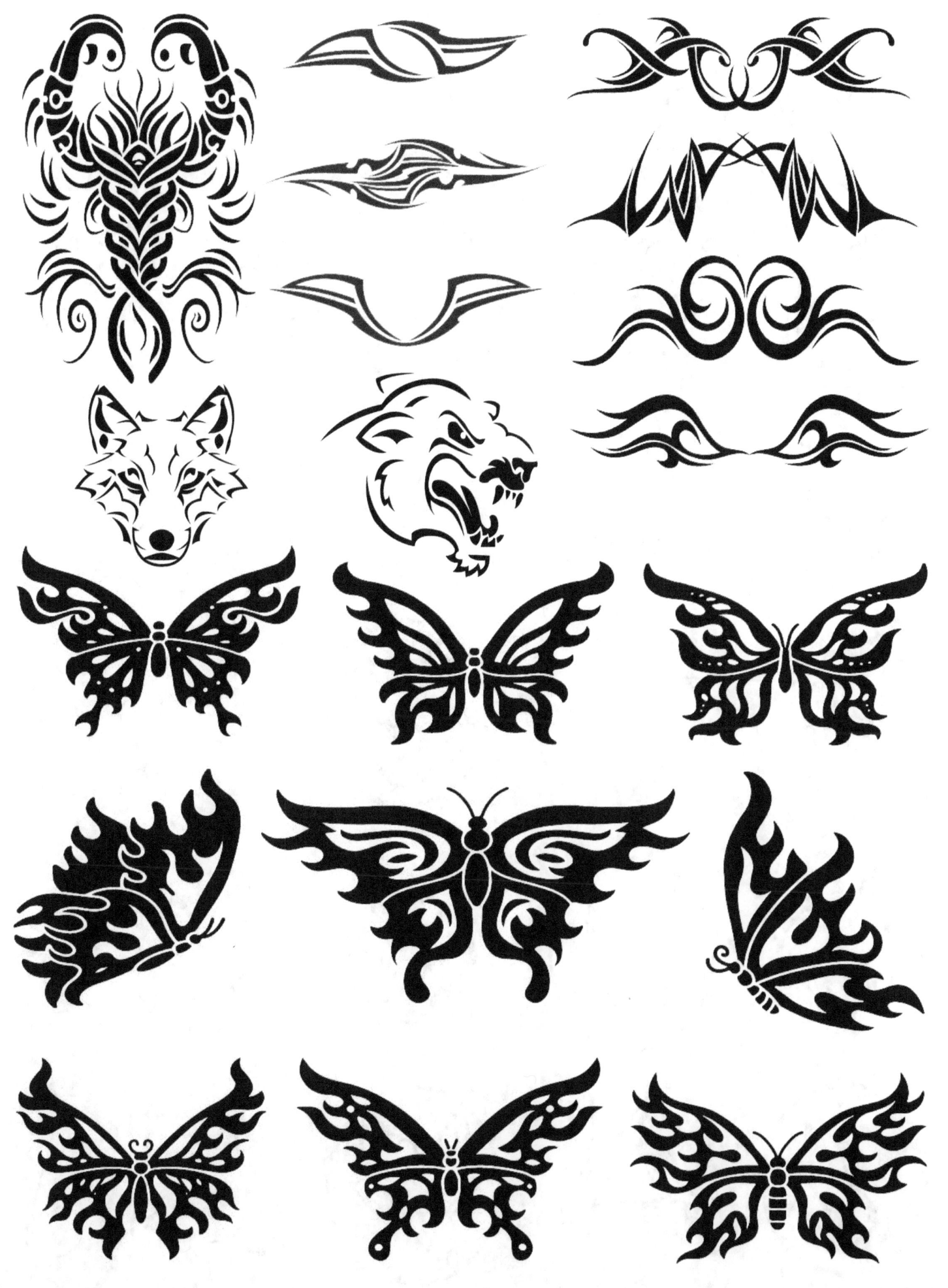

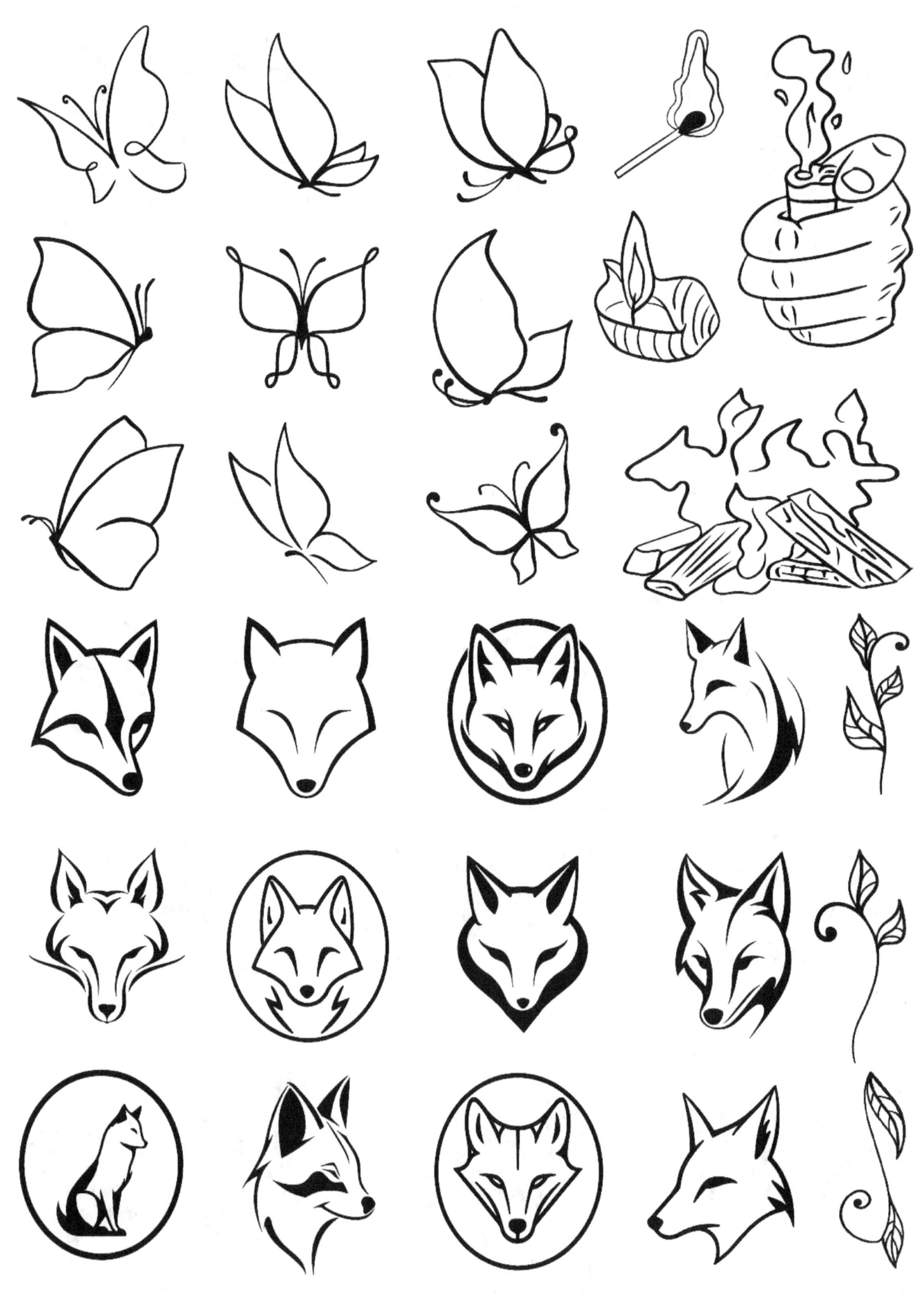

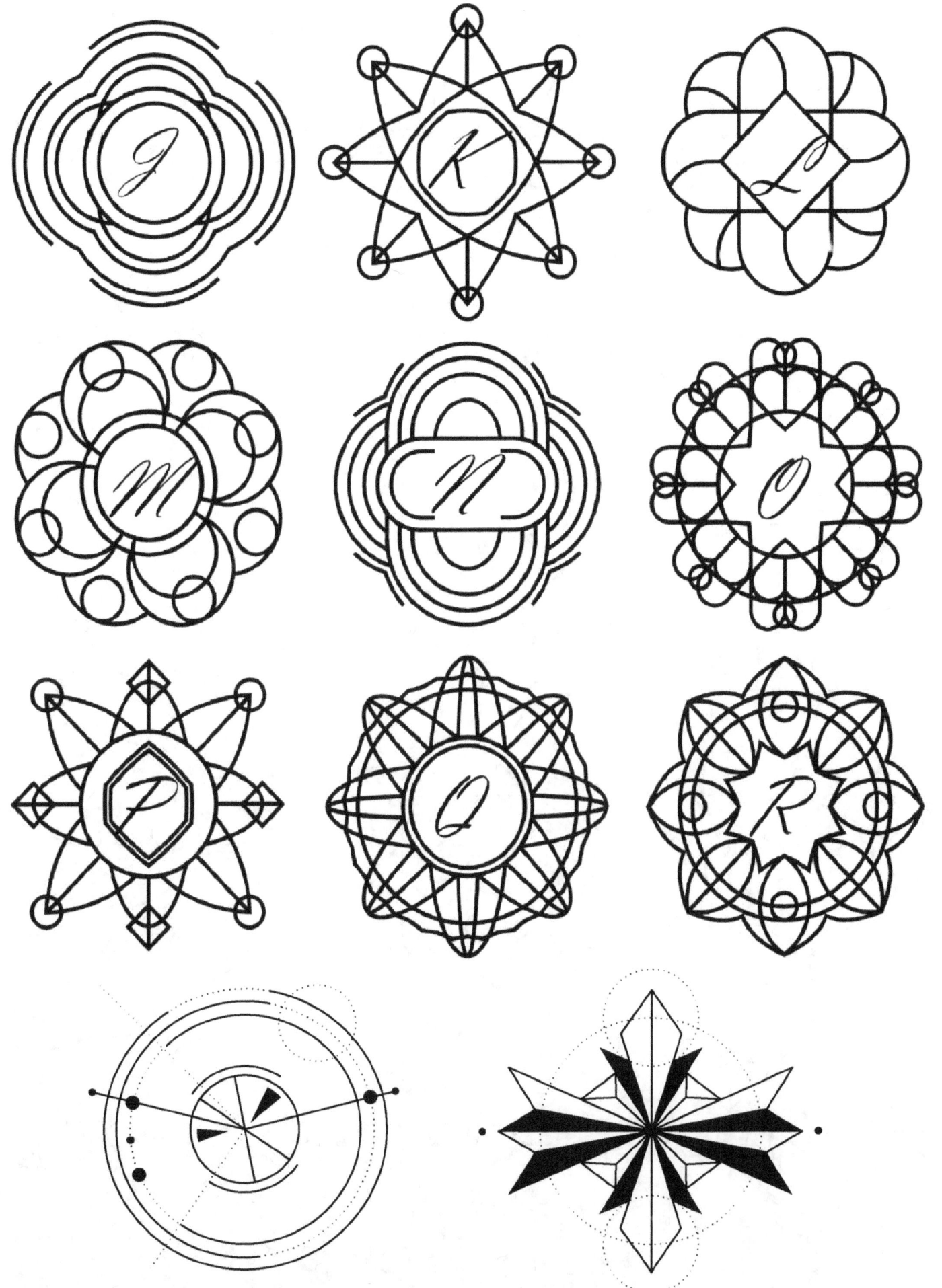

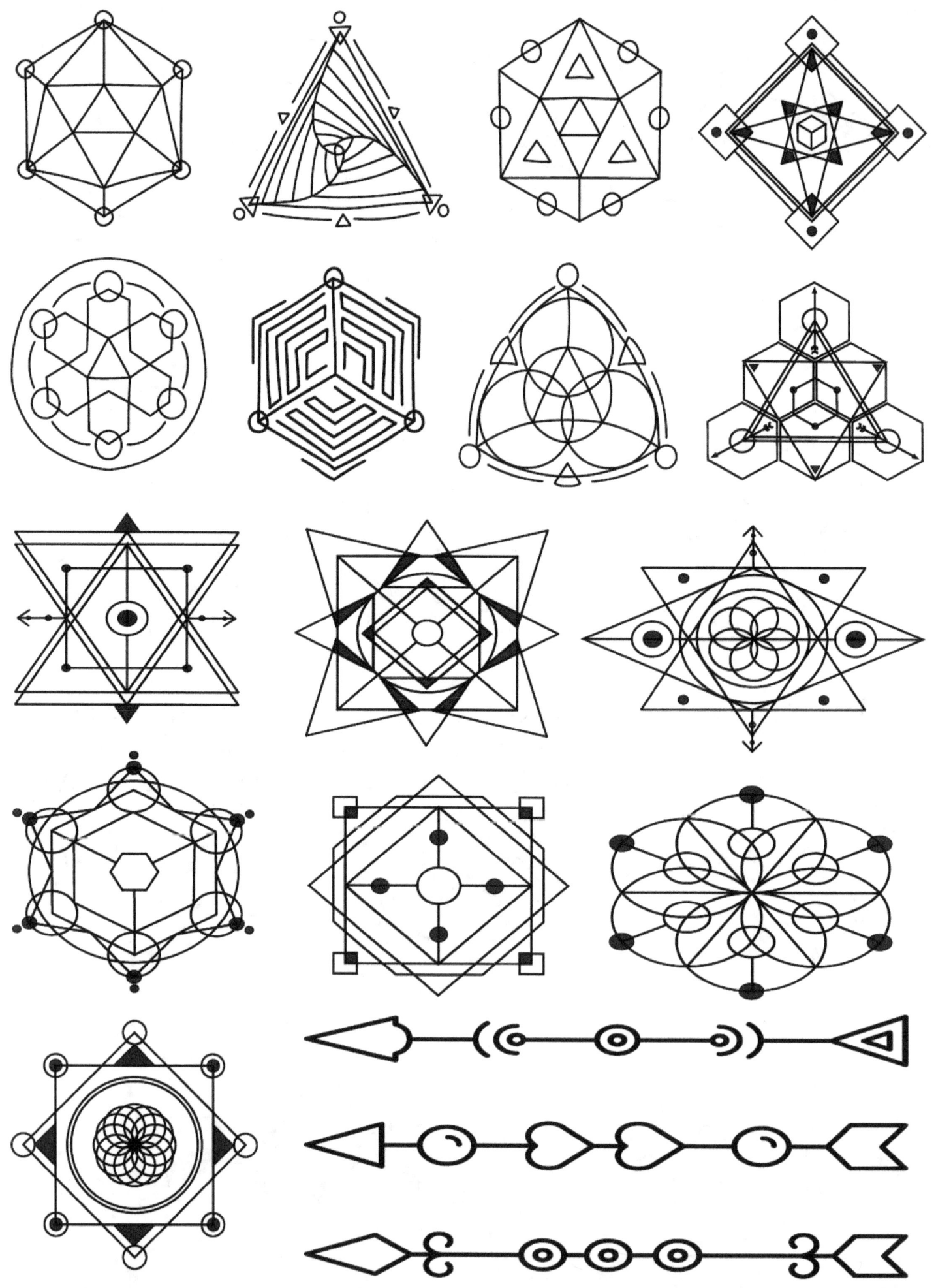

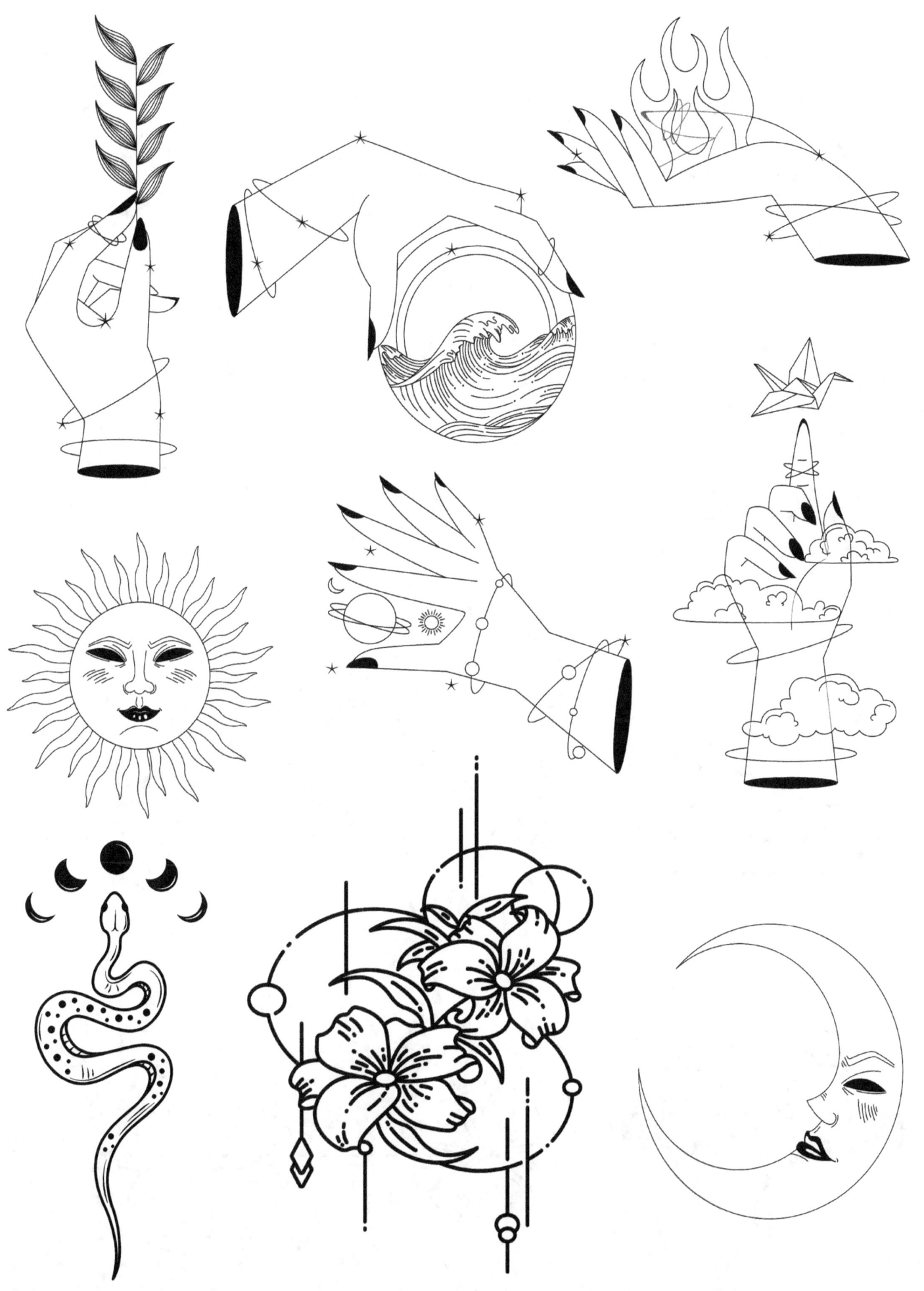

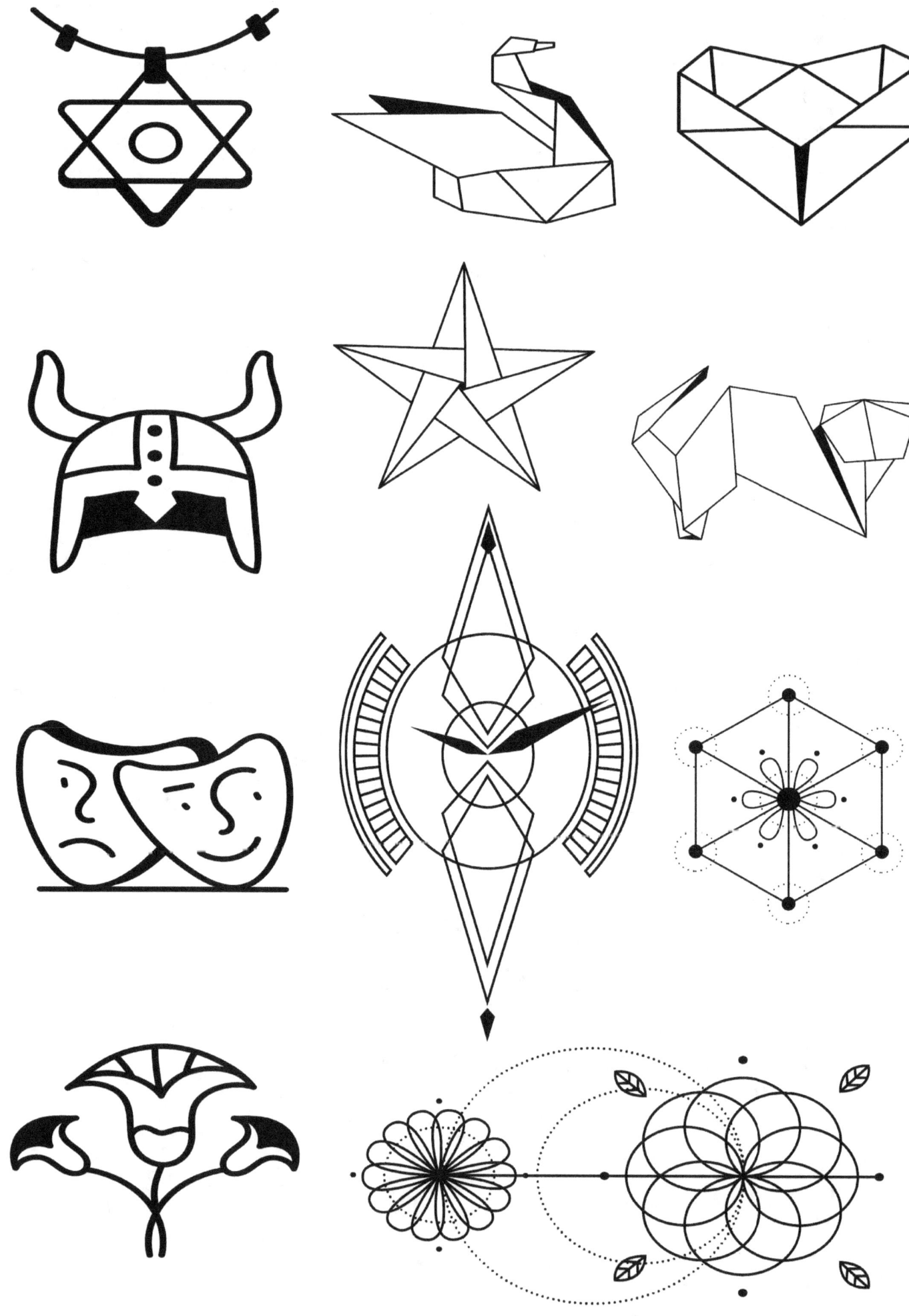

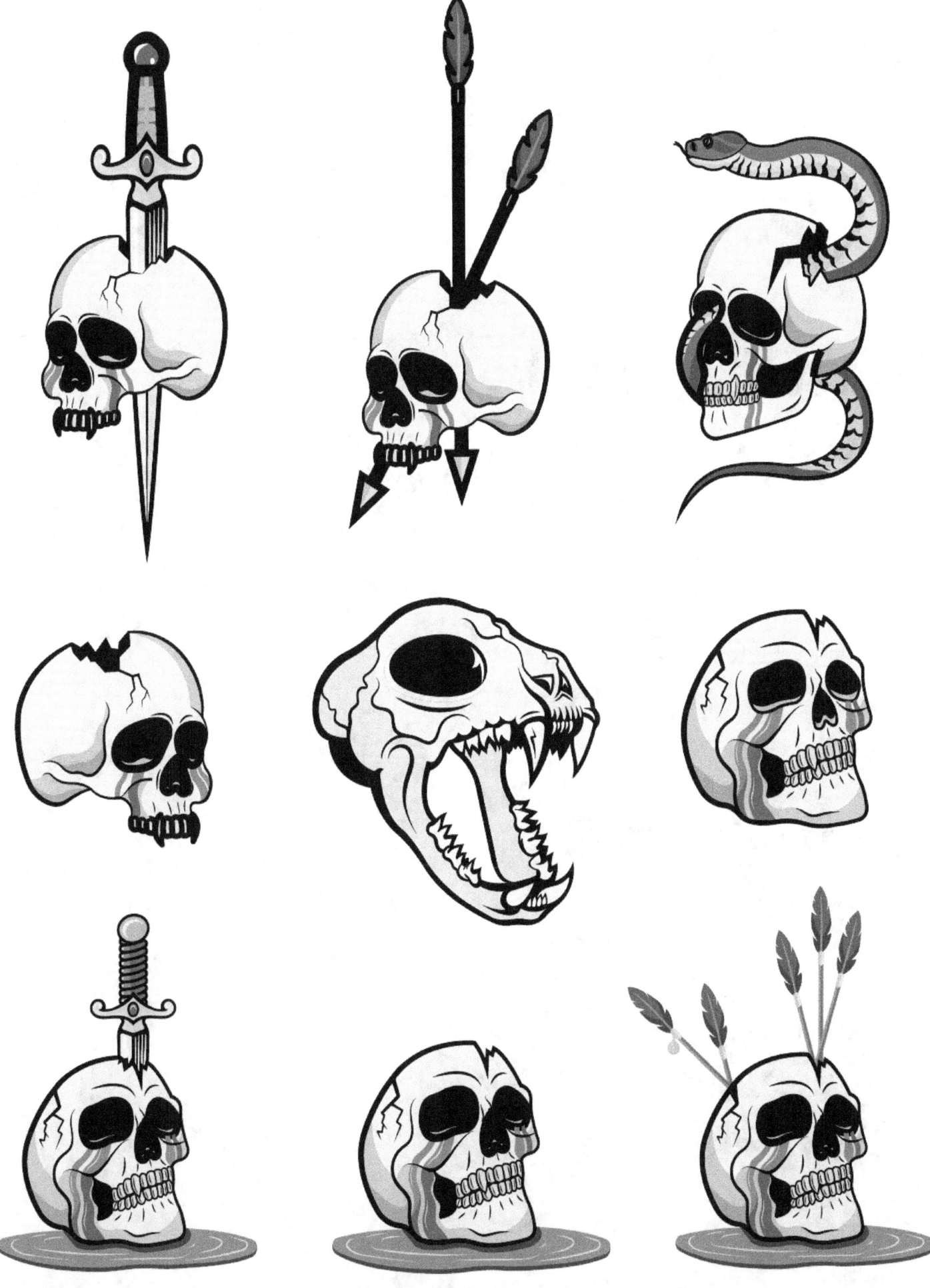

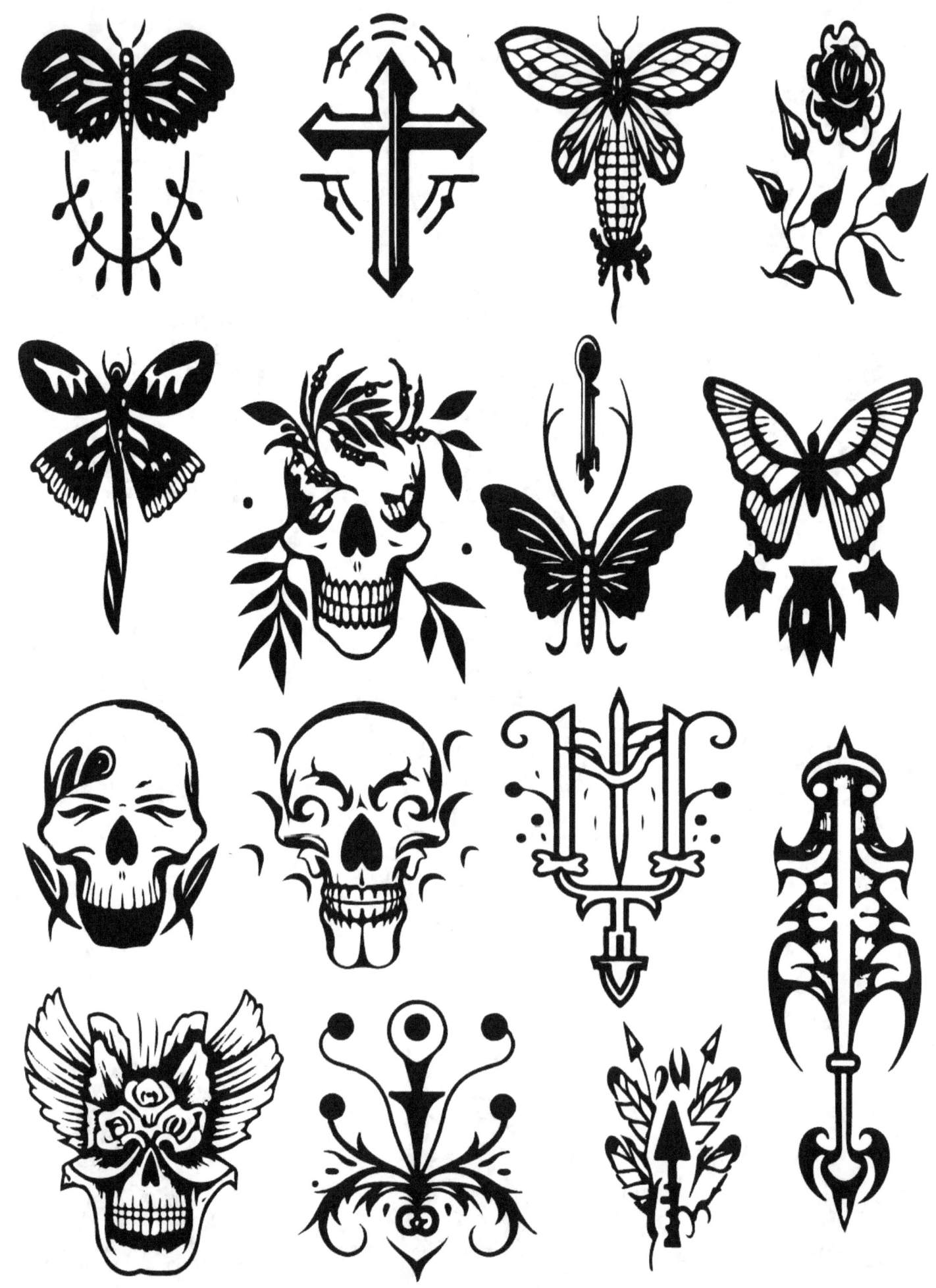

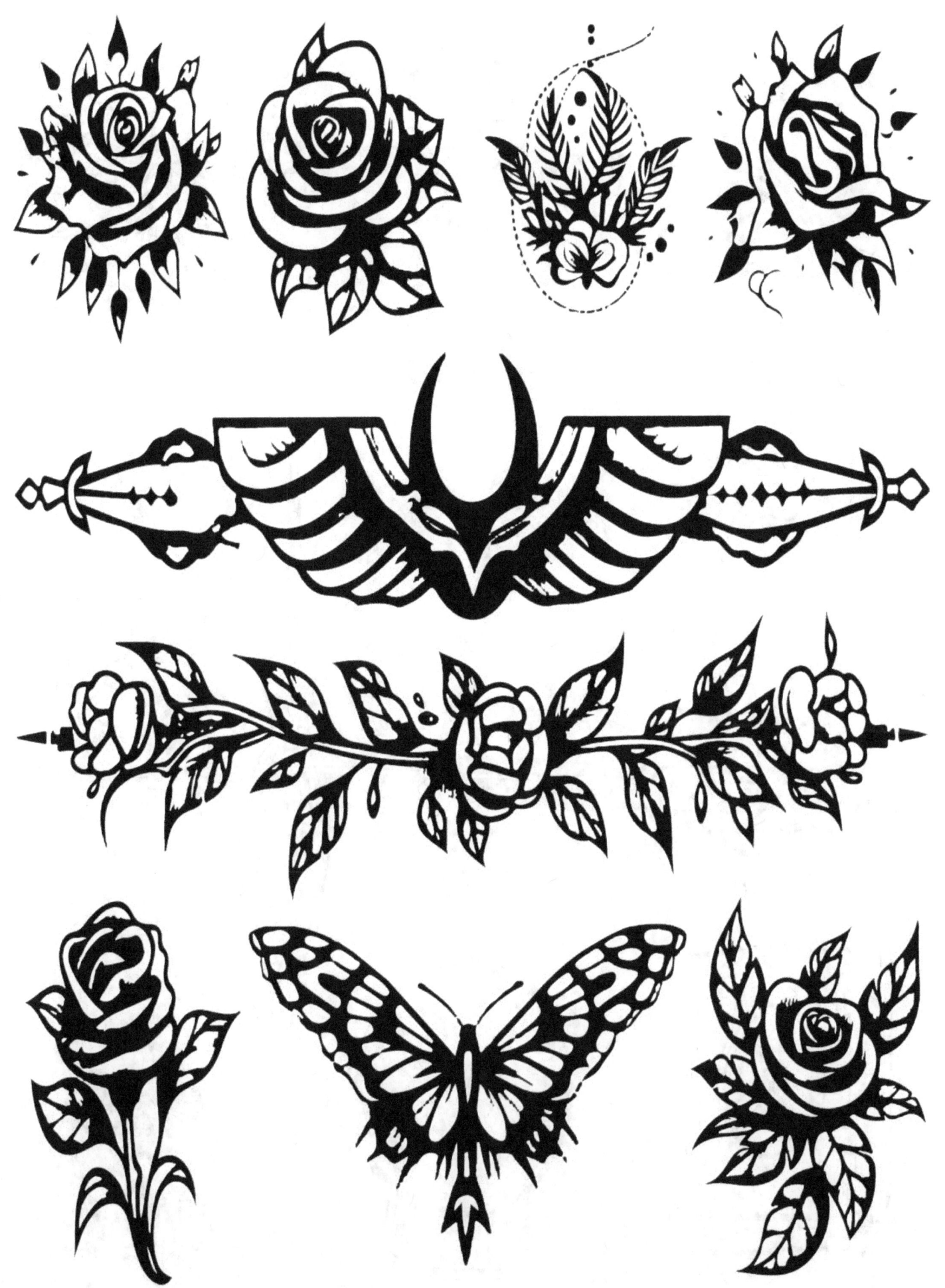

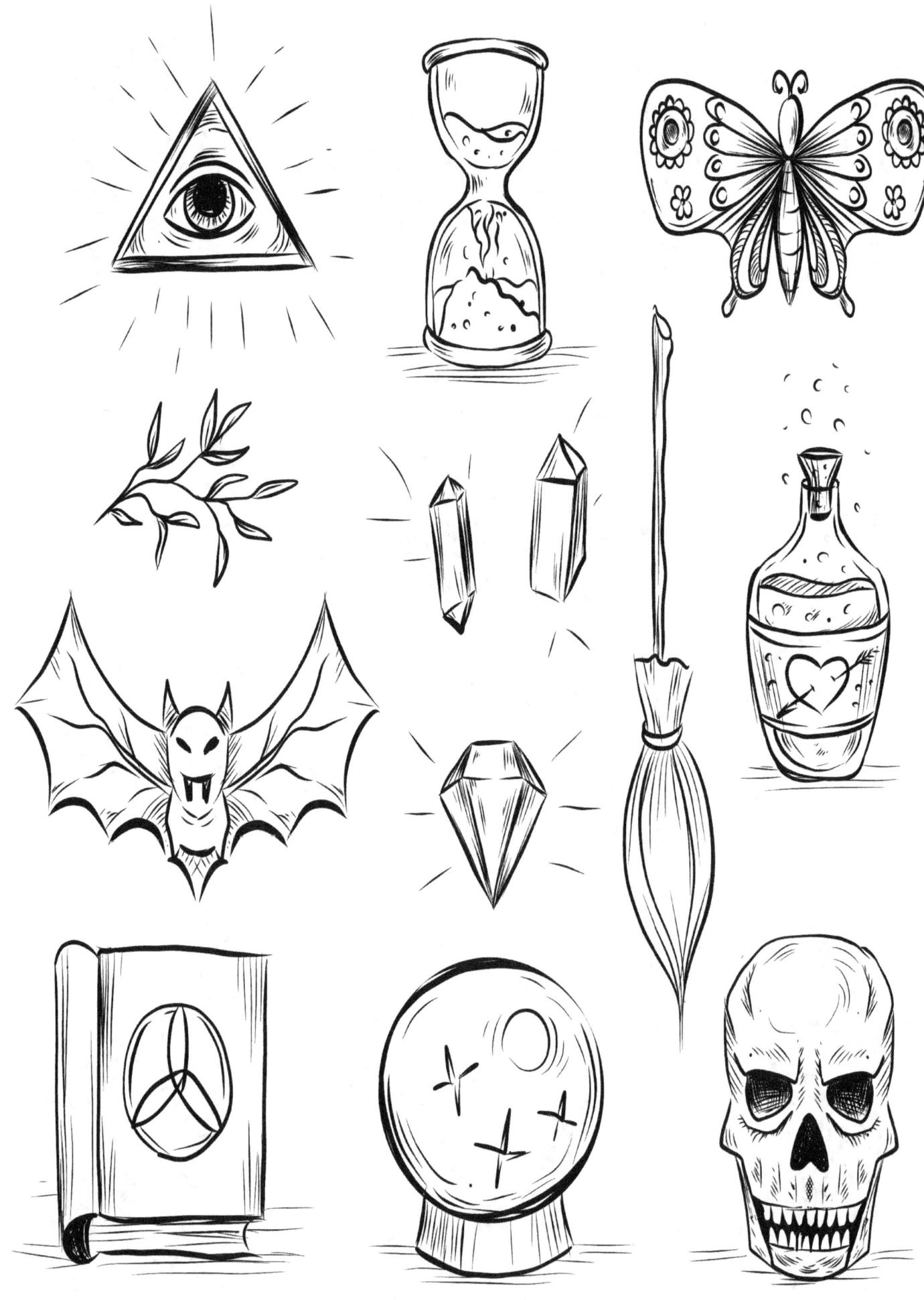

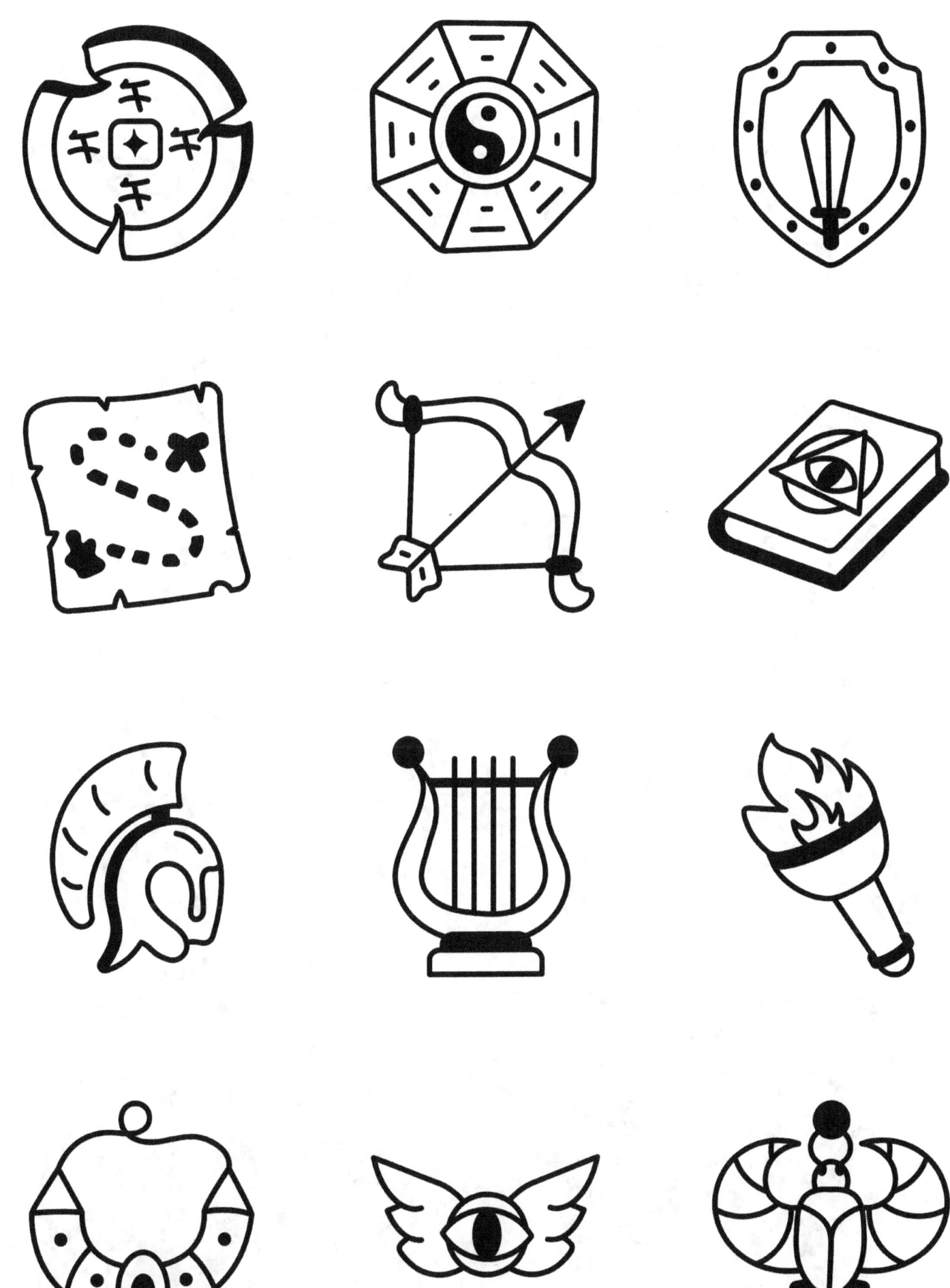

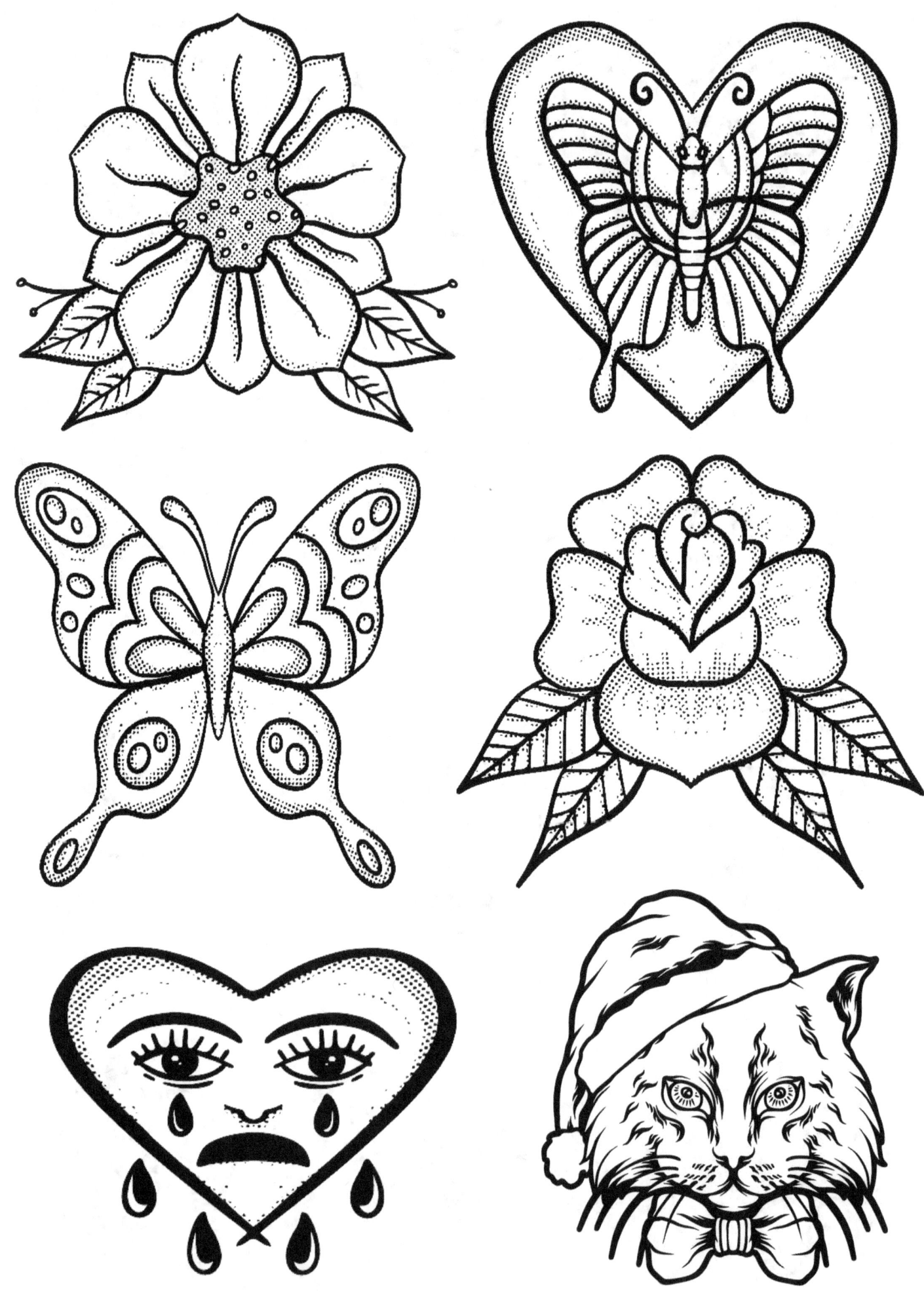

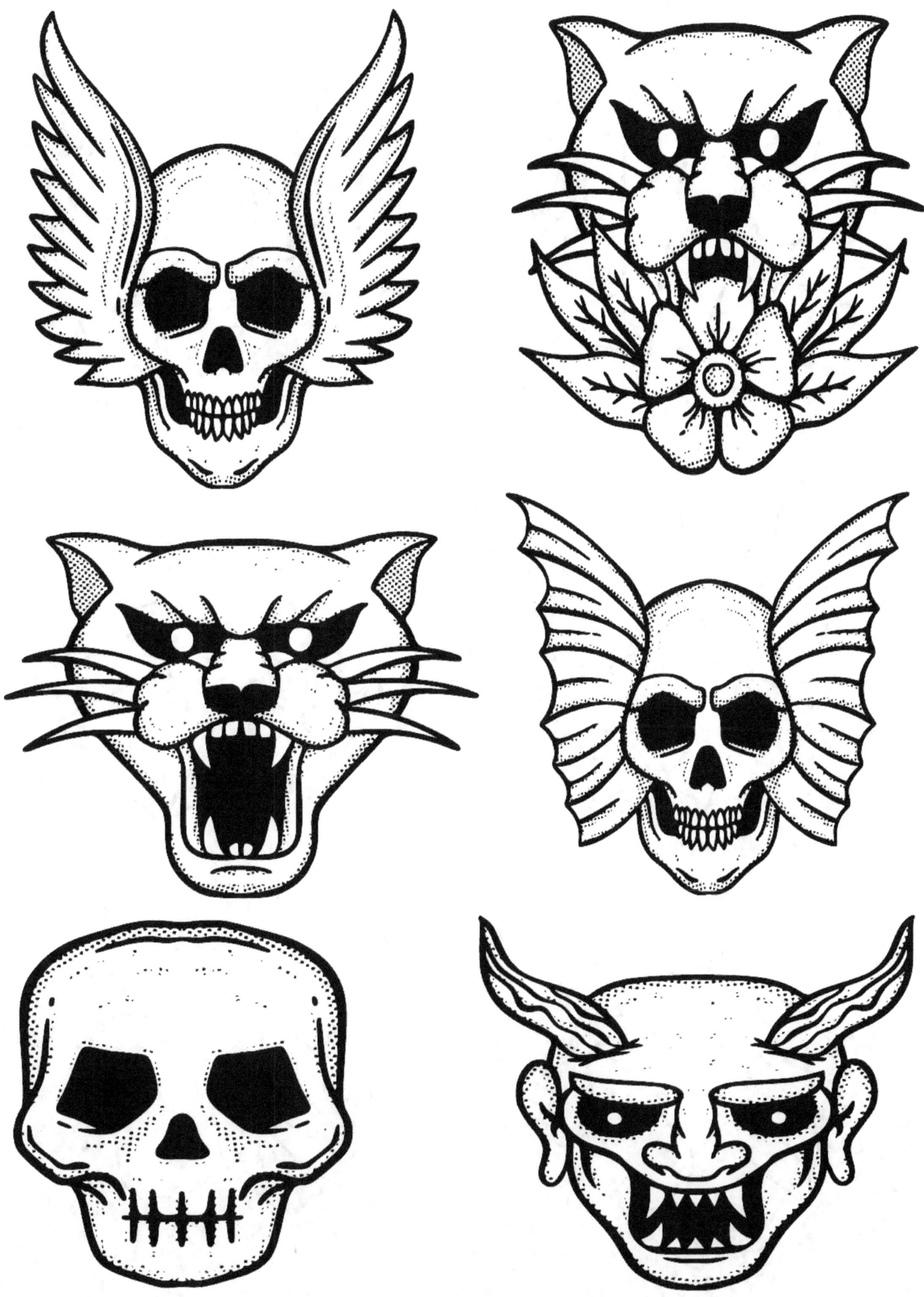

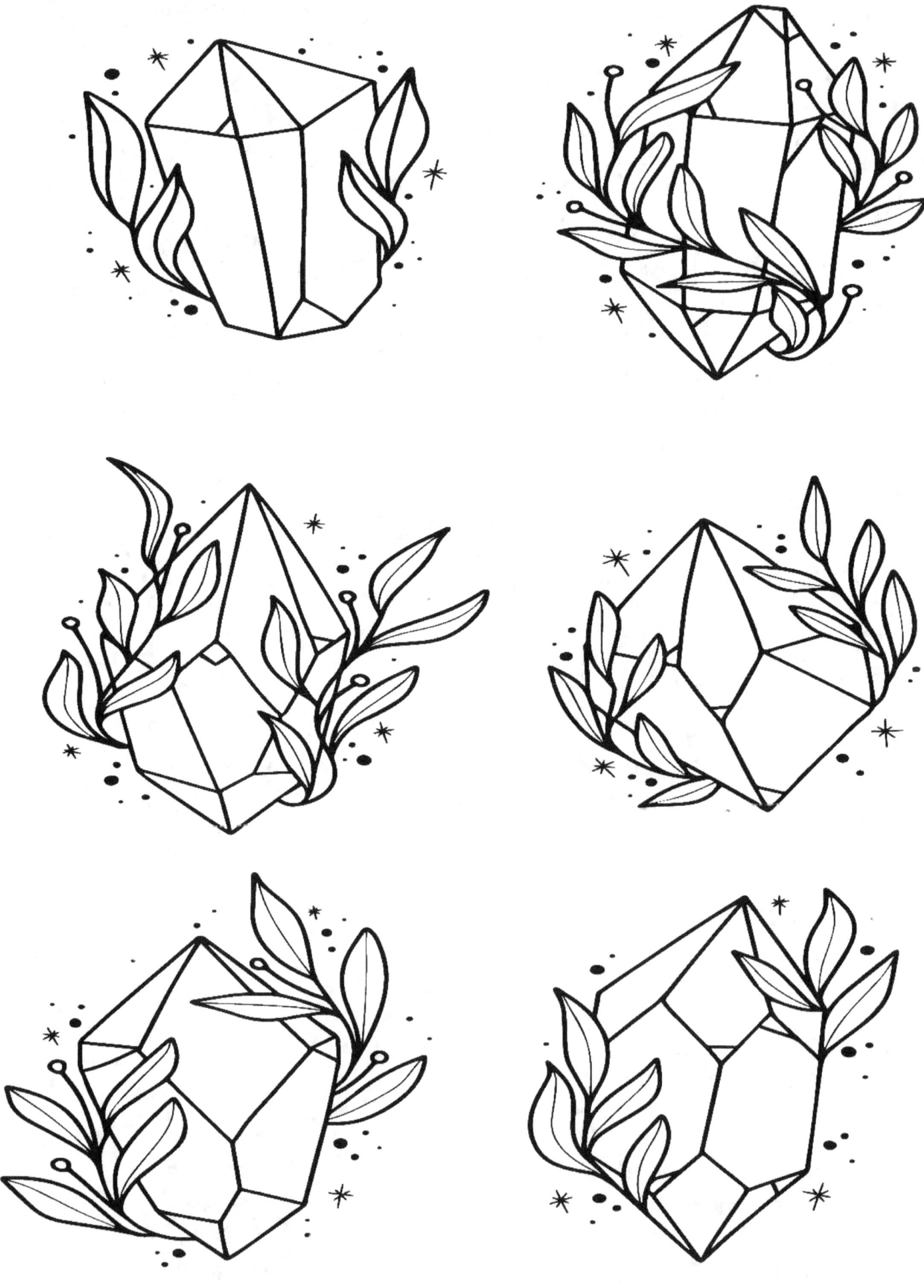

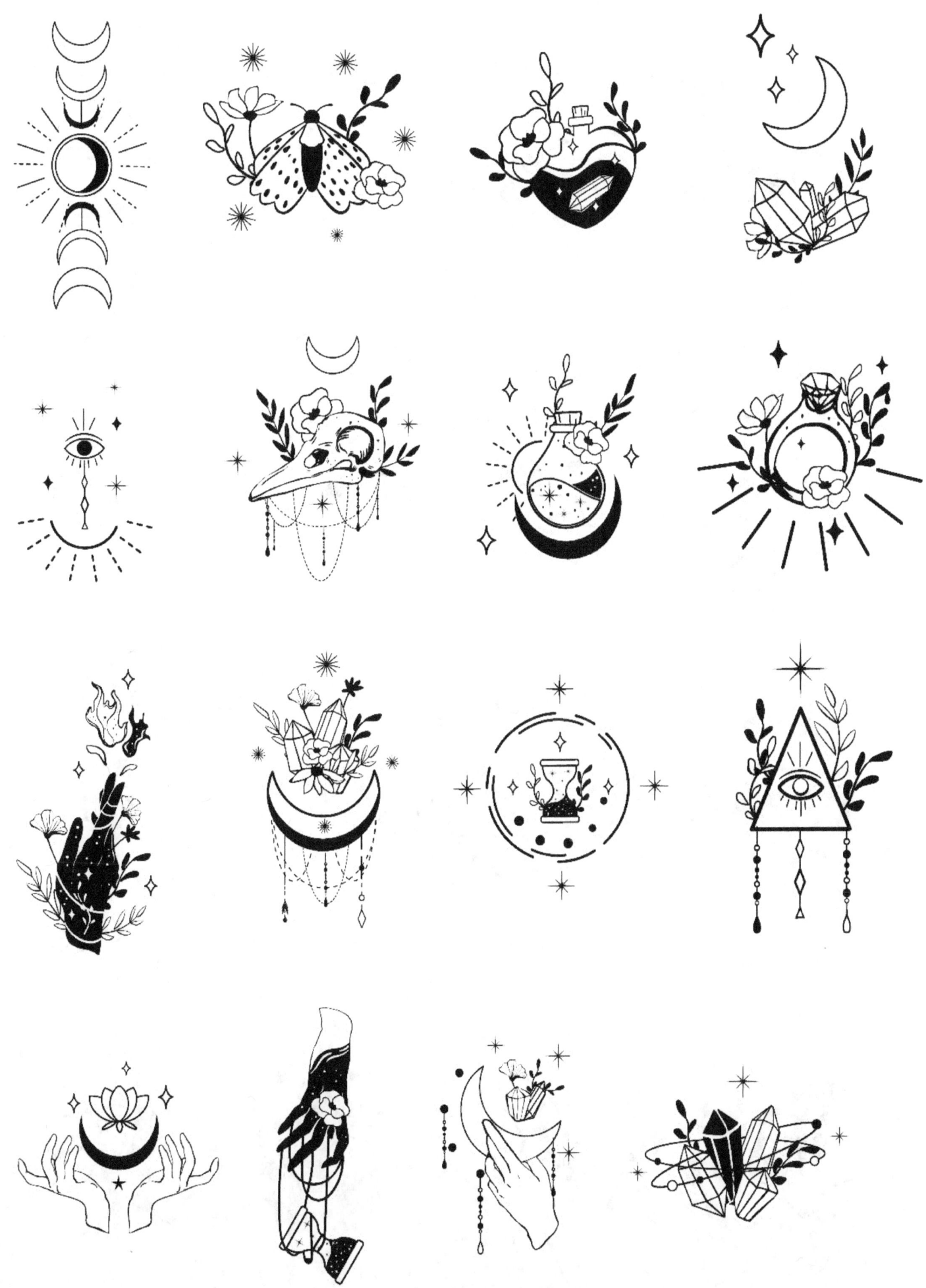

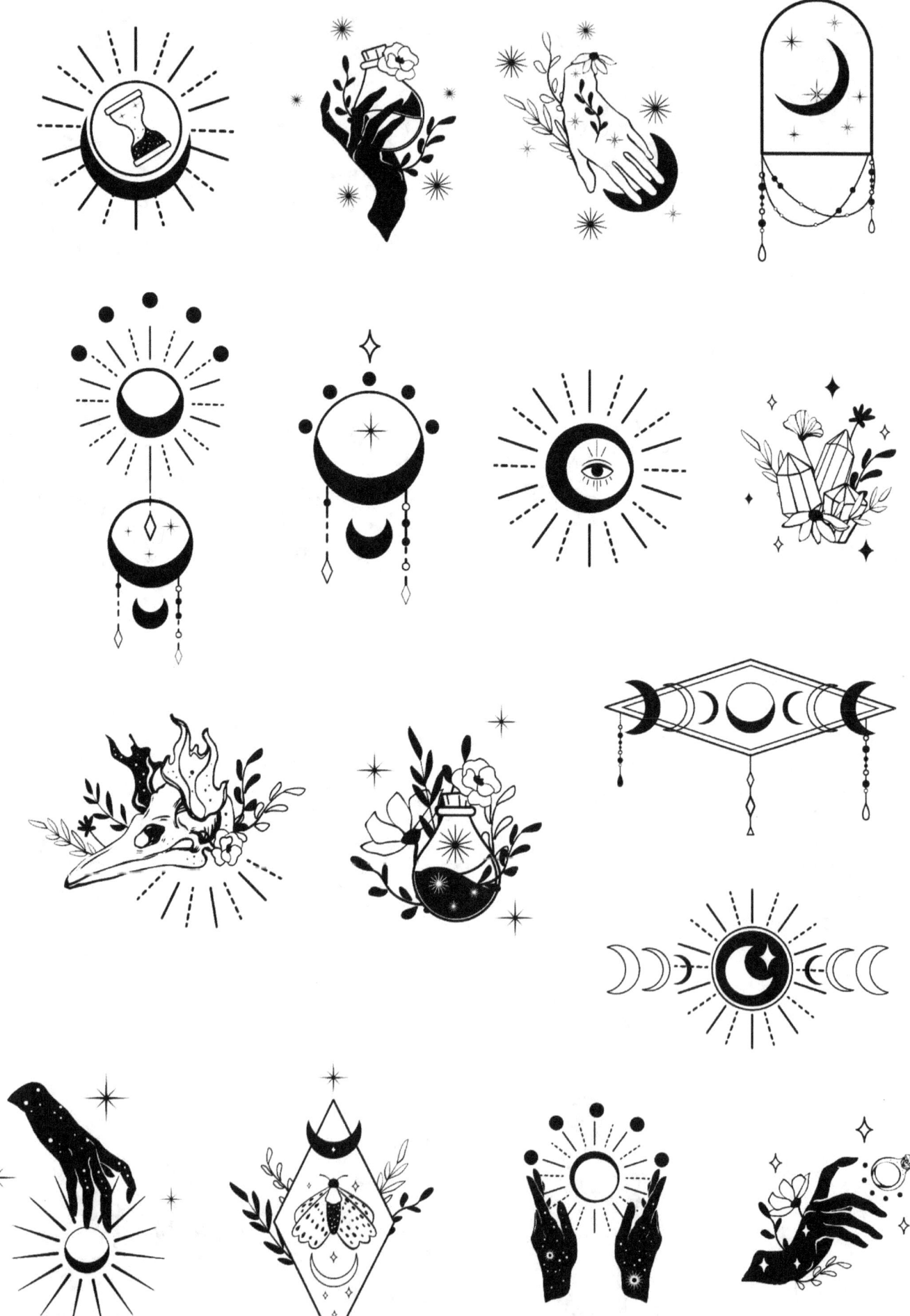

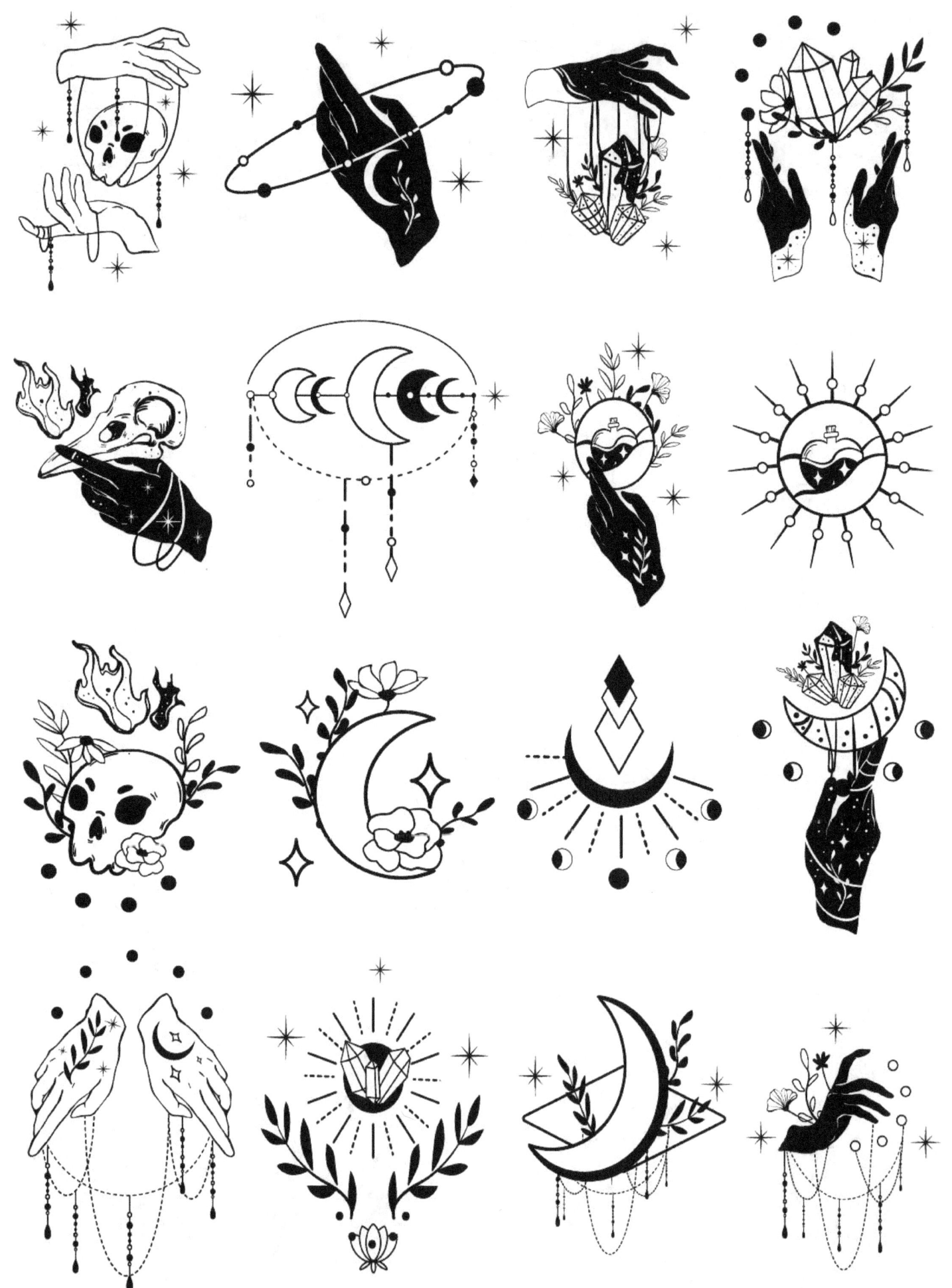

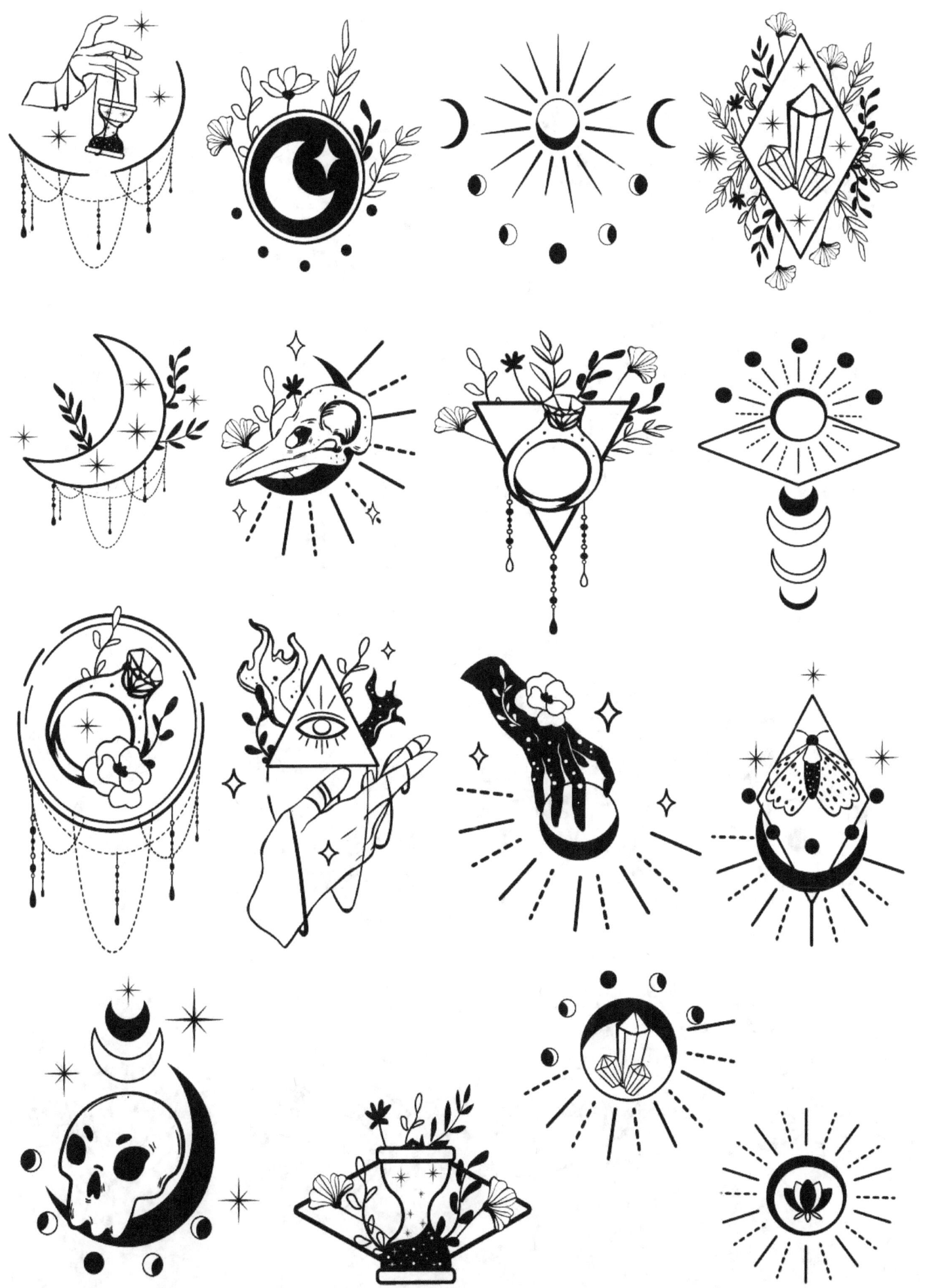

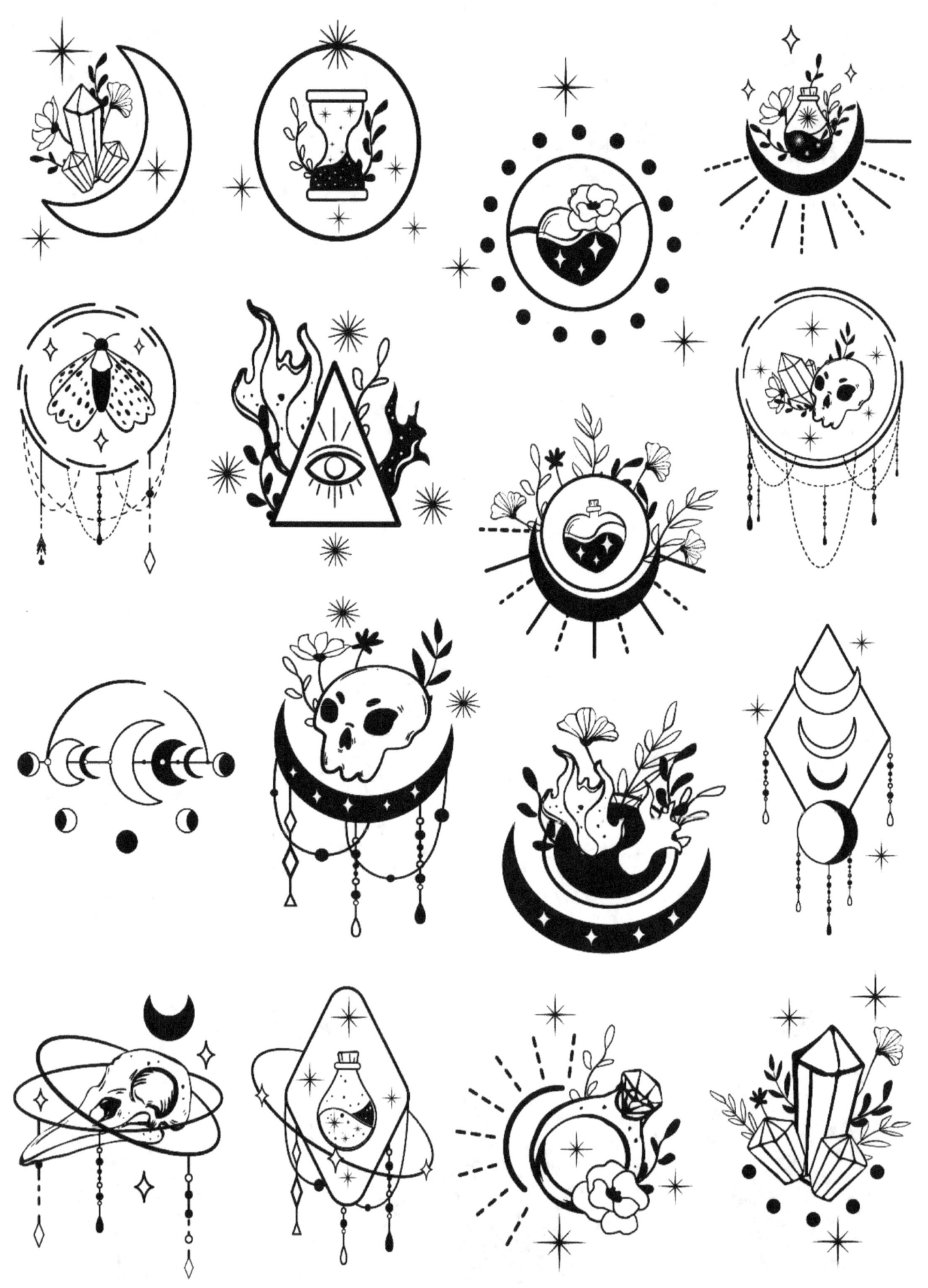

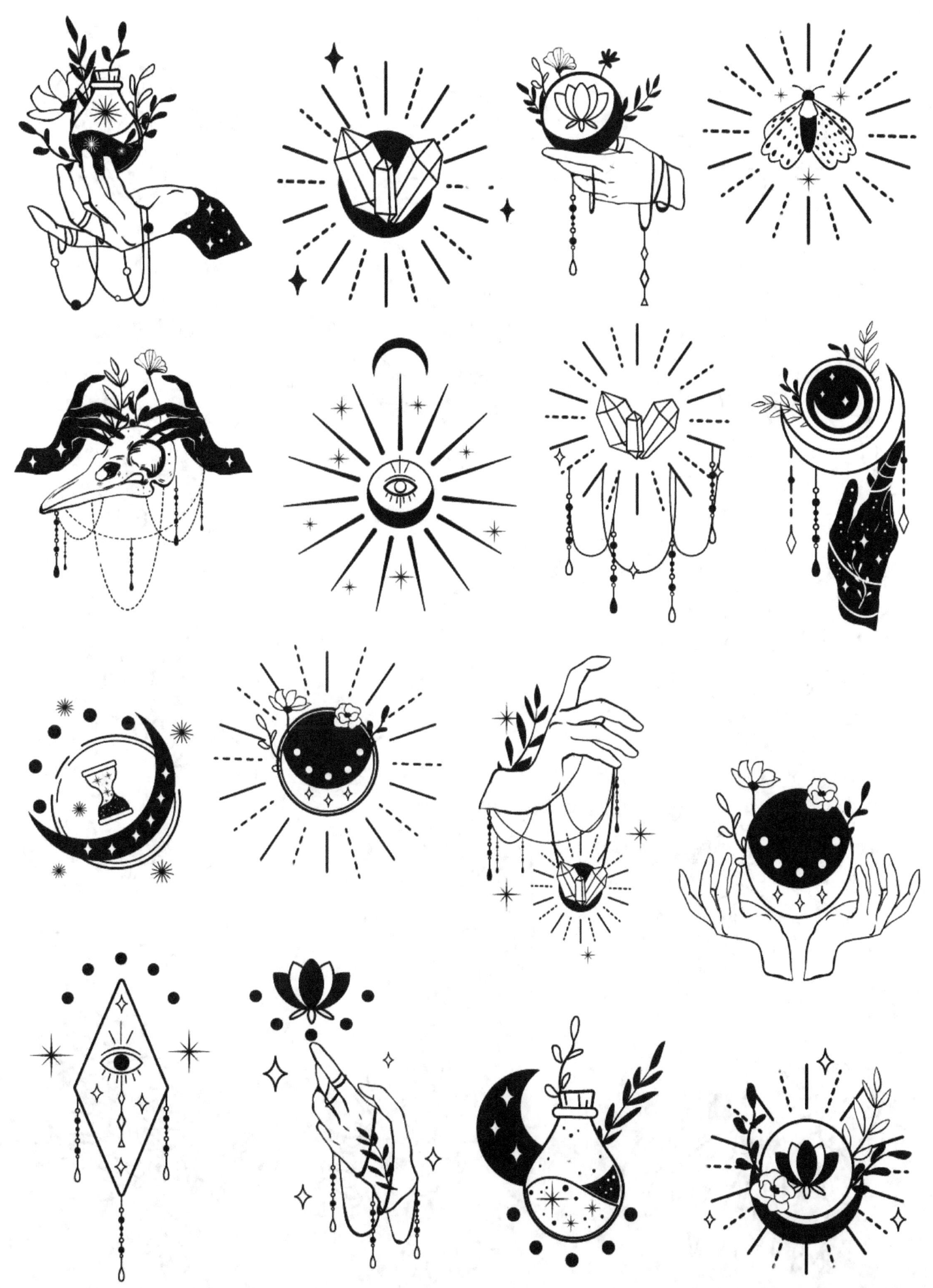

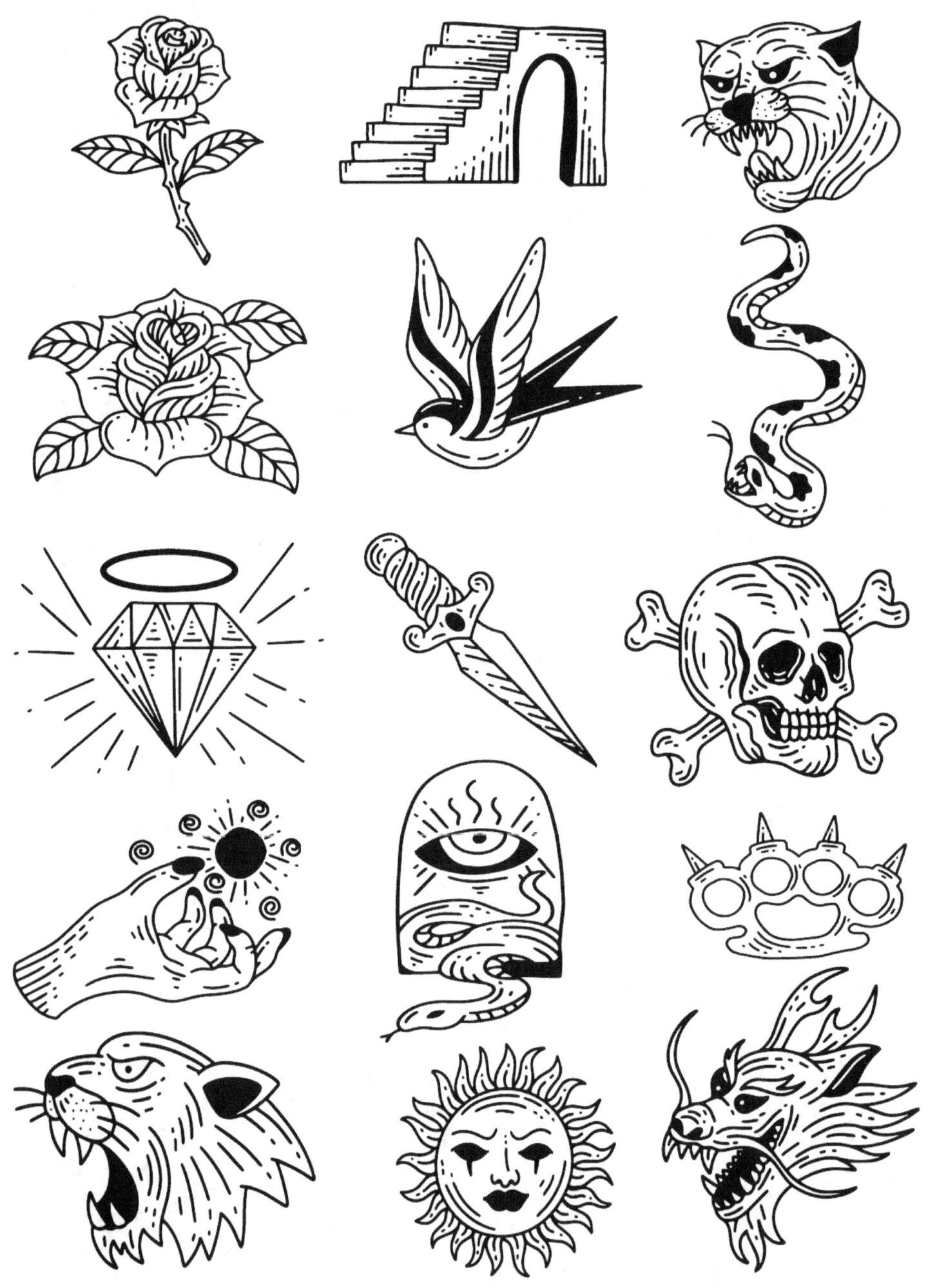

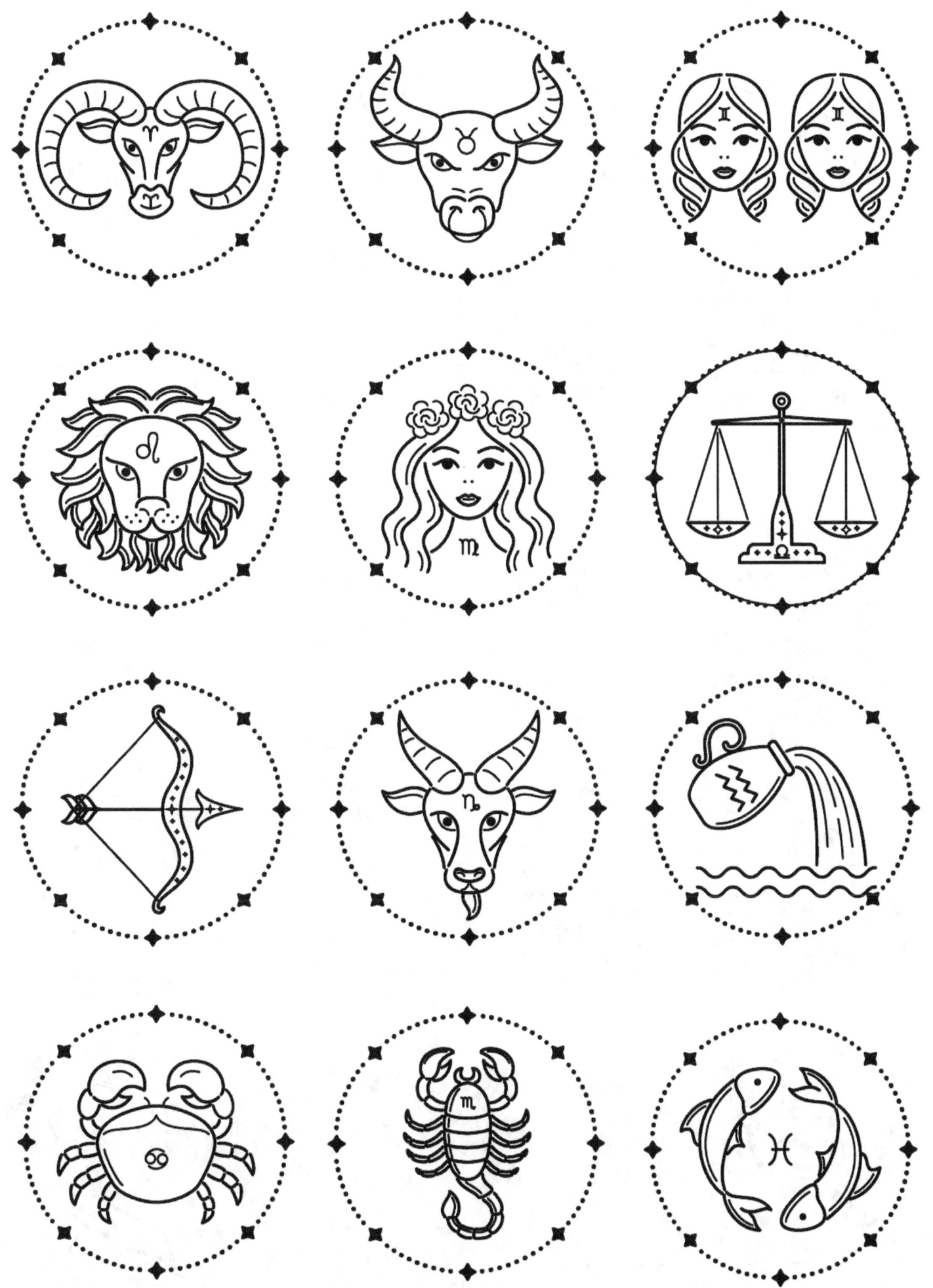

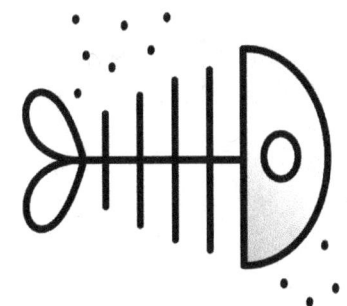
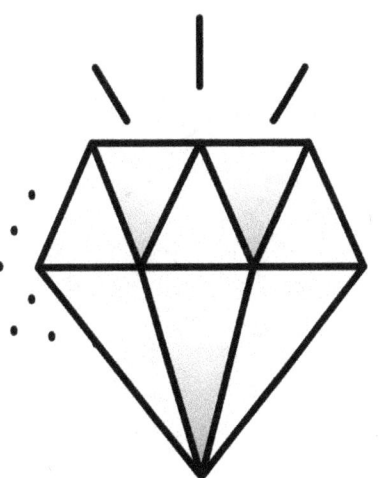
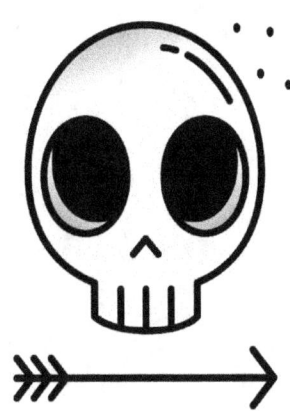
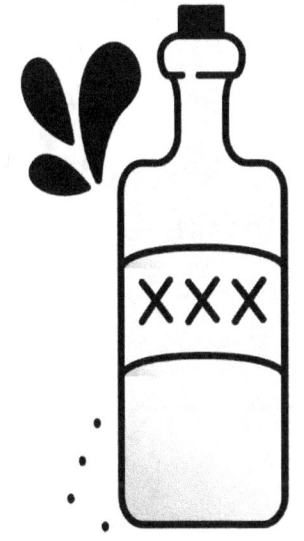
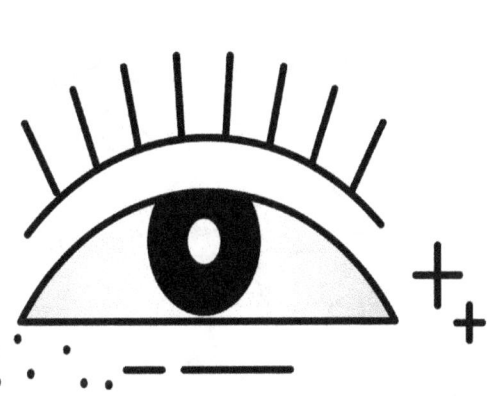
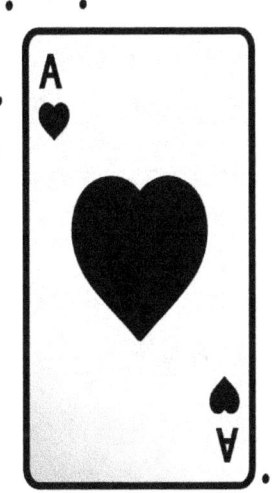
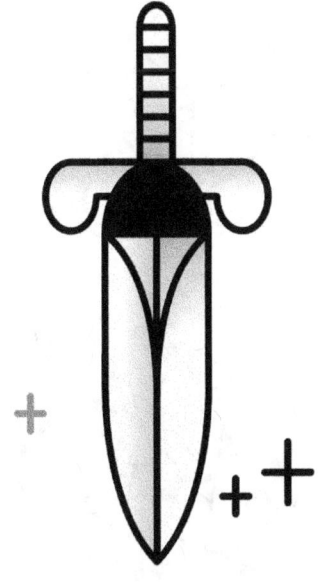
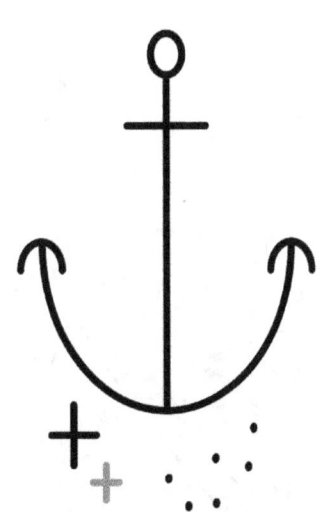
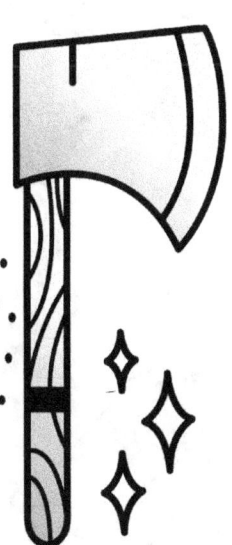

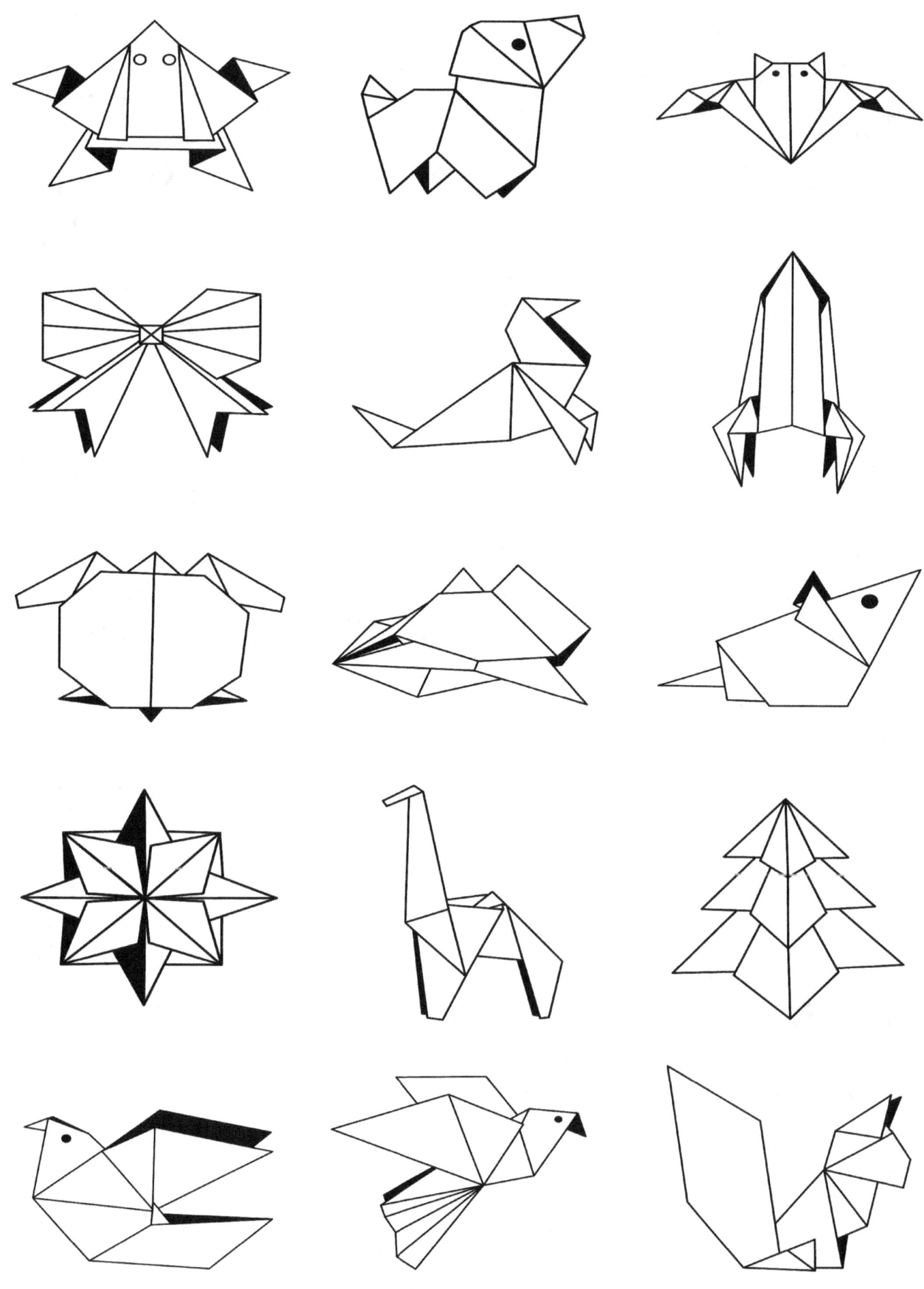

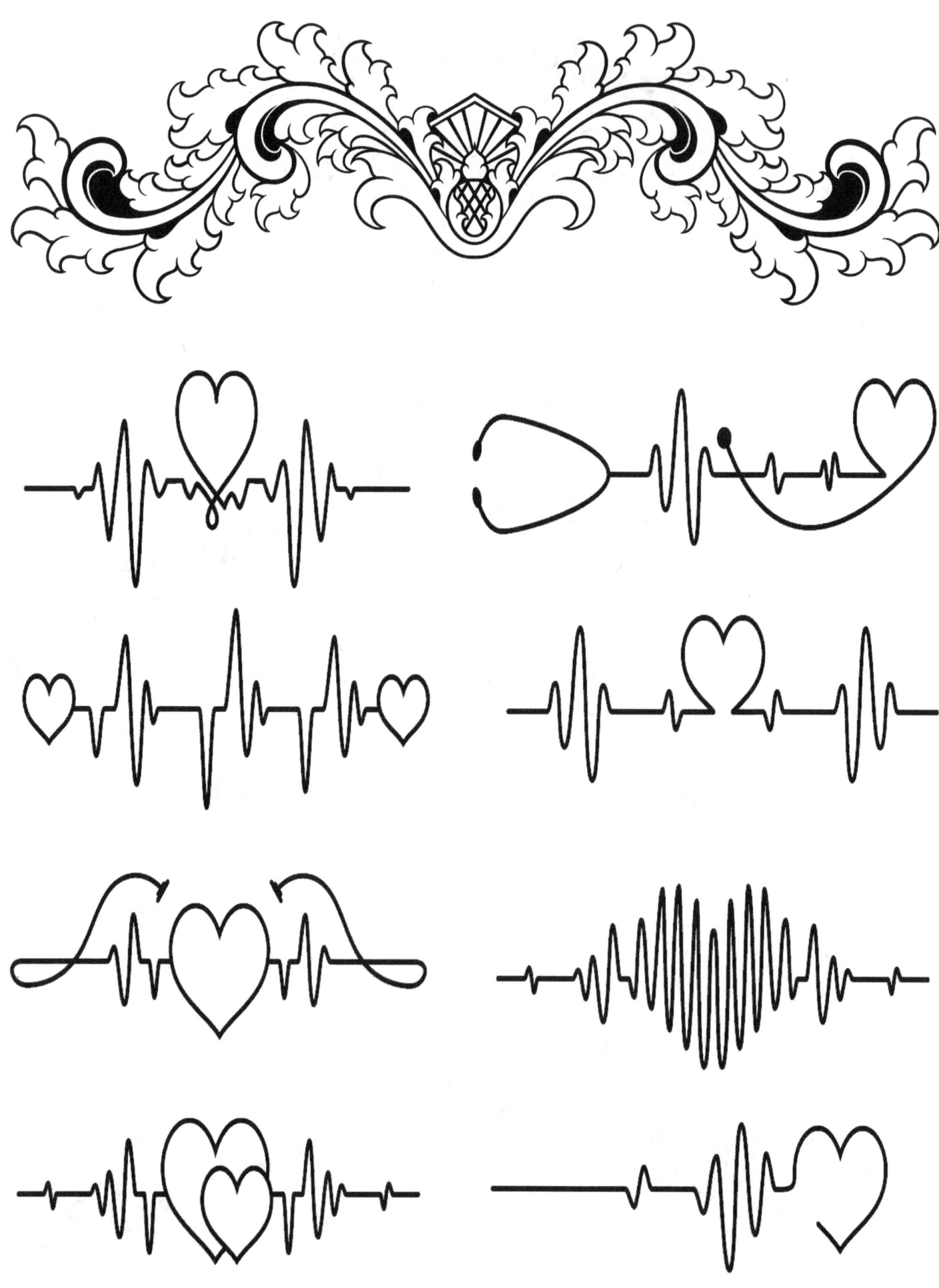

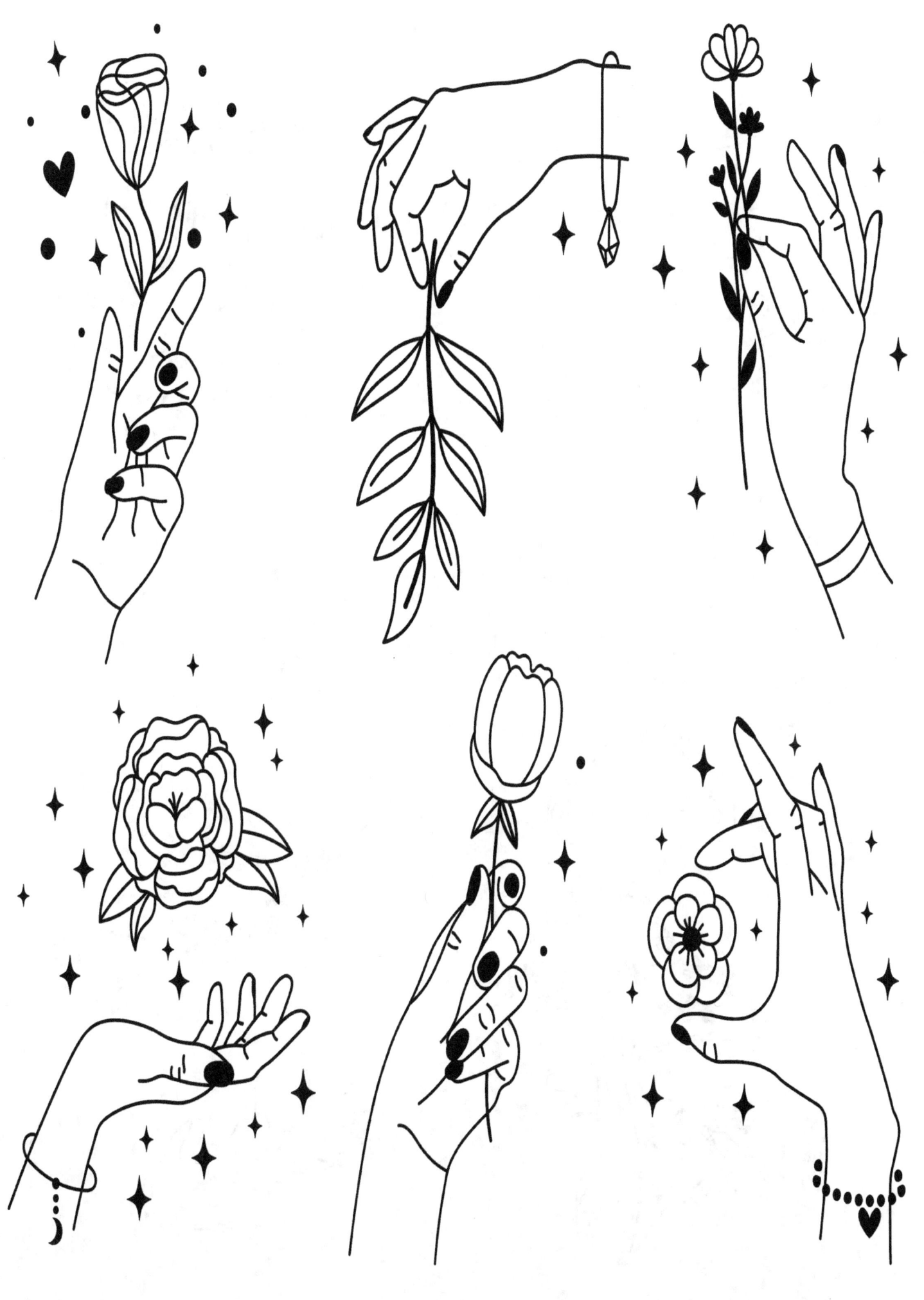

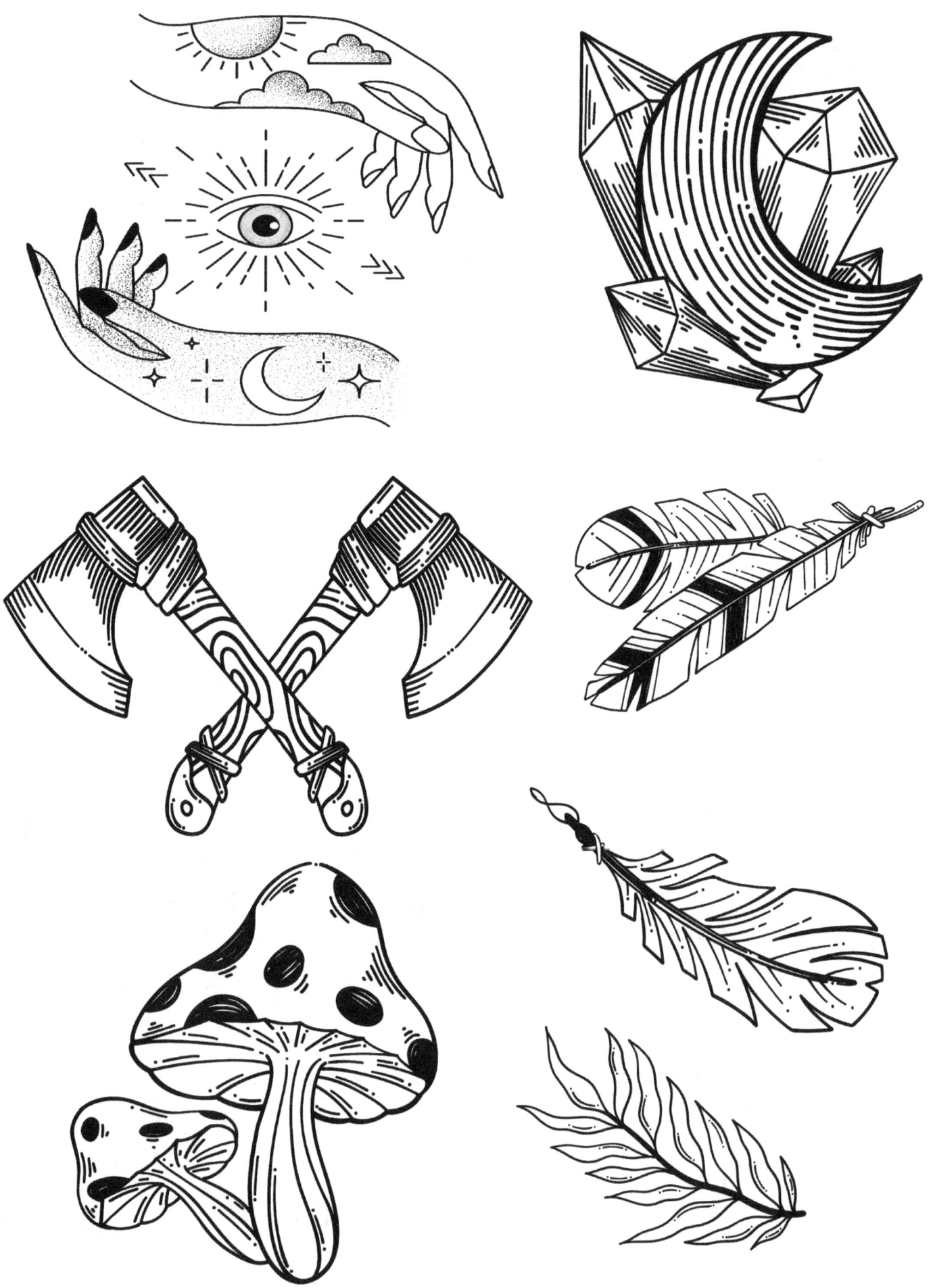

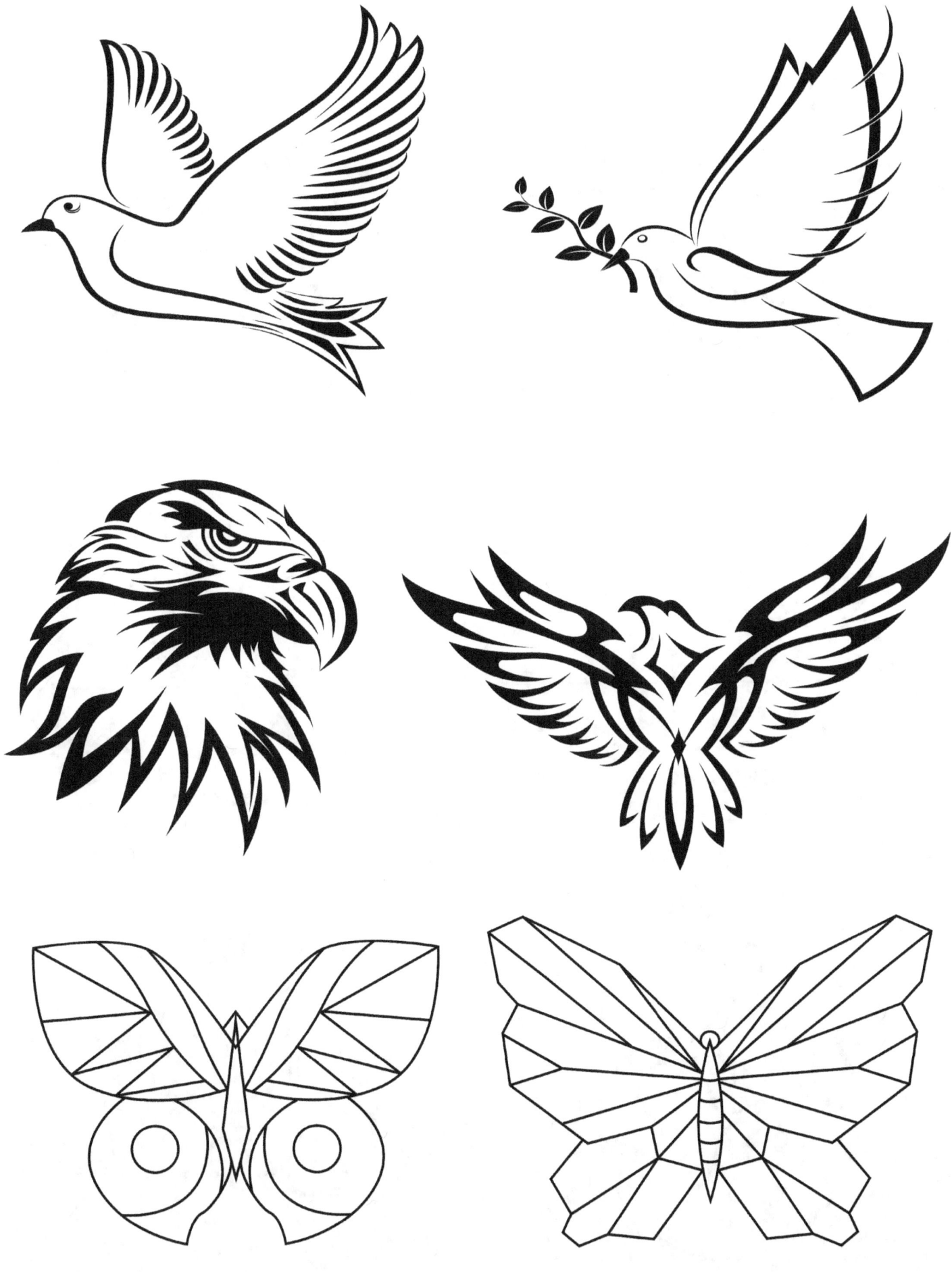

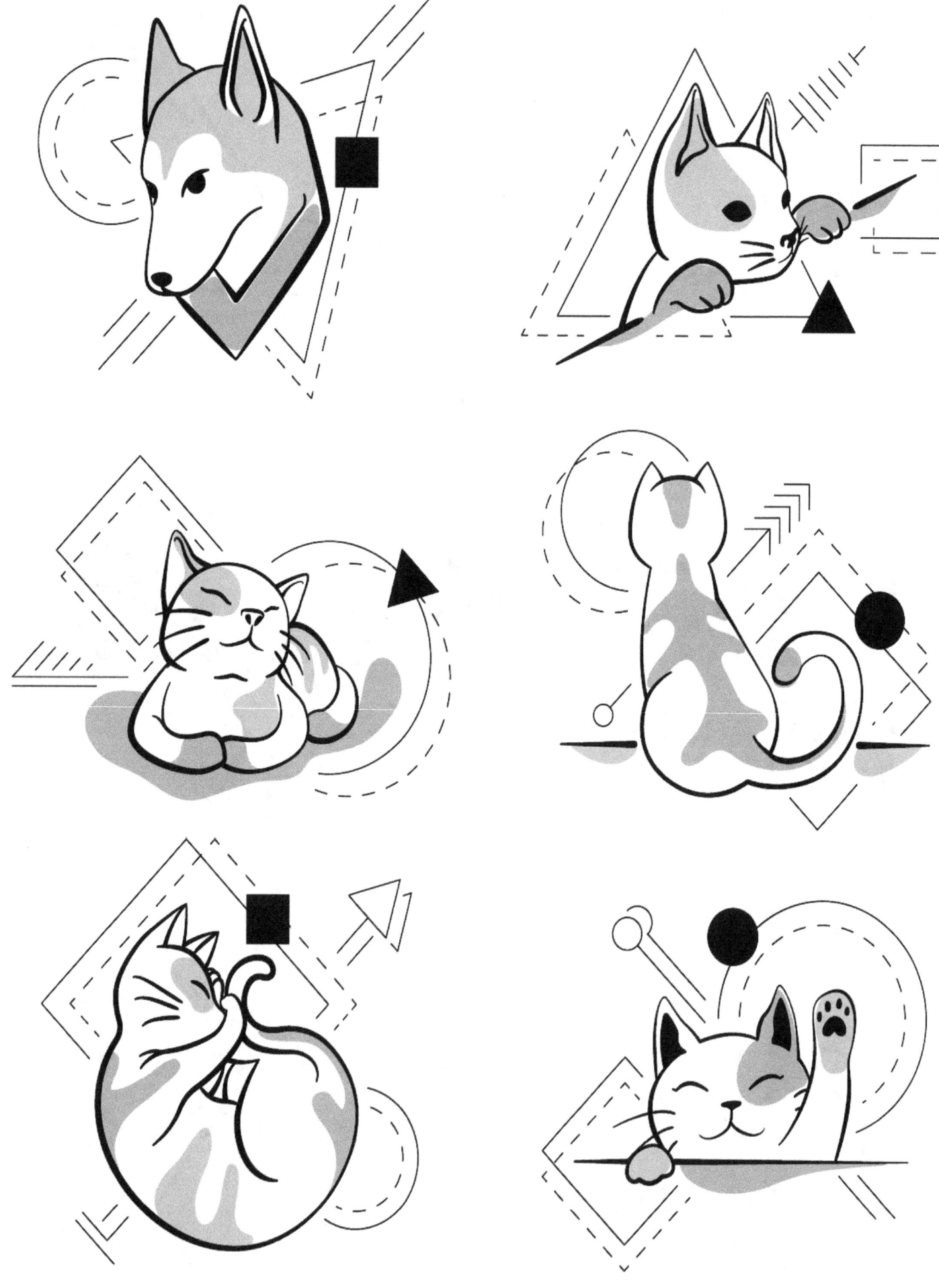

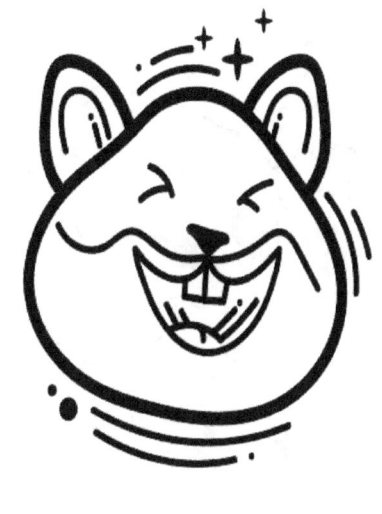
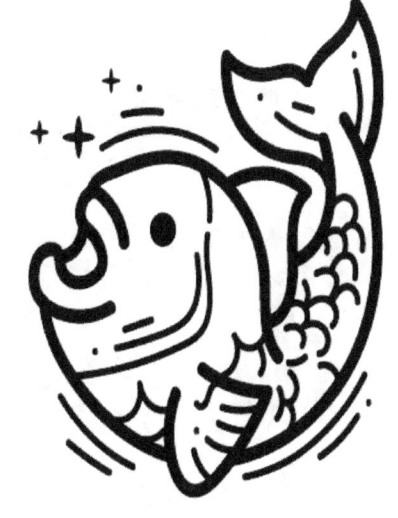
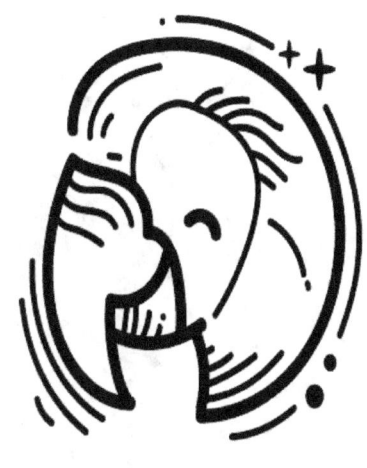
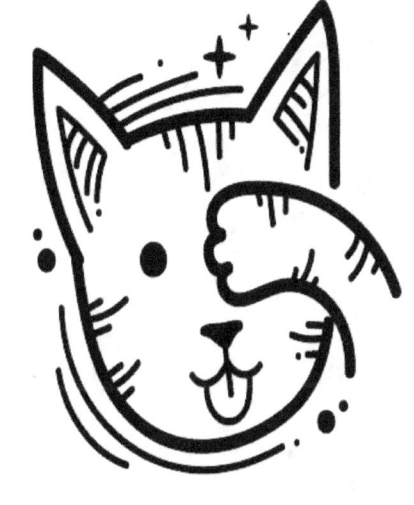
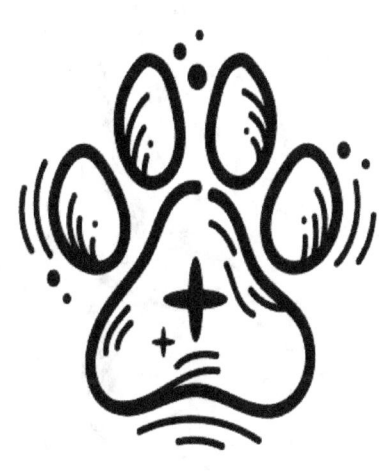
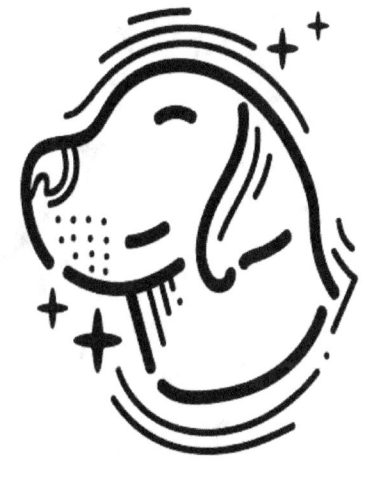
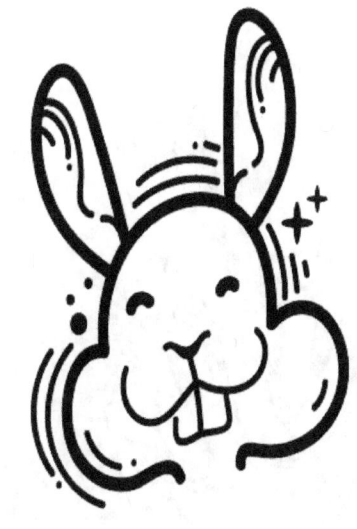
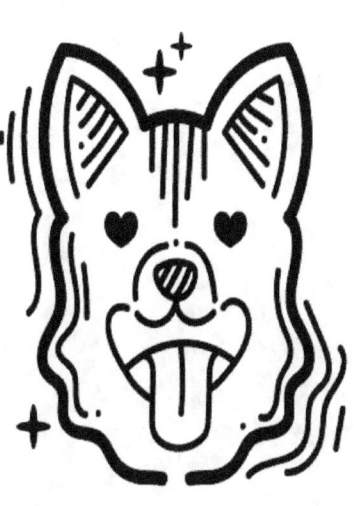
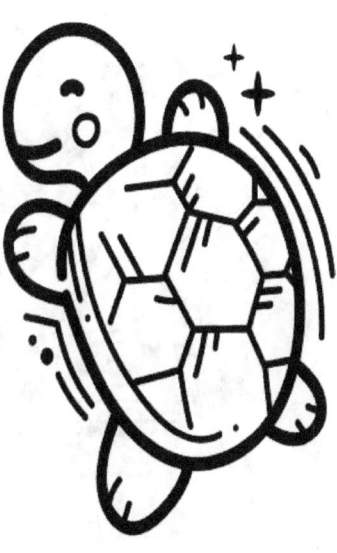

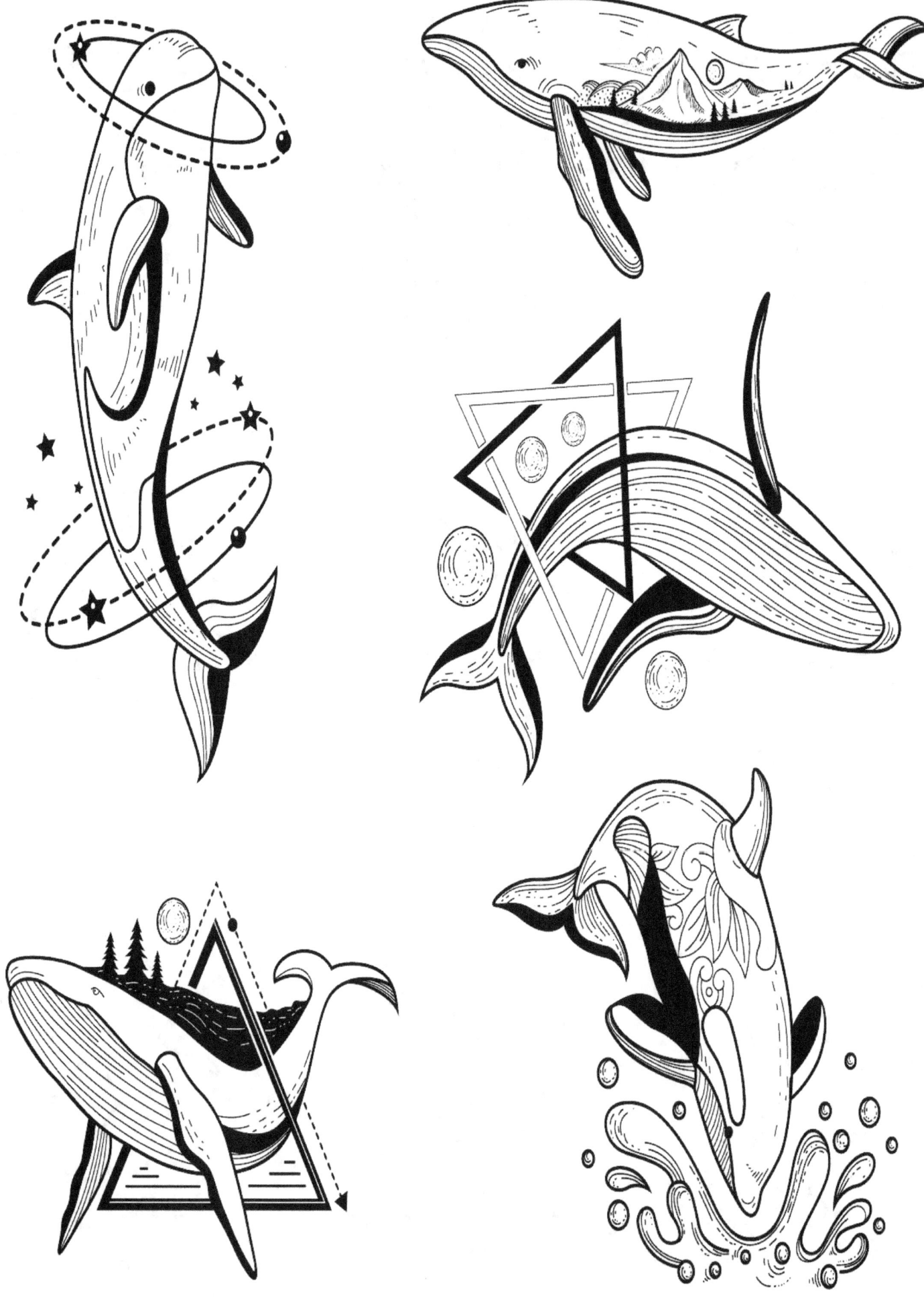

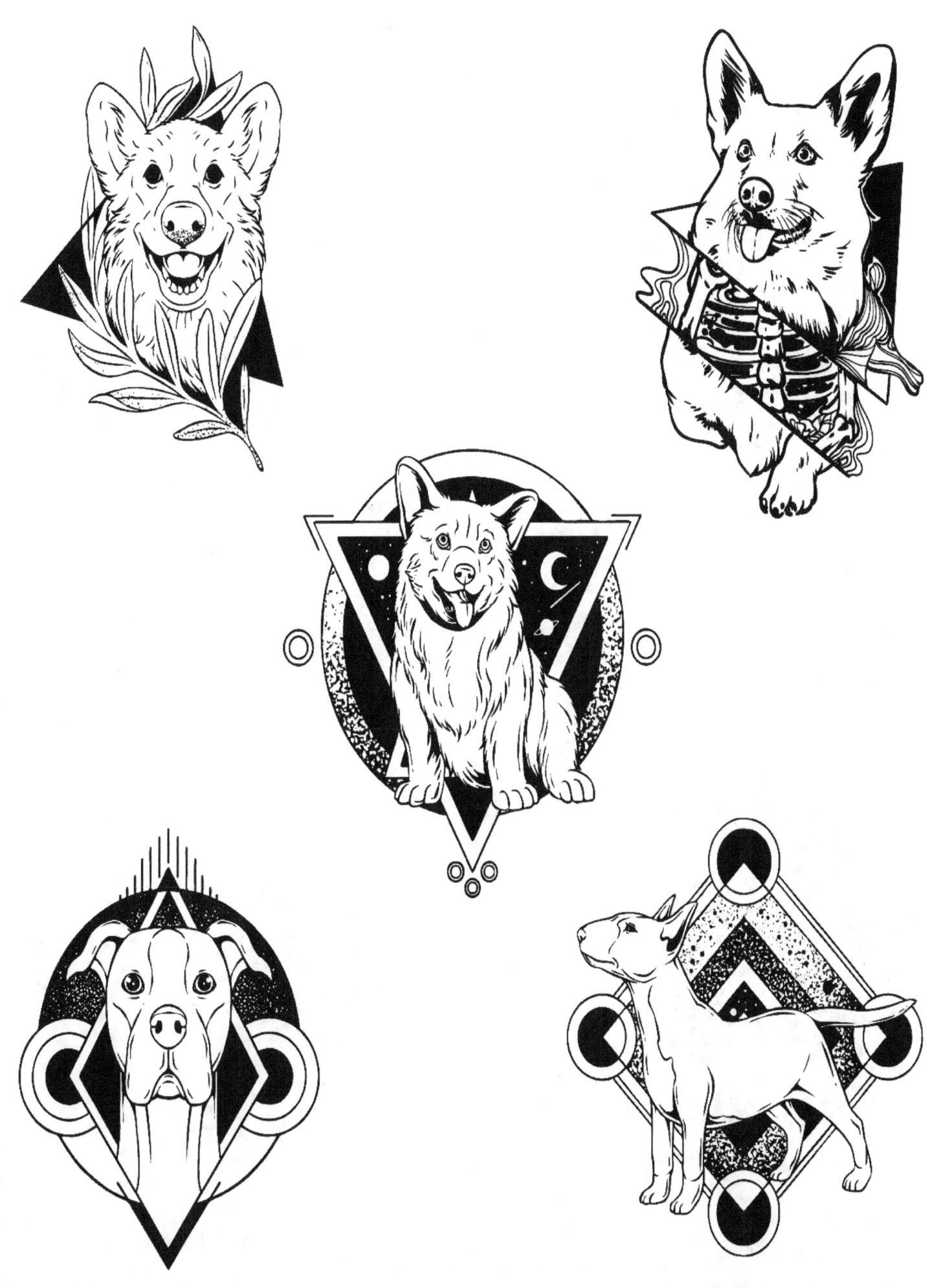

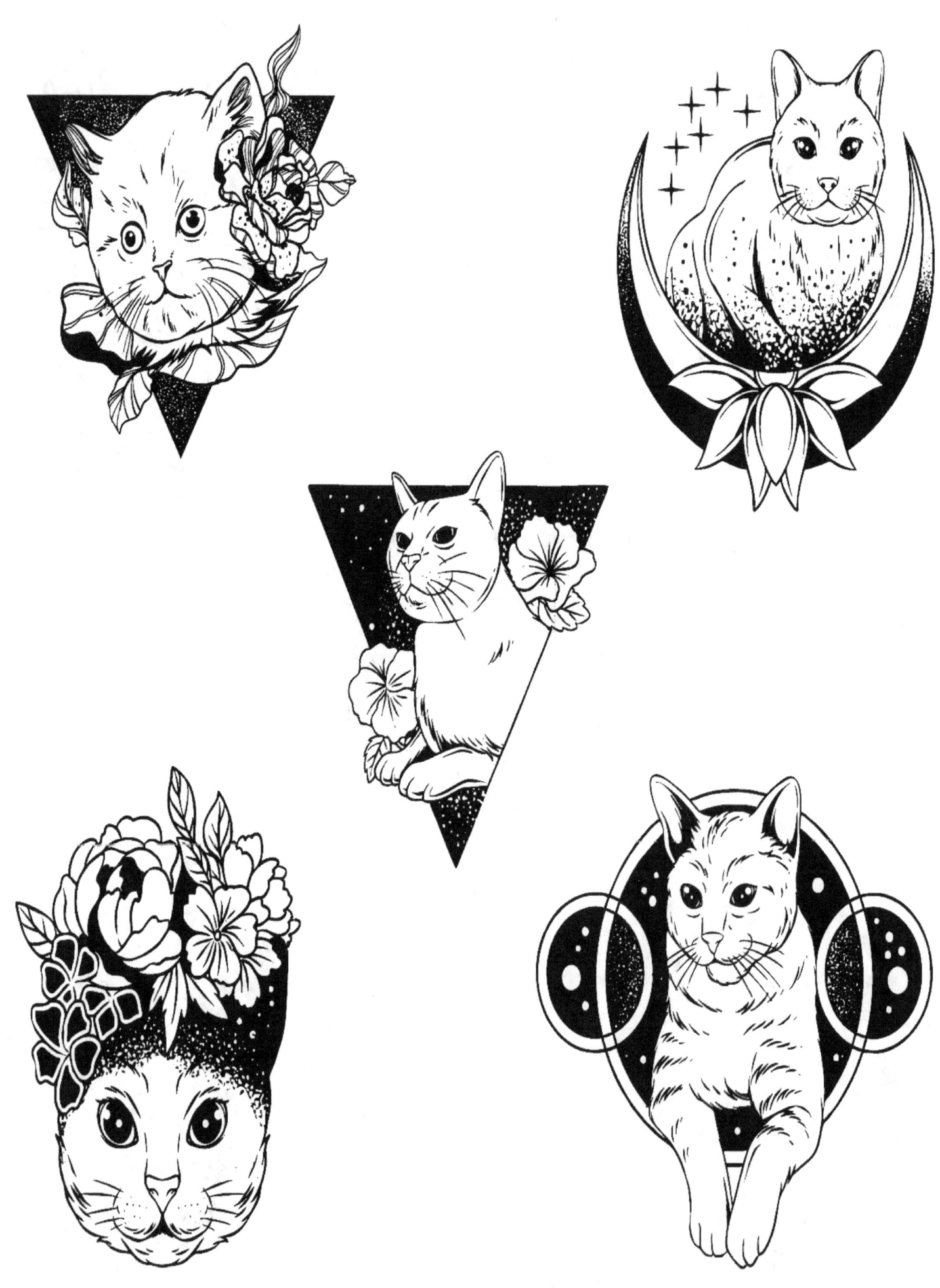

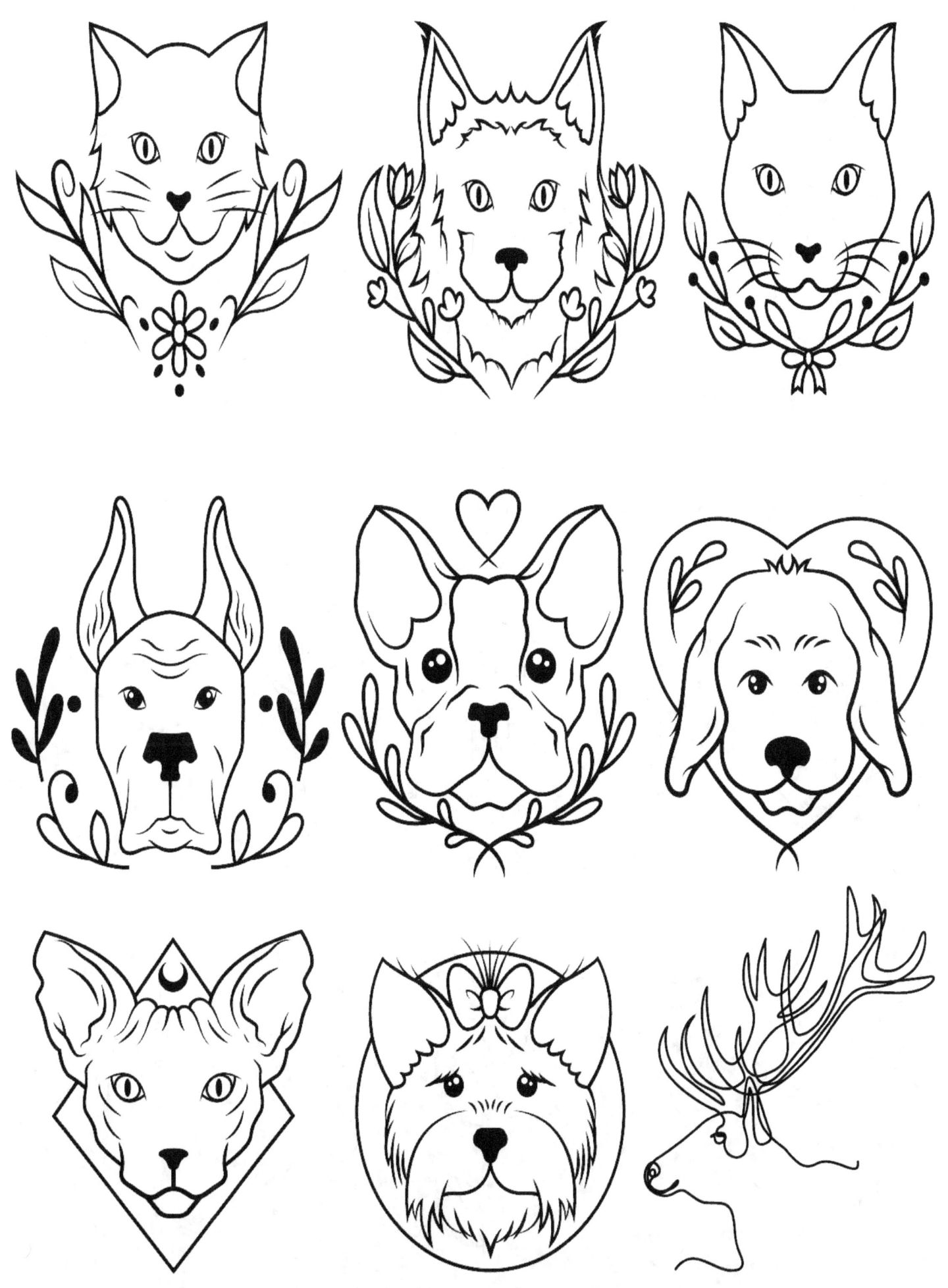

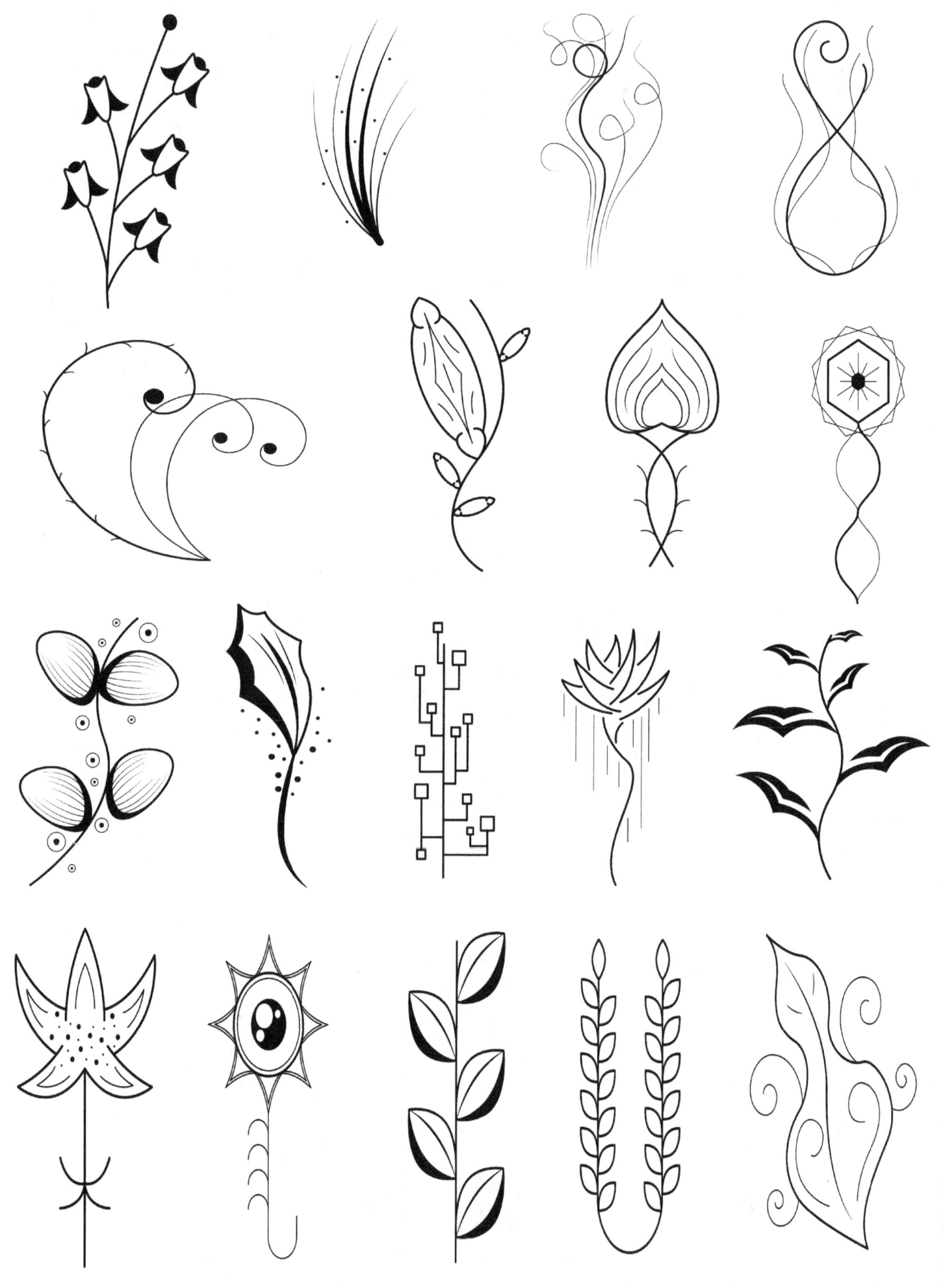

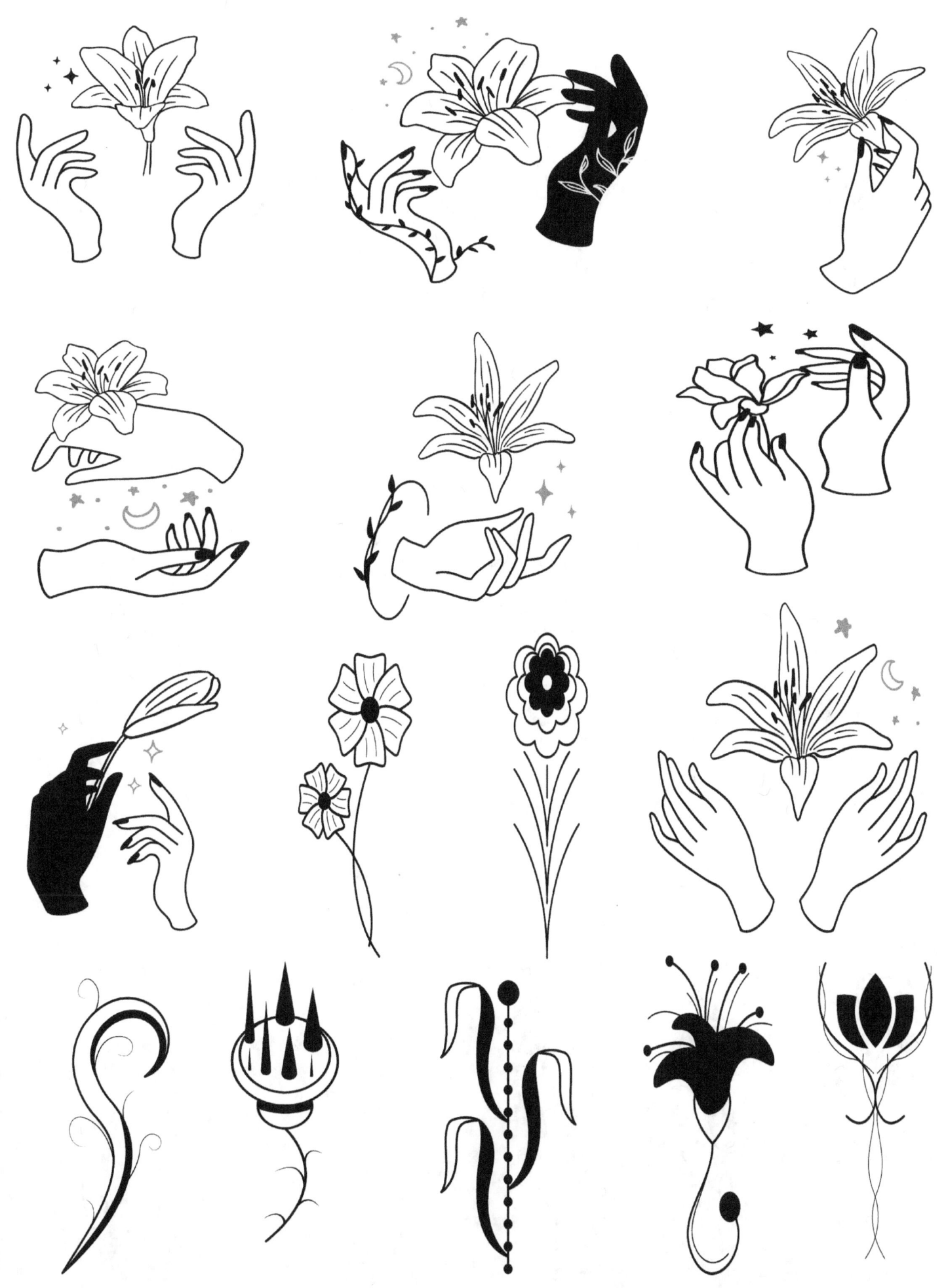

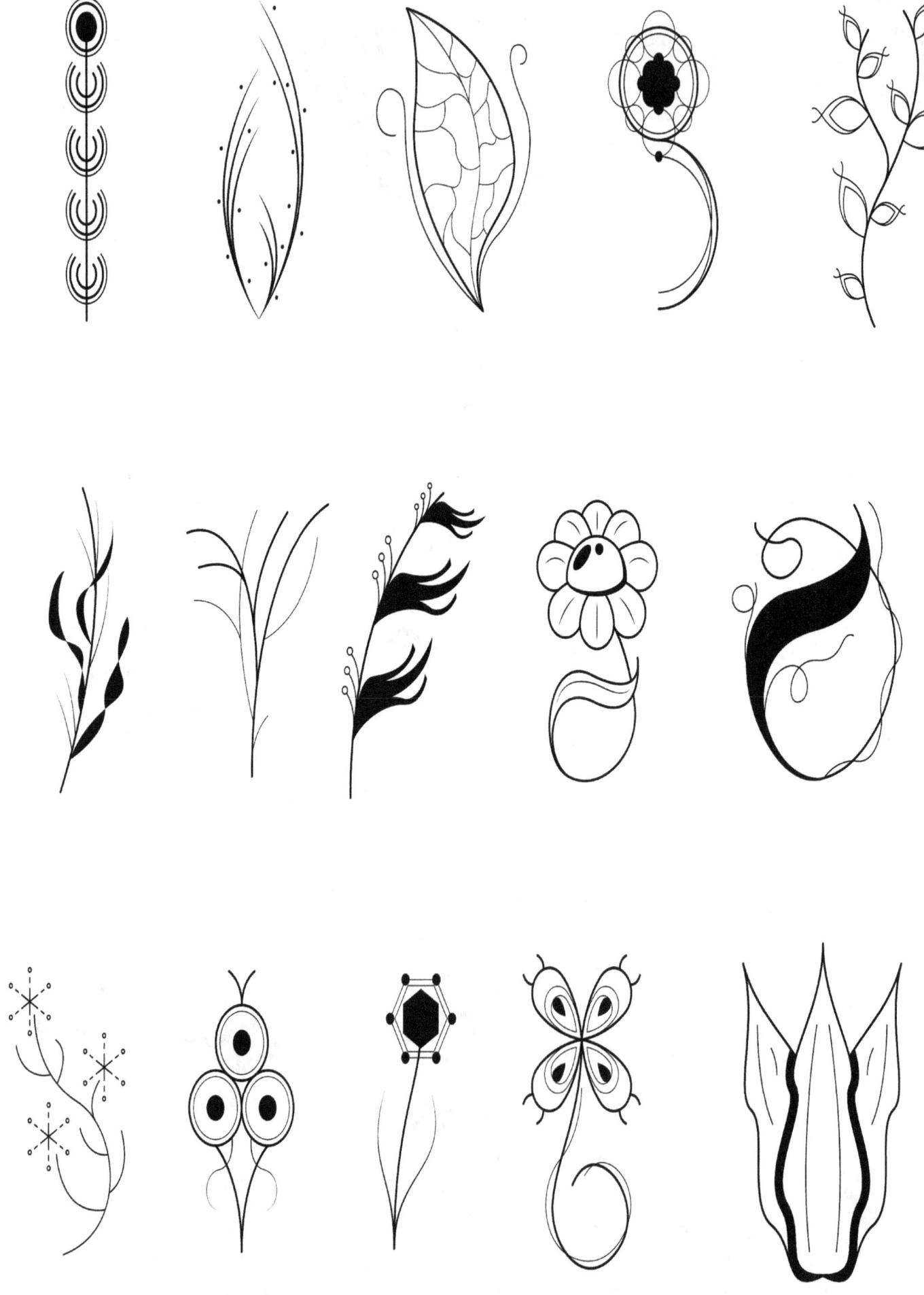

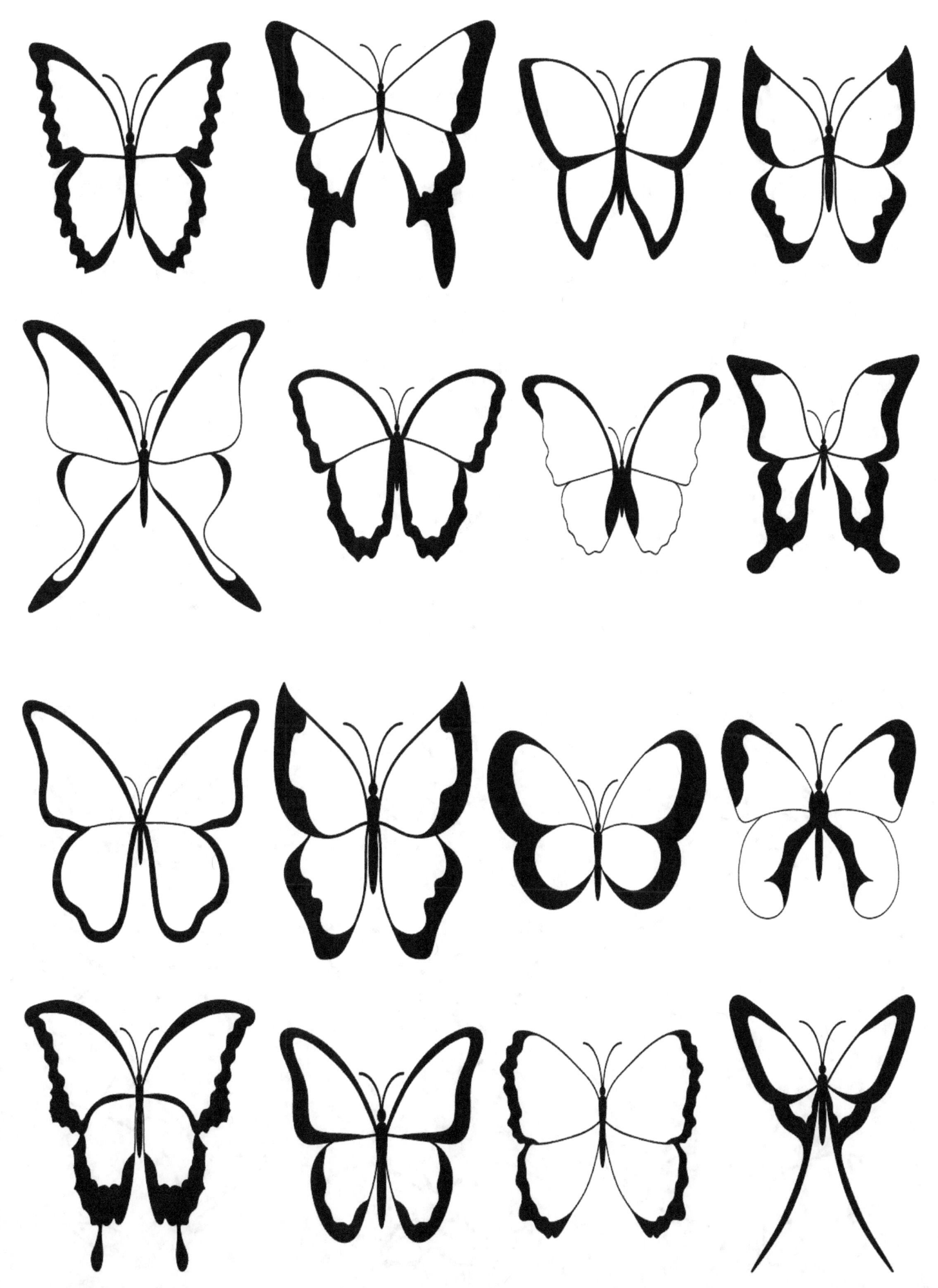

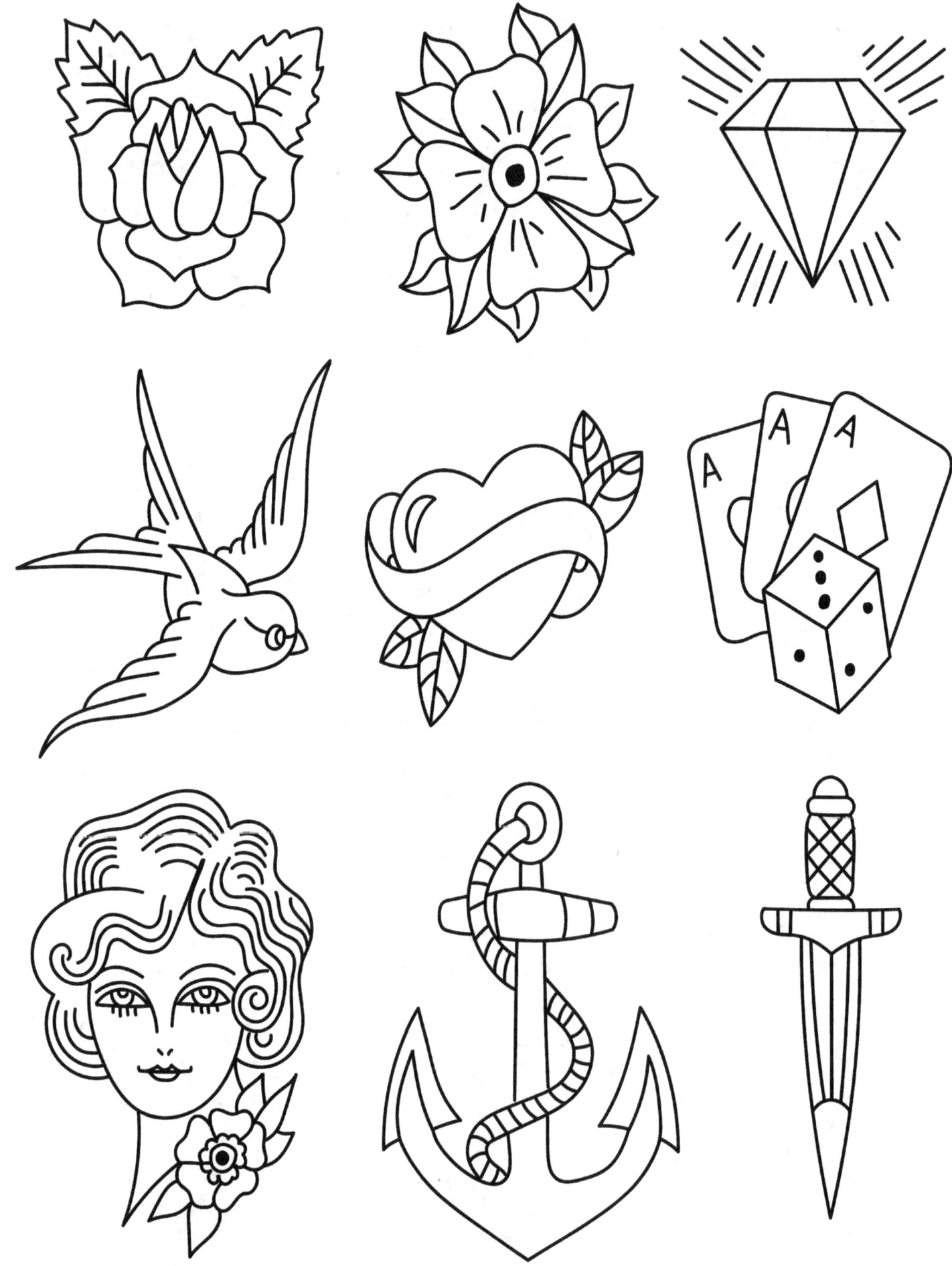

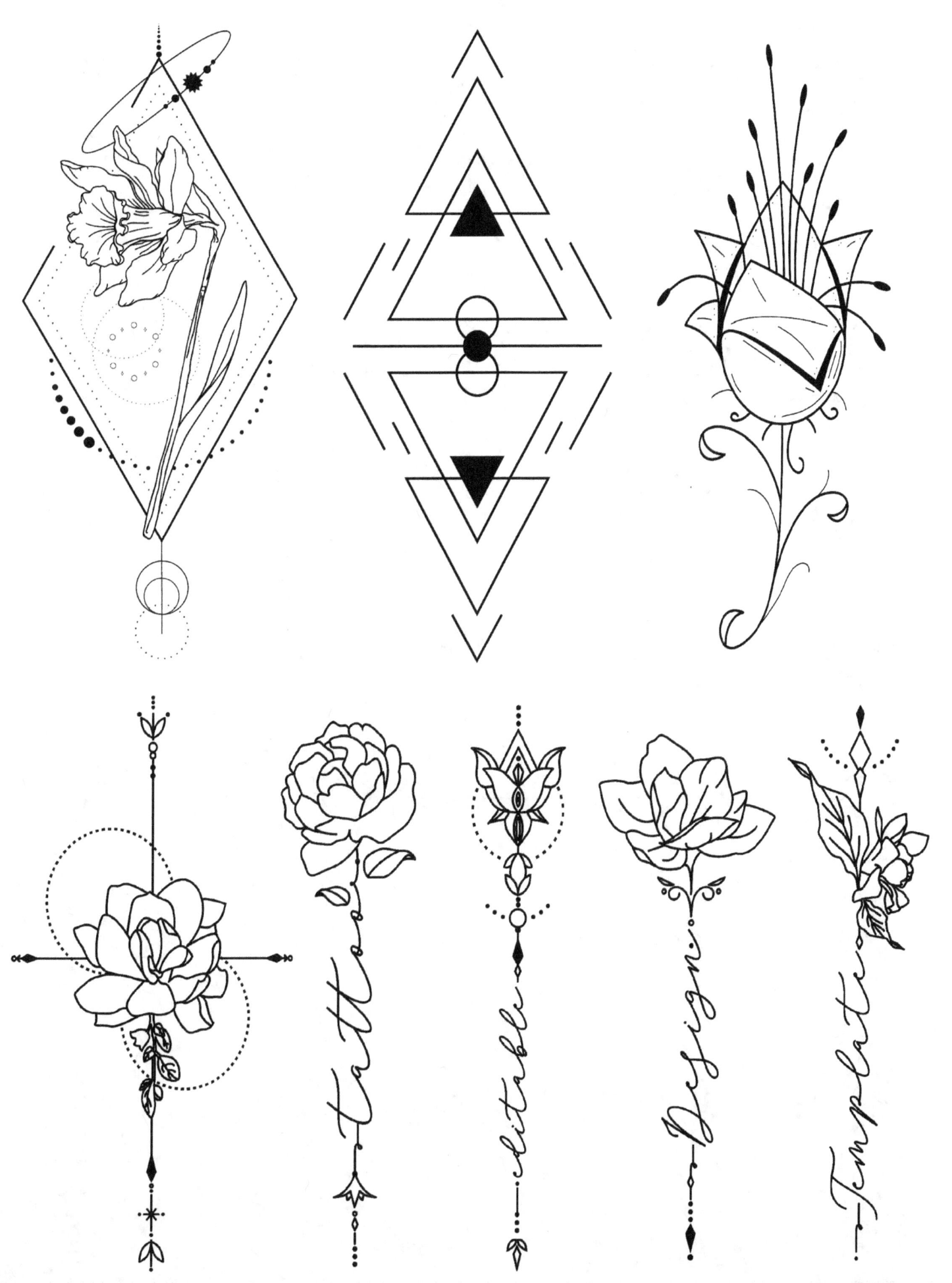

create

breathe

tattoo

love

dream

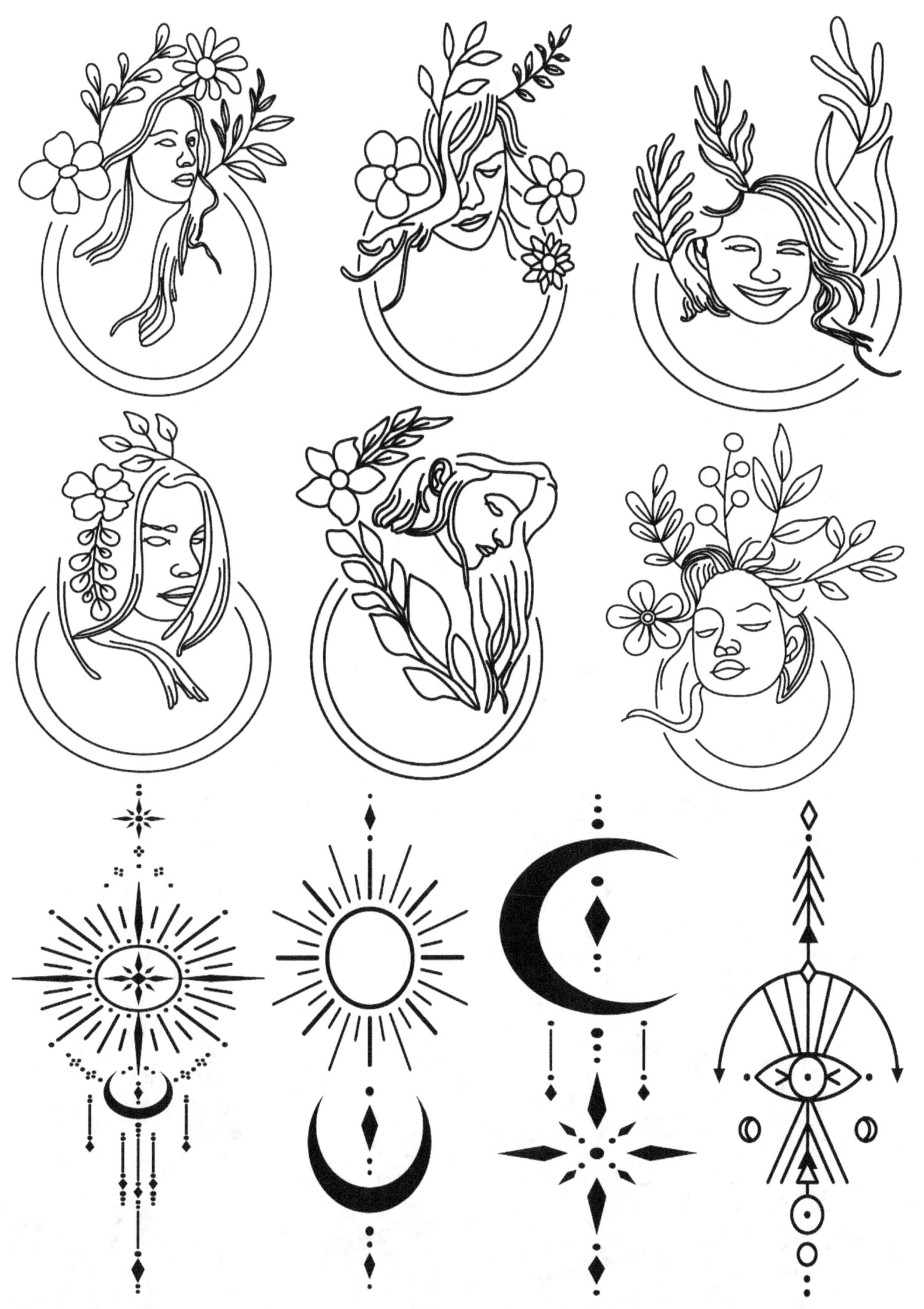

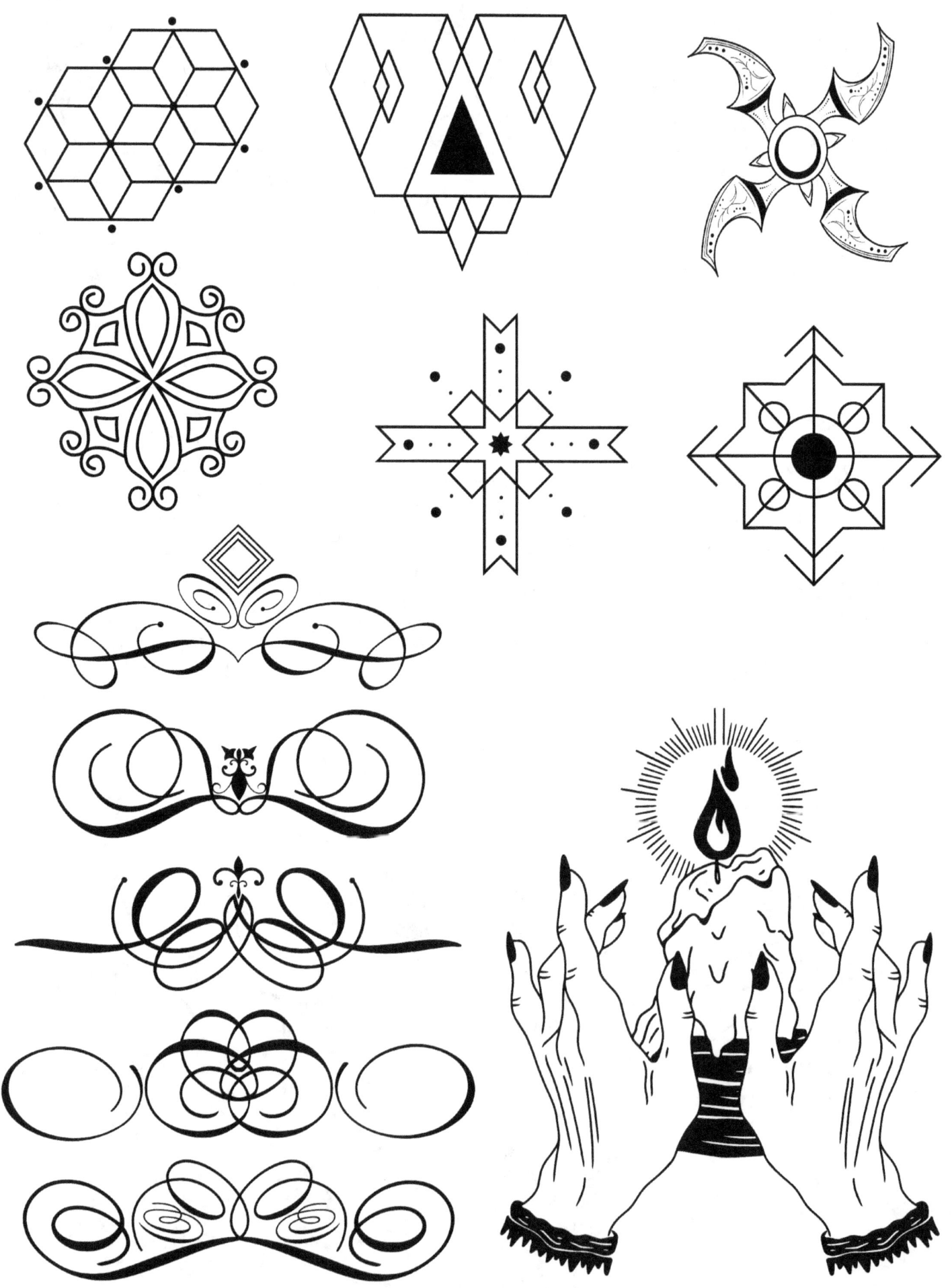

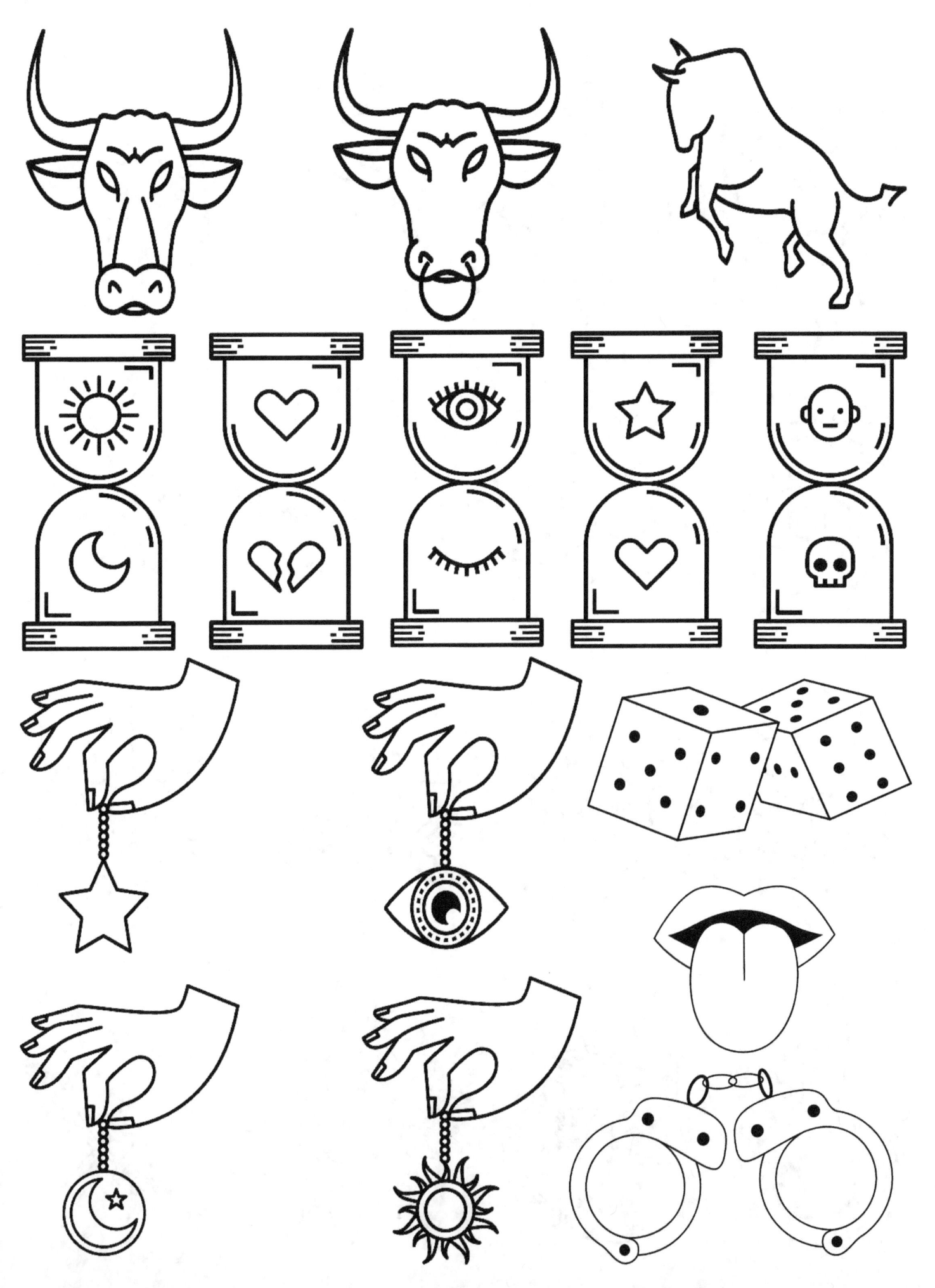

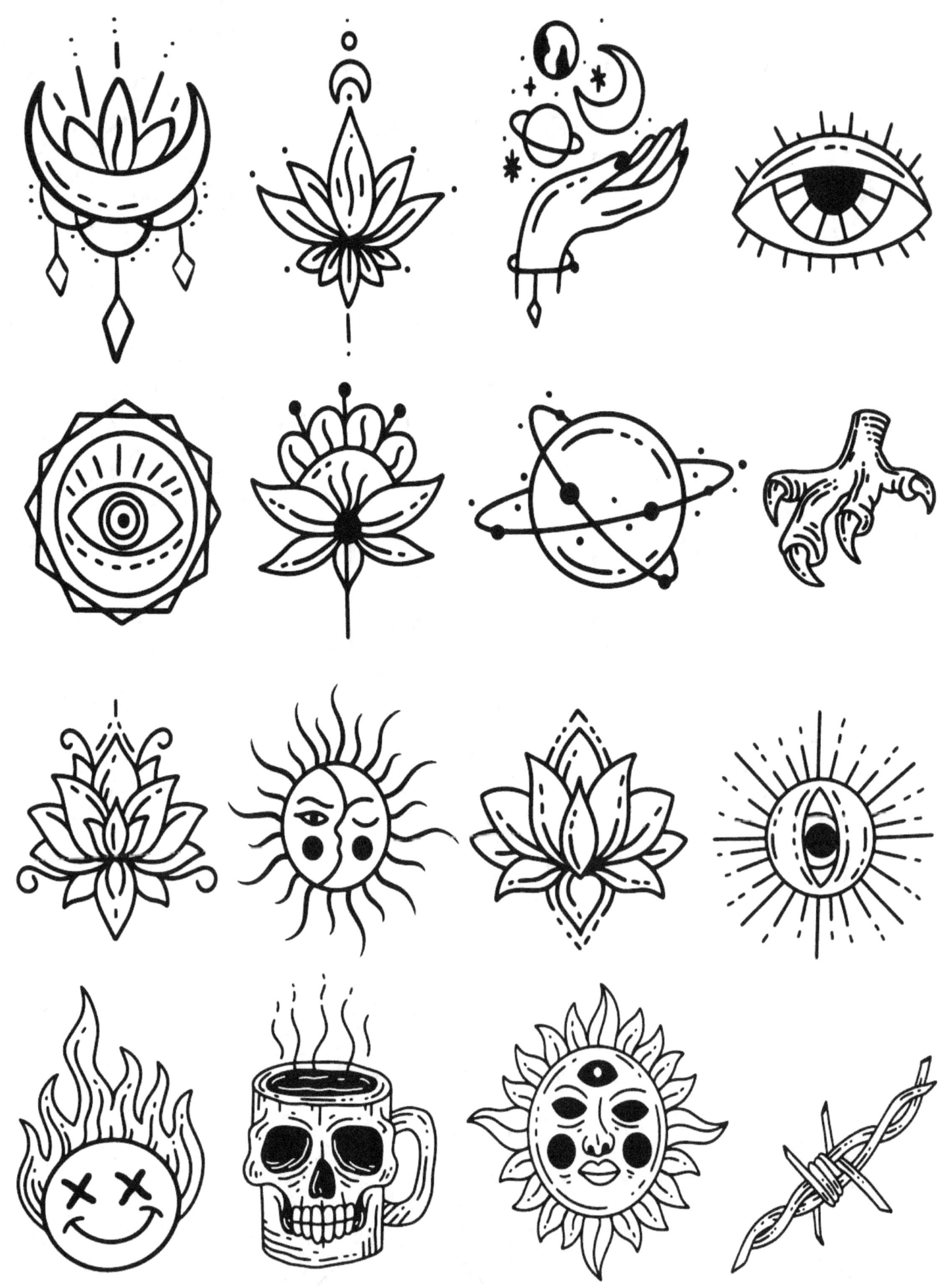

We create our books with love and great care.
Your feedback will help us improve this book
and create new ones.
Your opinion matters a lot.
Support us and leave a review.

★ ★ ★ ★ ★

Thanks for your purchase

BONUS

We have
some great
tattoo designs
for you to
inspire you

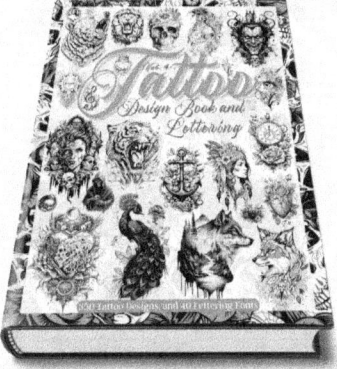

Tattoo Design Books

A. AGNES RAMA AND J. FABIAN RAMA

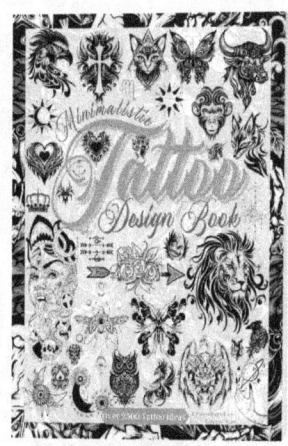

ISBN-13

979-8371492166

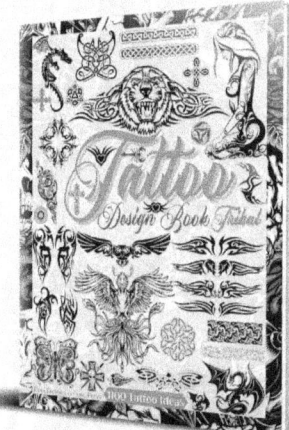

ISBN-13

979-8817137248

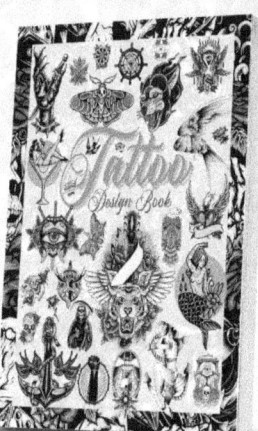

ISBN-13

979-8825575155

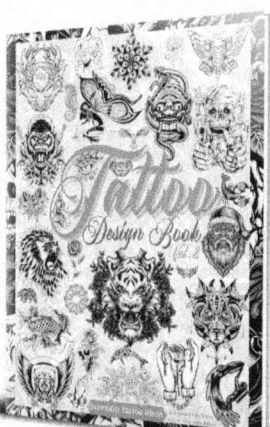

ISBN-13

979-8351925509